Christopher Wilkinson Knauff

Doctor Tucker, Priest-Musician

A Sketch Which Concerns the Doings and Thinkings of the Rev. John Ireland Tucker

Christopher Wilkinson Knauff

Doctor Tucker, Priest-Musician
A Sketch Which Concerns the Doings and Thinkings of the Rev. John Ireland Tucker

ISBN/EAN: 9783743402072

Manufactured in Europe, USA, Canada, Australia, Japa

Cover: Foto ©Lupo / pixelio.de

Manufactured and distributed by brebook publishing software (www.brebook.com)

Christopher Wilkinson Knauff

Doctor Tucker, Priest-Musician

DOCTOR TUCKER

PRIEST–MUSICIAN

A SKETCH WHICH CONCERNS THE DOINGS AND
THINKINGS OF THE

REV. JOHN IRELAND TUCKER, S.T.D.

INCLUDING A BRIEF CONVERSE ABOUT THE RISE AND
PROGRESS OF CHURCH MUSIC IN AMERICA

BY

CHRISTOPHER W. KNAUFF, M.A.

NEW YORK

A. D. F. RANDOLPH COMPANY

1897

Press of J. J. Little & Co.
Astor Place, New York

Dedicated

TO THE

GUILDS OF THE HOLY CROSS

OF TROY NEW YORK

UNDER WHOSE AUSPICES THIS BOOK

IS ISSUED

CONTENTS

CONTENTS

PROLOGUE

Bishop Potter once made the remark that Doctor Tucker's influence in Troy was absolutely unique. The Bishop of New York knew whereof he spoke: he was a long-time friend and former companion of the Rector of the Holy Cross.

But there was a wider influence. A multitude of others—outside the limits of his chosen city—have proved the quiet force and charm proceeding from the same source.

A new generation, however, is coming on, which knows the name only as designating a musical priest who was the editor of a far-famed Hymnal. It seems a pity that these should not make acquaintance with the features of an existence which was wholesome, good-humored, a believer in fun and yet not earthy; which was childlike and sincere, led by straightforward and lofty aims, and so lifted up to an unworldly level. It is not often that this sort of living is met with among the sons of men. When a favored few do find the rare example, it is the part of kindness that they shall tell their discovery to others.

His memory must be kept green. So it is determined in every case where nature has its unhindered working. In a family, the children take care

that the one gone before shall not be forgotten.
They inscribe one name after another upon their
household diptychs. These people in Troy who
loved their pastor with increasing affection all
through his life, and now love him better than ever,
they are his children—he had no others—and they
are the ones whose privilege it is to rise up and
call him blessed, and to recount the list of virtues
which had their dwelling in the earthly tabernacle
of their saint.

Again, we Christians believe in the Communion
of Saints, in a one life-fibre, a touch of soul with
soul. So strong is the hold of this article of faith,
that men and women parallel it by fond and harmless fancies of their own. Hence the present
thought about spirits gone before as inhabitants
of the planet Mars, and the effort looking toward
an exchange of signals with them. Hence another
speculation—that as long as any one is remembered, if only by a single heart, that one still retains
capacity for knowledge concerning human affairs.
However that may be, at any rate we feel, we are
sure of a relationship, not limited by earthly sphere,
established in and through the Lord and Head.
Many are they that remember, and that so believe,
gathered together in guilds at Troy.

As to the musical side of the question, there
is an ever-growing attention to the lovely art in
all its departments and manifestations. An enlarging band of devotees now ask, where shall we
find the early traces of this creation, this fair muse
that we love so well?

The whole art grows out from *Church* music as its primordial germ, and the ecclesiastical world of tone commences with simple psalmody. So it is that the hymn-tune becomes a prominent factor in history. As we follow the rise of religious melody, we note a struggling effort after purer art. On this side of the Atlantic, Doctor Tucker was a pioneer in the fight against bad music, against the admission of a debased sort within the sacred confines. In this cause he started out alone, a knight valiant and full of faith, and always a patriot laboring for the common weal. The story of his life affords a valued contribution to the new study —coming into vogue—which craves information about the increase and development of musical art in America.

Doctor Tucker, Priest-Musician

I

FOREFATHERS

" He was a saint from the day of his birth, and he, could sing before he could talk." So said a near relative of him who is here remembered, and who had known him, in the intimacy of family relationship, from the beginning until the end. It was an epitome fortunately expressed, a comprehensive summing up. It is corroborated by the experiences of a great multitude of devoted friends —by the companions of many years.

Doctor Tucker—the " dear Doctor Tucker," as those who knew him best were wont to style him— possessed an exceptional character. His was not an ordinary mind or heart. Although he lived an uneventful life of retirement, like Keble limiting his strongest activities to the quiet sphere of parish duty—to what the children of this world call a " humdrum existence "—yet, like Keble, his name became known on both sides of the Atlantic, and from the East even to the West. He became a recognized power in certain lines of thought and action.

It is right that the memory of his pure and noble living shall be set down for human encouragement. When one has felt as he did, and manifested forth such singular excellencies pertaining to an unselfish existence, when it so happened that the position occupied by him and the influence exerted became unique—having no exact parallel—it is fitting that we shall seek to know whatever may be told about the faithful course that has been run. Only natural it was that those who had been associated in sacred confidential relationship with him as pastor, should ask that some sketch of his life—a centre of their hopes and highest aspirations—should be shaped into permanent form that they might have it with them in their homes. Rightful it is that others also, outside of the charmed circle, may be permitted to discover some fraction of the fascination which never failed, and may find interest in the outline records of days which were not crowded with stirring incident, but which, nevertheless, were filled full of that which is of value to every soul that lives a true soul-life.

John Ireland Tucker was born in Brooklyn on the 26th of November, 1819.

At the time, Brooklyn was a rural suburb, as yet "in the country." Only three years before this had the hamlet advanced to the dignity of an incorporated village, having a scattered population of four thousand four hundred inhabitants.

Ancestry and environment are powerful forces, influential in the make-up of character. Our revered friend was blessed with progenitors for whom and whose dispositions he might well be thankful.

His maternal grandfather, Joshua Sands, was a prominent figure in the community, endowed with strength of thought and action in matters both of State and Church. He was a member and sometime President of the Village Board of Trustees, also the first Collector of Customs and a representative in the National Congress. One of the streets of the now great city bears his name.

We find the like inscription upon records which tell of religious activity. When an act of incorporation was passed, April 23, 1787, referring to that which bore the style and title of " The Episcopal Church of Brooklyn," we note the name Joshua Sands among the list of original trustees. This was in the days of ecclesiastical pioneers, when services " were held at the house on the North East Corner of Fulton and Middagh Streets; which house was fitted with pews." So says Gabriel Furman in his now rare pamphlet, printed by A. Spooner, at No. 50 Fulton Street, Brooklyn, in 1824. After this the primary congregation came into possession of the " Independent Meeting House, whose members had seceded to the Episcopal Church," a frame building located on the ground well known in later years as a place of burial. This is the structure which, at a time of revived interest, was painted blue, " which some of our older inhabitants well remember," says Mr. Fish in his Annals.

A few years after, the parish comes to be known

by a distinctive title, commonly called St. Ann's, for a cause interesting in its biographical association. Then and thereafter the name "Sands" appears upon the records with a regularity of recurrence that is remarkable. So it is set down that to this one of the chief inhabitants was entrusted constantly the duties of vestryman and warden, also of deputy to the Diocesan Convention. At the time of his death, in 1835, he was senior warden of the honored parish.

Wealth brought further opportunity for good to this progenitor. There was a time when he and his brother were endowed with large possessions. Their business ventures had prospered beyond ordinary measure. As far back as the year 1779 an act of attainder was passed against John Rapalje, by which his property was confiscated to the use of the State, and "that part of his property lying within the bounds of the present village of Brooklyn," so saith Gabriel Furman, "was, on the 13th of July, 1784, sold by the Commissioner of Forfeitures to Comfort and Joshua Sands, Esq's, for £12,430." A considerable purchase for that age!

However, as fate would have it, a serious setback came to pass in later days. It was before the time of the formation of insurance companies; as yet each merchant was his own insurer. During this unprotected period, on one sad day a disastrous conflagration destroyed immense storehouses belonging to the two brothers, and their losses were enormous.

But whether richer or poorer, Joshua maintained an even reputation for benevolence and public spirit. He and his good wife were acknowledged "friends of the people," known and welcomed by every one. Among other benefactions, they—the heads of the popular household—gave the land upon which the first Church building was erected at the corner of Sands and Washington Streets. Some years before the putting up of this—the "Stone Church," as it came to be called—the title of the congregation had been settled. Tacitly, by common consent, the style was changed from "The Episcopal Church of Brooklyn" to "St. Ann's Church," and it was so named on account of the one woman who was the "genuine Dorcas" of the settlement, that one who "went about doing good." The title was associated with her parish, by virtue of the character and influence of Ann Sands, wife of Joshua.

She, whose name is recorded as one of the three earliest communicants of the Church in Brooklyn, and who became a mother in Israel, was in the line of descent from Ann Askew—otherwise spelled Ayscough—who was burned at the stake in the time of Henry VIII. The family connection even now like to look back to the ancestor who hesitated not to hold firmly to her faith even unto death. The relative who gave me the information remarked, in reference to the subject of this sketch: "He came from that kind of stock, and really couldn't help being good." The name of Ann Askew is so highly prized that it still appears among the living; a daughter in one branch of the house to-day bears the title.

Here let it be remembered, too, that Archbishop Sandys is of the same line now known as Sands—another forefather who contributes to the stream of inheritance.

Anne Moore Sands was the daughter of Joshua and Ann. About her we shall hear further when we note a few brief selections taken from the letters which she wrote. She, maiden highly favored of the village, was wedded to Fanning C. Tucker, fit man of her choice. The groom was the son of a physician, Dr. Robert Tucker, the first graduate in medicine who received the degree of Doctor of Medicine from Columbia College.

Major Fanning C. Tucker, husband of Anne Sands, attained in his own way to high prominence in Church and State. He was active in affairs of parish as well as of the diocese. When Dr. Henry U. Onderdonk relinquished the pastorship of St. Ann's, promoted to the see of Pennsylvania, rumor had it that he was not well disposed toward Mr. McIlvaine—afterward the Bishop of Ohio—as a successor. The latter let it be understood that he would not accept the invitation to rectorship unless all members of the congregation should so desire. Then it was that Fanning C. Tucker gave evidence of his customary vigor; he took his carriage and went abroad visiting the entire region, securing the signature of every parishioner. The act was the more significant in view of the fact that in the current lively divisions of feeling as to matters ecclesiastical, the new Rector tended toward the one side and the prominent vestryman and ofttime warden to the other. Nevertheless, the chief parochial official worked ever in hearty unison with his ecclesiastical superior.

Major Tucker is described as a man of society, and a highly respected, successful administrator in business affairs. Later he became the president of a down-town bank in New York. He was of a lofty stature, erect, commanding, the sort of a personage to attract attention wherever he might go.

While yet a young and newly married man, Major Tucker set up his Lares and Penates in a house on Sands Street. There his son, John Ireland, subject of this sketch, was born in 1819. The name chosen for the child seems to have been of especial favor in the family. It had been given to a brother a little older. He died young, and a few months after his death the same name was bestowed upon him whom we recall. The original of the title was the Rev. John Ireland, Rector of St. Ann's at the close of the eighteenth century, and well known as a man of erudition.

Concerning the childhood of our John Ireland, son of Fanning, little may be told. He is described by one who knew him then as " a golden-haired, beautiful boy." His charm of face and form was remarked by all. The fond mother was accustomed to call him her " angel," or, adopting another equivalent exegesis, to name him now and again " her little Bishop."

When the boy was four years of age, the family

removed to a new home, erected on " the heights." The place is still remembered as containing a double mansion of ample proportions, built of frame, standing near to the spot where Grace Church is now located. The country homestead was known as " Bella Vista." It included some fifty acres, running down to the water, and comprising a fine garden of fruits and vegetables. There the household remained until after the death of the fond mother, when there was another removal, this time to the city of New York. Henceforth the family makes its abode among the dwellings of the Knickerbockers.

But before we leave the Brooklyn scene, let me pause to incorporate some information, imparted by Dr. J. Carpenter Smith, for half a century Rector of the historic parish of St. George's at Flushing, L. I. In his early years Dr. Smith was a resident of Brooklyn at a time when, as he says, the village consisted principally of St. Ann's Church and the Navy Yard. He remembers well both Fanning C. Tucker and his son John. He speaks of the stature and pronounced characteristics of the father : " wherever Fanning C. Tucker went he made himself known."

Another quality is referred to. The father was always a lover of harmony. He had a strong bass voice, which rendered good service, both in church and at home. In the former connection he was the forefront and backbone of the choir. At one and the same time he filled two positions, viz., warden of the parish and leader of the choristers.

It is easy to see whence the son, afterward famous for his musical ability and knowledge, derived his taste and tendency. They came to him by right of inheritance. To the father music seems to have been one of the essentials of living. As an example out of many, Dr. Smith recounts the audible performances, identified with a house next to his own, where lived a Madame Brichta, solo soprano and leading treble of the Church. Thither would come at times the director of St. Ann's choir to practise songs or take part in concerted pieces, and then, as my informant phrases it, " they made the neighborhood vocal."

By the same narrator the boy, John Tucker, is recalled, as he walks into Sunday-school, a tall and stately lad; there and elsewhere he always manifested a fine, natural propriety of deportment.

In the second or third decade of the present century the Sunday-school constituted one of the vexed questions. Opinions differed, and arguments were warm. A school had been established in Brooklyn in the early part of the ministry of the Rev. Hugh Smith, which began in 1817. The institution was continued, during two or three years, under the administration of his successor, the Rev. Dr. Onderdonk. Gradually, however, it languished, and at length expired. When Mr. McIlvaine came to the rectorship the school was once more started, and upon a career of renewed vigor.

Although Dr. Smith remembers his former schoolmate as a dignified and stately lad of erect carriage, yet the latter could unbend, showing the unchanging attractiveness of a cheerful mind. So it may be inferred from the designation " Jack," bestowed upon him by his father and by many associates. And so it may be witnessed, further, from a little exhibition of playfulness which is still remembered. The brief story was told by him, long after, to friends in Troy. He recalled an occasion when an assortment of cake had been placed in a " cake-basket " and covered with a doily. The boy passed the spot. By way of a prank, he removed the uppermost piece of cake, substituting in its stead an inverted saucer, again covering all with the doily. When the cake-basket was brought into action there was astonishment among the beholders. Of course the performance was a bit of harmless pleasantry at home.

To return to the benefit of forefathers. It is easy to perceive that in the case of him whose young life was bright and prosperous, certain definite qualities, running all through the fruitful years, may be traced back to their remote beginnings. Impalpable but real treasures, like that of a good name, pass on from father or mother to a child. So it is that we find a fittingness, a something expected not only in the stature and bearing, but in the piety and benevolence, the ecclesiastical tendency, the marked taste and ability in music, as well as the unquestioned respectability of Doctor Tucker. The entire list of attributes is in keeping with his antecedents. He was the worthy son of a worthy line.

II

THE BOY AT SCHOOL

There must be preparation for days to come. Accordingly, judicious courses of study are prescribed. For a time the lad crosses the East River, day by day, as he attends the Columbia Grammar School, then under the direction of the Rev. Dr. Ogilby.

When near thirteen years of age he is sent to Flushing, L. I., that he may be entered as pupil under the charge of William Augustus Muhlenberg, prince of philanthropists, who made an early start in his career of blessing, when he gathered about him a band of young disciples that they might be trained in knowledge and religion. By means of this, as well as later agencies, the head of the Flushing Institute inscribed an indelible mark upon his generation. Even at this late day Dr. Muhlenberg's school is not forgotten. Not infrequently one hears a reference to it, made in conversation; whereby it becomes apparent that the influences flowing thence have not yet passed away.

From the contents of letters—to which access has been kindly granted—we may gain a glimpse of the daily life at Flushing. The young student stands well in his classes; he exercises good judgment in the choice of his companions; he gains the express approval of the venerated instructor. From another source comes the further information that already a strong musical talent begins to manifest its presence in the youthful mind.

The mother, who loves as mothers do, opens her heart to the boy; she writes about the burden laid upon her by his recent departure from home.

BROOKLYN, Dec. 6, [1832.]

MY BELOVED BOY:

Your letter to your aunt gave us all a great deal of pleasure; I say us, for she was in the city. . . .

Thank you for the compliment you pay my letter. I should, my son, write much oftener; but to be candid, I don't feel quite as well after writing to you. The sacrifice I have made seems greater than I at first thought, and I almost shrink from the idea of our separation. Yes, my love, this is indeed the first birthday you have ever passed from home.

You were born a few months after the death of your eldest brother. He was everything that was good and estimable. When he died, I was afflicted, greatly so; but when you came, the void in my affection caused by his loss was filled up. With his name you appeared to inherit his amiable disposition, and I hope, also his talents. You will think I am dull.

We look forward with pleasure to the Holidays, when we hope to see you with your friend. I am sure I shall like him. Young as you are, you have always shown great discernment in the choice of your companions.

Don't, my love, expose yourself; your health is by no means robust.

God bless you, my dear John, and may you ever be the delight and comfort of your parents and friends as you are at present, is the prayer of your mother

ANNE M. TUCKER.

As we read and ponder the fervent messages, perchance the reflection may arise: " He could not help being a good boy when he had a mother like that—so loving, so trustful, and so sensible in her advice." Verily blessed are the sons that have a mother of the like capability, manifesting force and clearness of mind as well as enduring strength of heart!

The words now transcribed were written for private reading; but as both mother and son lie in their graves, it may not be accounted a breach of confidence to unveil their little conferences, immortal by virtue of heartful charm, and affording lessons of benefit for them that shall come after.

In the letter next following there is an especial trait of downright motherliness, in the passage where the writer refers to an article of clothing as having been made according to a style worn by the father, and this she knows will go straight to the heart of any boy.

BROOKLYN, June 1st. [1832]

My Dear Boy:

I have been prevented answering your last letter by an indisposition, which though slight, still from the unpleasantness of the weather I found some difficulty in getting rid of. This is the first day in two weeks that I have been able to write a line. I had flattered myself to have seen you before this; several days have been named for our family, with Mr. Carter's, to have paid you a visit, but something always turns up to disappoint us; then I was sick, then it rained, and then the gentlemen were engaged —thus has hope been deferred till I have lost all patience.

Today is to be your examination, I am told. I am confident of your doing your best, therefore am determined to be satisfied, whatever your grade may be. Don't think I wish you to relax your exertion to gain an honorable rank; but should you fail, don't think mamma and the rest of us will be mortified. Let me repeat it again, we know you will do your best.

It is really provoking that your bundles so often are detained. I always prefer Saturday as being the day when you are most at leisure, and the papers &c. will be acceptable. I have sent you this week the Monthly Repository. Fanning continues as much pleased as ever with his school. He hurt his hand, which will account for his not having written lately. The little girls are confined home with bad colds.

We purpose should the weather be fine, to have the little boys baptized next Wednesday morning at 11 o'clock. Do you think it would be possible for you to come down on this interesting occasion? They have both had colds, but have recovered.

Your Aunt M. has gone over to see little John. You never mention your nephews; their Mammas take it quite as a slight. I have a new stock for you, and have had a new shirt made for you to try, *full-bosomed* like your Papa's. I don't send them up, as I wish to see them tried on.

Here is a delightful bit of nature, the unfolding of a homelike affection; but the interest ends not with that. Here one may gain a view of the customs and manners of the second decade of the century. Would that a portrait were available, showing the youth, just waking to manly view of things, and clad in stock and ruffled shirt front! What luxury to him to come so close to the appearing of his ideal of human dignity!

But after the delivery of the message, of high import to the lad at school, the handwriting of the letter changes, and the father adds a postscript:

You see, my dear boy, that I am occasionally obliged to give your letters a finishing stroke. Your mother, as the day is fine, has gone to take a short ride. I think it uncertain if the children are baptized on Wednesday, as they both have colds. We had papers &c. put up for you, but have not an opportunity of sending them to the city; this you will receive through the Post Office.

Fanning went yesterday to Fort Hamilton, with the Kings County Sunday-school in the steamboat and safety barge. There were upwards of 5000 children. They passed a happy, delightful day. They had the Navy Yard band. Major G—— received them at the fort, had seats prepared for them, and every thing in handsome style.

Your letter, my dear boy, I received. This I do not consider as an answer, but intend writing you again shortly. All join in much love.

The matter of the student's standing receives attention in more than one epistle. Here, for example:

BROOKLYN, April 17.

MY DEAR BOY:

Your report has at length reached us, and a brilliant one it is, far, far above what I expected, though your last letter led me to anticipate something clever—but first rank, first grade, it is too much! If it had not been in Mr. Muhlenberg's own hand, I should have thought there might have been a mistake. Don't you think, Jackey, Lent has had something to do with your success? I shall really begin to be an advocate for simple diet (particularly when we have an object to attain.)

I am happy to find that all the days prescribed by our

Church, are so strictly kept at the Institute. You are right too, in changing the day of writing home; it has always been a matter of surprise why you should have selected Sunday.

I have nothing new to tell nor interesting to send you. Your sister Sarah has a periodical paper called the Casket, which she intends sending you, perhaps on Saturday. My respects to Mr. Muhlenberg and Mr. Seabury, and may you continue as now to be the delight of your parents and friends, is the prayer of your affectionate mother

ANNE M. TUCKER.

I intended sending this by the stage with your clothes, but it rains so hard; have therefore concluded on this by mail. Tomorrow you may expect a bundle. All the family desire their affectionate regards to you.

The art of music already comes into prominence. In a letter dated February 12 the good mother writes:

I think if you could without interfering with your more important studies learn the Pianoforte sufficiently to play an accompaniment, you would find it a source of great amusement. This, with the little knowledge you already possess and your great fondness for it, you will be enabled to do without much labor. And if Mr. Muhlenberg should not be able to obtain a teacher, why, during the vacation Mr. Boyle can give you lessons. I am quite anxious to hear how you make out with chanting.

The matter of chanting—even in regard to plain canticles or psalms—was then somewhat of a novelty in America.

The date was not far removed from the time when chanting was altogether unknown among us. The pre-revolutionary incompleteness of ritual had been perpetuated. Canticles as well as Psalter were read in ordinary voice. The issue of the Prayer Book in 1789 was framed to fit the use, or lack of use; hence the American rubric in the Post-communion allowing a metrical hymn to be sung in place of the *Gloria in Excelsis.* It was felt that some musical utterance was demanded in a service of high thanksgiving, but the whole American Church could sing nothing other than metrical psalm. It was not until many years later that Peter Erben, the organ-builder, played the accompaniment to the first singing of the *Venite* in the City of New York.

As in every case of reform or restoration, the subject became more or less a *quaestio vexata.* There was agitation among the Church folk about the innovation which had disturbed their peace.

There is no doubt as to the stand taken by Mr. Muhlenberg. An " Evangelical Catholic "—to use his own phraseology—he was keenly alive to the æsthetic side of religion, recognizing poetry, music, and painting as pertaining to the " beauty of holiness." Years before, during his diaconate, when he served as assistant to Bishop White at St. James' in Philadelphia, we are told that he formed a choir and published a collection of chants for their use.

When the " Institute " came into being, music was assigned a commanding position as a powerful auxiliary working toward the devotional mood. The wise Head-master lived out the Church year

2

after a fashion before unknown in the experiences
of the new land. He marked days and seasons,
upon occasion by sunrise services, by emblems and
lighted candles, by evergreens and flowers, but in
particular by hymns and carols and by appropriate
chantings.

Dr. L. Van Bokkelen had been for fifteen years
connected with the Institute and St. Paul's College,
first as pupil and then as teacher. Afterward he
writes:

It was the poetry of which evangelical truth was the
concrete. The Chapel was brilliant on the great festivals
with candles and emblems. At the Christmas services a
picture of the Virgin and Holy Child was placed above
the altar, wreathed with holly. On Good Friday, a picture of the Crucifixion, with drapery of black. On Easter,
O how glorious the service which began with the rising
sun! There were the bright lights and the fragrant
flowers ; among these always the calla lily and the
hyacinth.

Anne Ayres in her biography, referring to the
" peculiar services " of the College Chapel, quotes
Dr. Muhlenberg in one of his later utterances: " If
we practised more or less of ritualism, it was certainly not of the Romish type, but the product of
imagination in accordance with the verities of our
religion. As educational means, I believe these
services had only a happy effect on the minds of
the young, though some of my brethren in the
ministry, formerly my pupils, say that they were the
germs of their present taste for Churchly ceremonial and ornamented services."

John I. Tucker was all ready for the impressions which moved so many other young minds. Is it any wonder that he should follow in the footsteps of the saint who went before?

According to the testimony of the same Sister Anne, there was a " Choir of the School," appointed and drilled for leadership in Psalmody. Long after the period of which we speak, reference was made to the fact in a Convention Address delivered by Bishop Bedell, himself an alumnus of Flushing Institute. The Bishop is paying a tribute to his " dear old Master," and to the educational work accomplished by him:

During these years Dr. Muhlenberg laid the impress of his character upon some eight hundred boys. Those who survive are now men, most of them in positions where they touch the very springs of society, and direct the forces that are moving this age. One has played his part well in diplomacy, and still is yielding political influence. [Here a footnote gives the name John Jay, ex-Minister to Austria.] . . . Another, the sweet boy-singer, leader of the school choir, is now heard through his hymnal in hundreds of our churches and leads the devotion of thousands of souls as he learned to do when we were boys together at Flushing.

Here, again, a footnote identifies the reference this time recording the name " John Ireland Tucker, D.D., of Troy."

One can imagine the fresh avidity with which the youthful disciple would enter into this new garden of delight. He found himself in an atmosphere made glorious by tone and color. The tendency to which he surrendered himself fitted in with his natural temperament, his inborn love of music, and his lifelong devotion to the ideal majesty of that act which attempts to offer adoration to the high God. Gladly did he journey along the prescribed path. Æsthetics were never foreign to him, and he received his Catholic training from the Evangelical Master. As said Bishop Coxe, when the writer was conversing with him about the boyhood of Dr. Tucker: " Yes, Dr. Muhlenberg ' made ' him." In the Flushing days the bent was set which lasted to and through the end of the earthly life.

It has been written of the Monastery of Bec, school of Lanfranc and St. Anselm, that the enduring quality of its influence, and the brilliancy of its fame, were out of all proportion with the short term of its existence. So it may be said of the Flushing Institute during the brief period which covered its original condition. The effect seems incommensurable with the cause. Yet the reasons are not far to seek: the one man, the exceptional mind and heart, at the head of the establishment; also the wise methods adopted for the accomplishment of his ends.

Again, it is said of the same school at Bec, that it got its influence from the moral training there bestowed. It assigned a place of preëminent importance to moral and religious culture, while it did not forget the training of the intellect. Nowadays the tendency of systems of education is to drop out the moral. Not so with the Institute, where the Principal cared first of all for the religion of Christ, and defined that as including morals and sound learning.

Music is referred to yet further in the correspondence dating from the Flushing days. Says the father, writing on June 5, 1832: "I long to have a sing with you and Mr. Muhlenberg, and shall surely come and spend a Sunday with you for that purpose, as well as to ascertain whether you have gone ahead of St. Ann's choir in chanting the Church services." Was it possible that the example of the Institute had extended to Brooklyn, by way of the pupil and his musical father?

Again, on the 24th of December, 1833, the same writer speaks first of the child sisters at home who are "one, two, threeing at the piano." He incorporates a message: "Mr. Taylor, our organist, has politely said that he will yield the organ to you for a Voluntary, or a Psalm or so, when you come among us at next vacation." The musical programme for the Christmas services is mentioned as a matter of mutual interest. "Our music to-morrow, besides the ordinary portions, will be in the morning Kent's *Jubilate* and the *Gloria in Excelsis* of Mozart, introduced by the recitative, 'There were Shepherds'; in the evening, 'Go forth to the Mount,' to words composed by my friend Mrs. Embury, expressly for the occasion."

It is likely that the youthful singer was identified, not only with the choir of his school, but with that of St. George's parish in Flushing, of which Mr. Muhlenberg was Rector for a while. There, by an act far in advance of his period, the latter had introduced the singing of boys. So it would appear from a letter written recently by James S. Biddle, Esq., of Philadelphia, who in his youth was a pupil of the Institute. He says:

Flushing has a peculiar interest for me as I was confirmed more than 60 years ago in the old St. George's Church which is now in the rear of the new Church. And, writing to a musician, I must also confess that I was tried for a while in the choir and was not a success.

There is every likelihood that the " sweet boy singer, leader of the school choir," was a participant in the new venture at St. George's Church.

Mr. Biddle gives his remembrances of the old school-days as he writes, on February 5, 1896:

I was at the Flushing Institute under Dr. Muhlenberg from 1829 to 1833. Dr. Tucker was there with me, but I find that his name is not on the Catalogue of January 1st, 1831. He came probably in '31 or '32.

He was a very interesting and lovable boy, bright and handsome in appearance and a general favorite. Dr. Muhlenberg always tested the musical capabilities of a new pupil and of course soon discovered those of " Jack Tucker " as we always called him.

After leaving school, our paths led different ways, and I met him only two or three times during the sixty years before his death.

*   *   *   *   *

In 1889 I revisited the Flushing Institute after an absence of 53 years.

Yet another glimpse of youthful days, having to do with a momentous topic. The father writes to his " dear son " from New York, on the 9th of

January, 1834. . After a reciprocation of New Year's wishes, he continues:

I see that the Bishop is to administer the rite of Confirmation in the Chapel on Ash Wednesday, and you desire my opinion as to the propriety of your presenting yourself on the occasion. You are doubtless aware of the true character of the ordinance, and I myself should be willing to leave the subject to the exercise of your own judgment. I think you have attained sufficient age and discretion and cannot see any objection to your being confirmed. Yet if you have doubts which Mr. Muhlenberg cannot remove, then defer it, for it is neither necessary nor proper to be hasty in such matters. Upon the whole I hope you will prepare yourself and with a safe conscience be able to present yourself to the Bishop.

From your affec^{te} father

F. C. T.

P. S. I cannot but be delighted with your standing.

But the time draws nigh when the student must be promoted. The step is prefigured in one of the few letters at hand, written by himself:

FLUSHING INSTITUTE,
April 27th, 1834.

DEAR PAPA:

On my last visit, you mentioned that I had not said anything concerning that part of your last letter which had reference to the sentiments of Messrs. Muhlenberg and Seabury, respecting Columbia College and University. I have not yet spoken to either of the gentlemen, but will do so in due time.

Mr. Muhlenberg has informed me, since my return, that it is his intention to relinquish his present institution, on the first of August. He says he wishes it to be understood, that he does not then retire altogether from the instruction of youth; but that, after 18 months or two years, he will commence his contemplated St. Paul's College. In the meantime he will collect funds, and in other ways prepare for the establishment of his aforesaid college.

I hear that your horses still continue to please as much as ever. When you come to Flushing, I shall not be ashamed to own you.

    *   *   *   *   *

A person is now singing to the pianoforte. Therefore excuse the business faults of this epistle of your attached son

JOHN I. TUCKER.

III

COLLEGE DAYS—PREPARATIONS FOR A TOUR

The next stage of life is passed within the walls of Columbia College, where our student entered the Sophomore class in the fall of 1834. About the same time the entire family moved from Brooklyn to New York—except the fond mother, who had been called to go up higher.

College association begets congenial companionship. One of the intimate mates was John Jay, one year in advance of John I. Tucker, the former graduating in 1836. In later times John Jay became famous as lawyer and statesman, Minister to Austria, and Chairman of a Civil Service Reform Committee. A quartet of young men in New York were linked together in the bonds of especial friendship and in constant companionship. Two of these were Jay and Tucker, the others, Arthur C. Coxe—as his name appears upon an early Seminary catalogue—afterward the honored Bishop of Western New York, and John Henry Hobart, son of the former Bishop of New York. The members of this informal club were happy when they met together, severally or collectively. After their dispersal a diligent correspondence was carried on for a longer period than that devoted by most young-men friends to the service of the post office.

The class of 1837 graduated twenty-three in number. Samuel Blatchford was at the head, gold medallist by virtue of "general excellence." Later he rose from one judicial position to another, until he became Justice of the United States Supreme Court. John I. Tucker was among the elect; he was a double bronze medallist, receiving the two awards in special departments.

In an old scrap book, loaned for the purpose, I discover an undated cutting referring to the ceremonies of Commencement for the year. It will be worth while to see how they did these things sixty years ago; accordingly I venture to transcribe a portion of the article:

For the New York Daily Express.

COLUMBIA COLLEGE.

By invitation of a friend, I attended the annual Commencement of this institution. St. John's Chapel was crowded with the youth and beauty of the city, and everything was as favorable as the most ardent wish of the young men who were to receive the honors of the day could have made it.

I was particularly struck with the dignity and urbanity of the President, whom I had never seen before. He appeared to me to be a model of what an instructor of young gentlemen should be—able both to command respect, and to win confidence and affection. The prayer, at the opening of the exercises, was beautifully appropriate.

The literary exercises of the day were generally creditable to the young gentlemen who performed them, and to the College. The Greek Salutatory Poem, by Samuel Blatchford, was very beautifully and forcibly pronounced, so much so, that although I could scarcely make out the sense of a single line, I should not have been weary of it had it been twice as long as it was. The Latin Salutatory, by Charles Aldis, was also very well spoken, though it did not sound quite so musical to my ear as the other. The English Salutatory, by Nathaniel W. Chittenden, was a good performance, but not so well pronounced as it might have been. Indeed, I felt during the performance, that the gentleman was not doing himself justice. He made too much effort, which led him often to an incorrect emphasis and an unfortunate intonation of voice. His subject was " The Influence of Woman upon the Destinies of a People," and to his credit be it said, he had the good sense—while elevating woman to her appropriate sphere in society, to steer clear of fulsome adulation and unmeaning flattery. The oration on " The Poetry of Life in Modern Times," by Henry B. Fessenden, was excellent both in composition and delivery. The whole was highly poetical, and his contrast between the ancient and modern " Poetry of Life " particularly beautiful. . . . " The Limit of Civilization," by John I. Tucker, was very fine, one of the best performances of the day, both for sentiment and style of composition.

The Valedictory, by John Vanderbilt, Jr., scarcely equalled my expectations. By itself it would have been very creditable, but as the choice performance of so good a class, it did not appear so well. The farewell to his classmates was too cold and hortatory. An occasion which should have called for the expression of every kind and warm sentiment of the heart, was improved only as an opportunity of giving 'sound and wholesome advice to his classmates, whom he addressed as " gentlemen."

The music did not please me. It was a perfect chaos of sounds. It might have displayed great skill and science, but it did not touch the heart, neither did it well befit the sacred character of the place. If they would have the thing done as it should be, I would commend them to the Boston Brass Band.

According to the principles of internal evidence it may be determined that the critical writer of the article was a woman. She had an ear for music, for she liked the oratorical flow of the Greek verses, despite the fact, as she modestly phrases it, that she " could scarcely make out the sense of a single line."

Readers nowadays will be surprised to learn that the commencement exercises were held in a Church building belonging to the corporation of Trinity. From another article, printed soon after, it will appear that the occupancy of the Church was apparently unprecedented; it will be seen also that the music—at which offence was taken—found advocates in its behalf. An epistolary contribution is published in the *Evening Star :*

COLUMBIA COLLEGE.

MESSRS. EDITORS:—Having observed no notice in your valuable journal of the late Commencement of Columbia College, and thinking that some remarks thereon may be as interesting to some of your readers, as they are due to the reputation and intrinsic merits of an Alma Mater, which has reared her head above all difficulties and discouragements among the prouder seminaries of our land, allow me, though it be with a feeble hand, to dwell for a few minutes on its late celebration. Some such notice appears to be the more needed as in one respect at least, unmerited censure has been passed upon it by many of your contemporaries. I refer to the music. It has been said that " a poor and meagre band " supplied the place of the " rich and powerful organ " of St. John's Chapel. Be it known to the good citizens, in extenuation of this, that it was with the greatest difficulty that the chapel could be procured at all for the exercises of the day; and that when procured, it was only given one short week previous to the anniversary, and even then with an ill grace unbecoming the grantor. Of course it was out of the question to suppose that an effective choir could be engaged and rich music prepared in the space of one week; and as the Church was again and again refused by the Bishop of the Diocese early in the month of August, the senior class were forced to turn their attention to other sources than the sacred music of the Church. Let the blame then, if any blame there be, fall upon those who refused the use of the Church until it was too late to engage music appropriate to the place.

But again, when before was the rich music of Gambati's trumpet called " poor? " When before were the " Remembrances of Mozart," the " Overture to the Messiah," " Von Weber's Last Waltz," and similar strains, as performed by a large and skilful band, censured as being " meagre and weak? " Surely some strange infatuation has taken hold of our New York critics. The music, for intrinsic beauty and execution, was rarely so effective as at the late Commencement.

Besides, an organ sounds very poorly unless accompanied by a powerful choir. To engage one which would do honor to the occasion would insure an additional expense of near 250 dollars, while the very finest instrumental music would not cost more than 100 dollars. This is some object when it is remembered that the expenses of Commencement are not less than $600, as we know by former experience, exclusive of the dinner of the senior class—all which expense is borne by the graduating class, with the pitiful exception of $140, which sum is presented by the College. Let them not censure, then, the seniors for inappropriate music, at least until the College increase their donation and pay their moiety of the expense.

Let us glance for a moment at a subject more pleasing —the literary exercises of the day. They were such as to do full credit to the untarnished fame of old Columbia. The example so nobly set forth to the other universities of our country, we believe for the first time, by the graduating class of 1836, in exhibiting their classical attainments by a Greek and Latin poem, was worthily followed up on Tuesday last, reflecting no less honor on Messrs. Addis and Blatchford, than exhibiting in a marked light, the abilities and attention of without doubt the greatest classical scholar of our country, Prof. Charles Anthon. Her classical advantages have always been the boast of Columbia College, and fully have they been realized.

Among the pieces exhibited were many that struck us as peculiarly beautiful both in thought and expression. . . .

An oration on " The Limit of Civilization," was happily conceived, beautifully written and feelingly delivered by Mr. John I. Tucker. We like to see young men carried away by the enthusiasm of their subjects. It shows that their hearts are not rendered callous to all noble excitement by contact with the world. Well may their Alma Mater be proud of her sons, if all she yearly sends forth from her venerable portals, advance upon the stage of life, with the talent and the feelings that were displayed on Tuesday. . . .

No reason has old Columbia to hang her head at her late anniversary. Long may her fame and the abilities of her graduates attract the attention of the fair, the venerable and the great. Long may she be honored and revered as the Alma Mater of names distinguished alike in the walks of private and public life—at the bar, in the pulpit—in the senate house.

Long may she remain the pride of our city, unsurpassed in the various departments of literature, unequalled for the reputation and abilities of its Faculty, and for its opportunities of a classical education.

H.

It seems only rightful that the topic of music should be discussed in connection with the Commencement at which John I. Tucker was graduated.

As to the two opinions about the performance: " H " shows by his reference to the " rich music of Gambati's trumpet " that he was yet in a certain preliminary stage of musical development akin to that of parishes or concert audiences wherein the cornet is accounted the choicest instrument for solo use. So it was once with reference to the trumpet. Time was when the latter was called for on all occasions where music had high place. The hearers of stalwart nerve waived the objectionable blare, and considered themselves fortunate possessors and encouragers of lofty art. On the other hand, the independent thinker who writes the first article had nerves of her own, and so called for the Boston Brass Band itself.

Having graduated with credit, our young man begins to take a place in society, to make his mark in the social world, remembered to this day.

At the same time the attention is directed to topics higher and more serious. On the 23rd of September, 1838, his grandmother writes:

I believe my grandfather, John Ayscough, was the first Missionary that was sent out to this country after Quebec was taken by the English; after that he was Dean of

Bristol. . . . I see at times that his prayers were heard, at the throne of grace, in my behalf, and that I now receive a blessing from; I know of no other that ever put up a prayer for me. I hope my dear Son, your mind is fixed for the ministry. God intends you for it. You have my prayers for you. They may be heard when I am laid in the dust. May you, like me, look back and say—" My grandmother's prayer is heard in my behalf," as my dear old father's was for me. My father was a surgeon of the British service; was stationed on Governor's Island. He died in the year 1761. My uncle, Capt. James Ayscough, in the time of the revolutionary war, had command of the ship " Swan "; in an attempt to land on Long Island, he lost his leg. He retired; had a fine family. His son is now in the British navy. He had a daughter by the name of Harriet, about the age of your mother.

Your affectionate grandmother

A. SANDS

So good " Saint Ann " patron of the Brooklyn parish, makes her petition. It is well known that the mother also had hopes that her boy would enter the ministry. One of the pet names chosen by her to designate him will show the constant wish of her heart.

It will appear, however, that the young man had not yet made up his mind. Doubts must intervene, uncertainties about his vocation. There was to be a balancing of many questions before a decision could be reached.

The father said, " Let the boy go out and see the world. Let him judge for himself and then decide."

With brief delay the parental prescription was

carried out with a completeness unusual in human experience, whether of earlier or later times. Even now, when Americans are on the move continually, when a considerable fraction of them cross the great water every spring or summer, it is not customary to undertake a tour so grand that it shall occupy two years in the doing.

Preparations were in progress. It was agreed that young Samuel B. Whitlock, a college classmate, should be a travelling companion, but the father wished that some older head should be in the party, to act as adviser of the little company. Dr. Seabury and others were approached with the inquiry whether one or another would care to undertake the trip. Among the rest Dr. Muhlenberg was asked. His reply is at hand:

My Dear John:

From my continued connection with the Institute—which probably you have noticed in the papers—I fear you and our friend Whitlock have inferred that my going to Europe has been all a jest. Such, however, is not the case. I scarcely hoped at any time to sail this fall; and my renewed superintendence of the Institute (in which I have engaged rather than allow the school to be disbanded, to the disappointment of a number who calculated on its continuance until the opening of the College) will last no longer than the spring, when I hope to be able to realize the pleasure so long desired of seeing the old world. This, however, will still depend upon the contingency of my success in regard to the erection of the College. I expect to see the building resumed early in the spring, so that it may be continued and finished in my absence. In this I may be disappointed, and my voyage again be postponed—for I could not leave the country until things were in train for the completion of the College. Too much time would be lost if that were to be begun *after* my return from Europe. I am in *great hopes* of being able to get off in the spring, but I cannot speak with any more certainty. I have thought it proper to state the case to you, in order that if you are in earnest in wishing to accompany me, you may calculate accordingly. If you meet with an earlier or more certain opportunity, I would advise you to take it; but you must not misunderstand me in saying this, to imply that I should not regret the loss of your company—on that point you need have no doubt. If you are satisfied with *my* company, I certainly shall be with yours ; but the former, I suspect, requires a little more consideration than you have given it. Two gay young fellows going to see the world, under the conduct of a parson, are not likely to have all the enjoyment they anticipate. Not, of course, that I would expect you to restrict yourselves in the way of amusements, etc., to what I might think proper for myself: but still, I fear that we might differ sometimes on questions of propriety. But of this we can talk more, when we meet, should you still think of waiting my uncertain movements.

Remember me kindly to Sam, and believe me

Sincerely, with much affection, yours

WM. AUGUSTUS MUHLENBERG.

PITTSFIELD, MASS.

    Sept. 4, 1837.

I expect to reach Flushing by Wednesday next.

The revered instructor and friend was sorely disappointed. He had to abandon all thought of travel on account of the death of his only and beloved brother, who had become his coworker at Flushing. Dr. Muhlenberg had to wait six years before he could find realization of his hope to visit

Europe, and then he went abroad only for a brief summer holiday.

The Tucker contingent intermitted not their preparations. No co-traveller, who would at the same time fill the place of director, could be found. At last said the father: " Let these two boys go by themselves; if they are not now old enough to take care of themselves they never will be." So it was determined.

While the plans were making, the attention of the future voyagers was directed to the possible benefits and satisfaction to be derived from the keeping of a daily journal. To Mr. Tucker a connection writes at length upon the topic, giving explicit suggestion. One part of his letter runs thus: " Keep a journal of everything you see and hear. Let this be done every day. Do not postpone it from day to day with the hope of posting up at the end of the week. If you do so, the interest and much of the benefit to be derived from it will be lost. The advantages of keeping a journal are so great that I would urge you particularly to attend to it. It will improve your habit of observation."

The date of the letter, April 31, 1838, will help to fix the time of the commencement of the grand tour as presumably in the spring of that year. Then began the long-continued wanderings over the continent of Europe, including the less frequented pathways in the Holy Land, in Egypt, and wherever there was something to be learned. Mr. Tucker made a temporary residence in Paris, and again in Italy, that he might study the languages of the respective countries under competent instructors. In the former capital he paid attention to the cultivation of the voice, under the tutelage of Lablache. So impressed was the instructor with the ability of the pupil that he urged the young man to prepare for the operatic stage.

The suggestions about a journal were remembered and reduced to practice. By way of witness we find two fragments, portions of journals of travel, among the manuscript papers now preserved. Would that there were more!

IV

THE FIRST JOURNAL OF TRAVEL

It would be interesting to note the many and diversified details of the grand tour, of phenomenal extent, but our attention must be limited to a small fraction of the whole. Fortunate it is that we have any record.

The earlier of the two journals is included in a little book whose pages are closely covered with manuscript. In these the traveller sets down his daily doings in so far as they relate to portions of the months from April to August of the year 1839, passed in the Orient and along the Danube. The entries in the journal are especially valuable, as they take the place of letters, ordinarily relied upon as the basis of biography. Herein the voyager tells his own story.

Already does it become apparent that the young student has an opinion of his own; he goes back of human actions and considers the explaining motive. On the 29th of April, at Cairo, he writes:

Accompanied by a Janissary we visited the Citadel. It is situated on a projecting point of Mount Mokattam, in the eastern part of the town. After passing the mosque of Sultan Hassan, you commence an easy ascent to the grand gateway, passing near the spot on which was perpetrated the massacre of the unfortunate Mamelukes. In considering the deed, so bloody and cruel in appearance, we should remember the cause that prompted the act, and the circumstances that compelled the manner in which the act was accomplished. Mahomet Ali, by forethought and perseverance had placed himself in the situation to which his ambition had long spurred him on; his enemies were all vanquished, save the single band of "white slaves." He had none to fear but them, but they were sufficient to deprive him of his hard-earned possession. In open warfare, they were invincible; their destruction was necessary for the protection of his throne and life. Secret means, *treachery* could alone effect the object. The mind untutored by religion's pure law is not liable to judge correctly of moral questions. Means to an end were not weighed by the rules of Christianity. The end was necessary—the means so far *good* as they effected the end.

We went through the Palace. The Divan was a large room about 140 feet long. The furniture of the whole palace reminded us all of the decorations of a country ball-room. The ceiling was decorated with paintings furnished by Greeks, generally representing the Pacha's fleet. They are now putting up in all the rooms, handsome chandeliers. The passages are lined with Egyptian alabaster, which has a rich appearance. In the large room, there is nothing but a divan all around the room, except a place on the side near the door, which is a kind of throne, or platform with a low railing, on which the Pacha reclines when receiving company. From the windows of the Divan, you obtain a fine view of Cairo and the environs.

In the Citadel the Pacha is building a splendid Mosque of Egyptian alabaster; the stone is rather too coarse. The Mint is as rude in its working as the metal is bad; in the gold coin there is about 75 per cent. of alloy; the "pressing out" of the metal is done by oxen. The men leave their work, and join the usual cry for "bakshish."

There are three or four pillars left of Joseph's Hall. The Pacha is at present building another edifice on its site. Joseph's Well, or the Well of Saladin is more singular for its size and depth than its good water; at the top it is 45 feet in circumference; the depth is 270 feet; you descend 120 feet by a kind of road, when you arrive at the first wheel, which is turned by oxen.

The Mosque of Sultan Hassan was visited next in order. We were obliged to take off our shoes, as in our churches we would remove the hat. We proceeded through a narrow passage, dirty and gloomy, ornamented with a few wooden lanterns and ostrich eggs. In a short time we arrived at a door leading to a court. Here we removed our shoes, and found ourselves in a wide court, in the middle of which was a large fountain. Opposite the door by which we entered, was a covered passage; along that side of the court, there was a pulpit, from which on Friday, the priest leads the prayers and adorations. Near the side of the pulpit is a door leading to what appears more like a Church than any other part of the building. In the centre is the tomb of the Sultan, which is surrounded by a railing. The ornaments of this chamber are exceedingly rude, approximating however to the Gothic style. On the floor, several spots were pointed out to us, as the blood of the Mamelukes. One of our friends who could not remove his boots without taking off his French pantaloons, soon after we left him made his appearance with rags about his feet. With all the toleration and kindness of Mahomet Ali, there is still some difficulty in visiting the mosques, without the protection of a Janissary, as nothing can remove the violence of a fanatic.

Mad-house. Going through a small passage off the Bazaars, we entered an open court around which were cells. There was a maniac in each cell. They were all miserably clad each with a chain about his neck. One poor fellow, a mere skeleton, appeared to droop under the weight of the iron collar, which hung round his delicate neck. A Nubian struck us all with the dignity of his air; it appears that he had, unprovoked, killed two men, one after the other. Even here we heard the universal cry of Arabs "Bakshish." The Pacha formerly had a band of Arab musicians to play for the amusement of the poor lunatics. Instead of bettering the condition of the inmates of the Asylum, by the introduction of cleanliness, kindness, freedom, etc.—the main features in the management of similar institutions in Europe—he satisfied himself by merely taking up something which struck him as being exceedingly singular. The rude, Arab music! The persuasive notes of Orpheus themselves, would find a Herculean task to tranquillize the wretches that here wear away a miserable existence. By particular favor, and by our providing some rolls of bread to bestow upon the women, we were admitted to the "female department," which was much worse than the one we had just visited. One poor creature really had nothing on her, except the iron chain. We were more startled by what we saw here, from the circumstance of our having visited previously the Pacha's lions and double-horned rhinoceros, which had princely habitations in comparison with the filthy asylum of these poor, unfortunate beings.

Slave Market. The same disgusting sight as at Alexandria! Here however we saw some Abyssinian ladies, quite pretty as well as costly—$1000—or $500—perhaps. These young women appeared quite happy, and anxious to fascinate a " Frank."

April 30th. Went to Tourah, and the quarries in the neighborhood, from which the stone was procured for the Pyramids. They are now worked by the Pacha, who has constructed a railroad in the neighborhood to carry the stone to the water. This railroad is perhaps one of the best in the world, but executed at an enormous expense; the Pacha instead of importing iron from England for £8 a ton is content to manufacture it for £40. A singular policy—independent, no doubt, but certainly an expensive system!

At Tourah is a military school for Cadets. The young men were engaged in drawing designs in engineering, and going through demonstrations of Euclid and calculations of Algebra. They study ten hours a day; the teachers are Turks, the principal a Frenchman. Everything, their dormitories, kitchen, eating room, accoutrements, are extremely neat and cleanly. Through the carelessness and ignorance of our Janissary, we could not find the Petrified Forest.

There are entries made in the beginning of May, first about the experience of a " horrible wind," by means of which some thirty or forty vessels were lost, houses blown down, and lives destroyed; again, about the performance given by a famous Algerine conjurer, professing occult power, who had deceived many, but who proved himself a mere charlatan. The next entry records the traveller's observation anent the pioneer of the recent incubating machine:

May 3rd. In company with Capt. McC. and his mate, we visited today the chicken ovens at Ghizeh. To get into them, we crept through a small hole, and found ourselves in an extremely warm and " fleay " place, a chamber about 20 feet long and five wide. On one side were ovens or small chambers, in which eggs were deposited; some were bursting the shell, others not so far advanced. On the other side of the passage were chickens just hatched, others three or four weeks old. They manufacture 4000 a month, and are employed all the year with the exception of four months. The chickens are all small, as is the case with the eggs in Egypt, which may account for the curious system of making hens.

The Cavalry School, at the same place, is well worth visiting. It being Friday—their Sunday or Holyday—the cadets were nearly all absent. The school is under the charge of a Frenchman, and is complete in every respect. They have a class in wind instruments. The horses are in good order, everything clean. The uniform is a green coat, ornamented with gold lace, and European pantaloons, made extremely full, of red cloth, with boots; it is really quite pretty. At old Cairo, we visited the ancient Church of the Copts, in which they show a spot, where—they say—the Holy Family reposed in their " Flight."

4th. Dined with Dr. Abbott; a real Arab or rather Turkish dinner—fingers instead of forks, etc. Introduced to the room of the Egyptian Library, a capital collection of books on Egypt. Rosonelli's drawings and paintings of the Tombs, etc.

5th. Furnished by Dr. Abbott with tickets for the Amateur Theatre here. The room is exceedingly well arranged; sufficiently small to secure a full house. There was much beauty among ·the Levantine women. The play was an Italian farce, extremely well acted. There were a man and a pretty modest-looking girl, who were public actors.

6th. Tomb of Mahomet Ali, or rather of his family. Much to our surprise, we found it all carpeted and arranged with divans. There were several tombs. Instead of the turban, we noticed the "tarboush" cut in stone, and placed on the exterior of the tomb, or on the headstone. The tombs themselves were gaudily painted; but notwithstanding this, I was taken with all of it. Here was no breaking of the social ties; no committing the body of a beloved friend to the sole company of gnawing worms. Here was a retreat, in which to mourn over a beloved parent, a faithful friend. It removes the gloomy thought of death; it keeps in remembrance the deceased. On our way home, we passed round the other side of the Citadel, and visited the tombs of the Caliphs and Mamelukes.

7th. Rode out to Shoubra Gardens—a perfect Paradise! Met the Pacha's post, going along on a donkey.

The gardens are beautiful, laid out in French taste. The Palace which the Pacha is now building or repairing, is exceedingly beautiful and well adapted for a summer residence. It is built in a square, forming a simple colonnade, with rooms at each corner. The palace is to be lighted with gas. It is tastefully gilded, and ornamented with paintings executed by Greek artists. The columns are of Oriental alabaster, the pavement of white marble. Near this palace, we saw ostriches and some gazelles. In the neighborhood of the gardens, the elephants are kept, which were presented to the Pacha by the East India Company. The Pacha doesn't like the present much; too expensive to keep the animals! He has endeavored to make them of use by carrying a steam-engine over to Suez; but it was " no go "! the animals could not move it.

8th. Went through the principal factories at Boulak—manufactories of arms, cotton, hardware, etc. The steam-engine has been found not to answer, and was consequently given up, for manual labor, three or four days ago. There is great difficulty in keeping the engine in order, in consequence of the sand which is almost always in the air, and the great liability to rust to which iron is subjected; something quite singular in this dry climate! Then again, there is much expense. To work an engine of twenty horse power, costs per day £6, whereas the labor of 300 men costs but £4, the highest wages being four piasters a day or twenty cents. The moving power is generally or universally, oxen. Throughout the different establishments, a cleanliness and niceness were observable.

Two days were spent in preparations for leaving. On the eleventh they departed, bound for Alexandria. The journal continues:

On the river the Pacha's steamer, being aground, endeavored to seduce some of our men, promising to tow us to Atfih if we could give them assistance; but we were too much of Yankees to be seduced by an Arab's promise, and left them to get off as well as possible with their own labor. We arrived at Alexandria, at midnight of the 14th.

15th. Early in the morning, left our boat and went to the Hotel d'Europe. All full! Obliged to go to Hill's Hotel, kept by Reynolds, situated pleasantly out of town. They say that it is an unhealthy place; commodious and clean. Today young Glidden dined with us—a clever fellow!

16th. A large party of us went on board the Pacha's corvette and one of the ship of the line. They were in beautiful order, the accommodations for the officers good but small. The decks are so arranged as to be very convenient for action. Visited the palace to see the Pacha, but it was too late; however, we had a sight of him sitting on a divan near the window, apparently earnestly engaged in conversation. The plague has broken out.

17th. Left in the French steamer, with 45 passengers. Found on board an American, a Mr. Calhoun, a missionary. 18th. The weather continues delightful; no sea. 19th. Weather still pleasant. A great contrast to what we experienced on our voyage from Civita Vecchia to Scyra. Mr. Calhoun we find an agreeable companion; in fact, our company is as agreeable as we could wish.

20th. Arrived at Scyra at 4 o'clock. Quarantined for 14 days, our passage included, in consequence of the plague at Alexandria. Before we left, a person said he had seen the funeral of a man who had died from the plague. Two men proceeded in advance, with swords drawn, and another with a wand, crying out in a loud voice to keep away.

21st. Still at Scyra. The Lazaretto here is so bad that we shall all go to Athens, with the exception of Clot Bey and others who sail for Malta. In the evening, left for the Piræus; arrived there early in the morning of the 22nd. At nine o'clock we understand that we had 17 days to perform quarantine. At twelve o'clock, left for our new quarters, situated behind the Custom House. Here we found everything much better than we had anticipated; the rooms are small for two or three persons, but at the same time convenient, furnished with beds, bedstead and sheets. We have a pier about 40 feet long, which affords us a pleasant place for exercise. Everything is extremely neat about the establishment. In front of the middle of the house is the " Parlertorium," a small, covered place, divided by three partitions. Communication with your friends is carried on through two sets of bars of iron. Along the front of the establishment, a few flowers are cultivated. We divided the rooms amongst eight of us, and are comfortably settled for 13 or 14 days. Each room has a guardian, under whose special charge are its inmates. You don't stir without being faithfully attended by him, as a prisoner by his gaoler.

22nd. Mr. Hill was here this morning, waiting for his wife, whom he expects daily from Constantinople. Mr. Benjamin and Mr. King likewise called to see us this morning.

23rd. Mrs. Hill has arrived, in a small vessel chartered at Scyra. A most ludicrous sight—the reception of her ladyship by her husband, who could not come within six feet of her, without subjecting himself to quarantine. 24th. Our prison is becoming quite gay. Mrs. Hill's friends are here constantly. Lady C., Mr. Leeds, Captain Forbes and hosts of children are here frequently. We have brought a *restaurateur* into quarantine and two servants, and consequently make out very well. 25th. We find our time well employed in reading, writing, eating and sleeping.

28th. On this day we had a slight shock of earthquake. I believe it is an everyday occurrence in the Morea. It afforded some excitement, and therefore was better than nothing.

31st. This afternoon we left our quarters at quarantine and our English friends. I hope I may never see the former again; the latter, it would afford me much pleasure to meet. As for Mr. Calhoun, our Missionary at Smyrna, we like him better each day. He is certainly an estimable man—I might almost say faultless, for so I believe he is. Mr. Hill came alongside to bid us good-bye. We had a delightful sail; passed by the tomb of Agamemnon. Ægina, once the rival of Athens, the place where they say money was first coined, was seen in the distance. June 1st. Arrived at Scyra at four o'clock this morning; our fourth visit to this curious place. A grand fête-day in honor of the King's saint. A royal salute was fired from the Greek gunboat, and from the five steamers (four French and one Austrian) lying in the harbor. The steamers all hoisted their national colors, and gave the harbor a gay appearance. We went on shore at eight o'clock. The Greeks were making preparations for a glorious time. Processions etc. were getting under way. Met Mr. Perdicaris our Consul at Athens, who has just returned from an excursion through the Morea. He speaks of returning to America; says that Greece will do for one or two days, and then tires. He longs for the luxuriant foliage of America. At two o'clock we left for Smyrna; saw in the distance Andros, Tenos, Delos, Paros, Naxos, Mycene. Delos is celebrated by the nativity of Apollo and Diana; Naxos interesting as being the spot where the heartless Theseus left Ariadne, his benefactor and lady-love. At twelve o'clock we passed along the coast of Scio; too dark to see objects.

June 2nd. In the morning found ourselves entering the Gulf of Smyrna. Delivered despatches to some vessels of the line (French) lying at anchor, about 20 miles from Smyrna. The English and French fleet are expected daily; they are to act conjointly in preventing an engagement between the fleets of the Sultan and Pacha. It is a beautiful sail up the Gulf, which is hemmed in by mountains on either side. It reminded us much of lake scenery, but the mountains are not like those of Scotland. About six miles off we saw the city, distinguished by a smoke rising up from its centre, and the dark foliage of the cypress. As we approached Smyrna, we distinguished two or three American flags; an English corvette and two or three Austrian vessels were lying off the city. The agent of the steamers came alongside and said we could communicate, there being no plague. We accordingly determined to land, and to remain a few days at Smyrna, and perhaps make an excursion to some of the seven Churches.

It will be noted that the traveller, although yet a youth, is well acquainted with his Bible; he knows " the mystery of the seven golden candlesticks." Although a young man of society, the very " pink of courtesy," still he cares enough for sacred subjects to seek out certain of " the seven Churches which are in Asia," to which St. John delivered the Revelation of Jesus Christ. The record proceeds:

At ten o'clock, we took leave of our friends on board the steamer, put ourselves and luggage in a small boat, and rowed to the American consulate; Mr. Oflin was absent from the city. We procured porters, who carried on their backs almost as much as a camel, and proceeded to Mad. Rosa's hotel. These porters are celebrated for the weight they can carry; sometimes they may bear 400 or 500 pounds. They have a padded apparatus fitting to the back, on which they place the heavy burden. As we walked up to the hotel, we were surprised to see the doors and windows of each house filled with beautiful faces. They appeared to have turned out to receive us; on inquiry, however, we found that it was no particular honor to us, but a universal custom of exposure on each returning Sunday. They were all beautiful, or at least appeared so to us, who had not seen a woman for some months.

They have a speaking eye, all eloquent, and love seems their only language. They were all prettily dressed. Braided in their dark tresses is the scarlet tarboush, richly ornamented with gold, forming one of the most beautiful head-dresses I have ever seen.

Mr. Calhoun saw us to our quarters; he met us again at four o'clock and took us to Church. They have a nice Chapel attached to the Dutch consulate. The pew of the consul was mistaken for a pulpit; over it are the arms of the Netherlands. There are four or five services performed each Sunday in this same chapel, and accordingly you find every variety of book of prayer in every variety of tongue. In our pew we had a hymn-book in English, a Book of Psalms in Greek, a Bible in French, the service of our Church adapted to the Church of the Levant, in Italian. The service on the present occasion was the Presbyterian. The Rev. Mr. Temple of America preached a very good sermon. The audience was not large, in consequence of most of the Europeans or Franks, at this season of the year, being in the country. Mr. Calhoun was kind enough to introduce us to the *congregation*. Dined at six o'clock; good dinner; amused ourselves the rest of the evening by seeing the people pass our door on their return from Caravan bridge—a grand promenade on Sunday.

3rd. Mr. Agger, a Missionary here, called on us this morning, and with Mr. Calhoun accompanied us through the bazaars. They are much better, as far as the building is concerned, than those of Cairo, though there is perhaps not an equal variety of Oriental goods. We wandered through the bazaars, passing through the heart of the city, and wound our way up along the streets, until we had almost reached the height of the hill on which the old city was built, when there came on a violent rain, which forced us to take shelter under the low hanging eaves of a house in the Turkish quarter. The rain continued so hard, that we were compelled to give up our ascent to the old castle; so we returned, and being somewhat hungry, went into a *café*, and regaled ourselves with a dish of Kabobs which we found exceedingly nice.

You constantly pass graveyards in the very heart of the city, beautiful and gloomy at the same time—with their cypress and poppy—like the hectic flush on the consumptive patient. In one of the large graveyards a place is walled up and kept as it were sacred, in consequence of a tradition cherished by the Greeks and feared by the Turks. There is the base of a fine pillar, which the Greeks say belonged to a Church dedicated to St. Peter. For a time, the Turks defiled the sacred spot, by burying there their unsacred carcasses. Night after night, St. Peter removed the bodies; the tombs were found empty, the bodies were found in the public road, and the Turks were compelled to respect the sacred spot.

Spent the evening at Mr. Riggs'. Mr. Calhoun has rooms with him. We met here Mr. Agger, and in company with him, Mr. Calhoun and Mr. and Mrs. Riggs, spent a pleasant evening. Their house is well built and pleasantly situated, so as to have a fine sea-breeze almost continually. Mr. Riggs has the reputation of being a very superior man, a capital Greek scholar, etc. We had intended to go to Ephesus tomorrow, but horses cannot be obtained. Perhaps it is all for the best; our friends were extremely opposed to our going, as there is great fear of the fever at this season of the year.

4th. Mr. Temple called on us this morning; he is something of a croaker, but, I believe, a good man. He has been fifteen years in the Mediterranean. Invited us to his house to spend the evening. Mr. Calhoun and Mr. Agger we see constantly.

In the evening took a walk with Mr. Calhoun, and passed along the barracks. Saw the soldiers exercising; a better looking set of men than the soldiers of the Pacha. Passed the Governor's house, and ascended the hill by the Jewish burial ground. The tombs consist of flat stones. There were some Turkish women taking the air, sitting on the tombs; I believe it is a fashionable resort.

From the top of the hill, we obtained a beautiful view of the town and harbor; the sun was just setting. The houses appear to be built one upon the other. You see the remains of an old Roman road, the site of the Stadium, the buttresses of the theatre and a part of its side, also a small part of the old wall. A solitary cypress with a tomb at its base, marks the spot associated with the martyrdom of Polycarp, who was killed on the Stadium. It was too late, so we hurried down through the Armenian quarter; being thirsty, stopped at a *café* and sitting down under a broad shady plane-tree, drank a capital cup of coffee.

5th. Remained in the house in the morning. At three o'clock, accompanied by Mr. Calhoun, we took a ride on donkeys to Bûja, a place where most of the English pass their summer. We had a delightful ride. Our road passed along by the celebrated Meles, near whose source tradition affixes the spot that gave Homer birth. It is a small stream except during the heavy rains, when it becomes quite a torrent. Passing round the castle we ascended the hill. We soon obtained a beautiful view of the valley of the Meles, "which by a livelier green betrayed the secret of its silent course." There was a rich luxuriance, a beauty of foliage, a gentleness or serenity which was extremely pleasing. At a distance we saw the Gulf. After passing the mountain, we reached a beautiful plain, and continued in it for a mile, until we reached Bûja. It is very pleasantly situated; the houses are particularly comfortable and neat in appearance. We went immediately to Mr. Halleck's, printer to the Mission. He has here a delightful summer residence, and an agreeable wife. Mr. Agger and Mr. Calhoun when here, live with him. Mr. H. received us very kindly, and introduced us to two American girls, one about 17, the other 35, I should think.

They have a pretty little chapel, which they have made from a room in the upper part of the house. We passed an hour here very agreeably. The donkey boy had gone off to feed his donkey, and we could not find him; consequently we were obliged to walk almost halfway home. We met many merchants, on their way to their country-seats. Mr. Calhoun and Mr. Agger dined with us, and gave us much information connected with the Mission here. Their influence is increasing so much at Constantinople, that many of the Armenians are frightened and commencing persecution. The Patriarch of the Greek, or of the Armenian Church, the Rabbi, and others of equal ecclesiastical right, have the whole and exclusive government of people of their nation—can banish, or punish them as they see fit. There is a Jewish prison in Constantinople, which has never been opened but to Jews. Having this power, persecution is an easy thing, and consequently they banish the disaffected of their Church. They have lately exiled two or three very estimable men, merely because they read and expounded the Bible; in word or action, they never slandered their Church. There is now here a young man, a converted Jew, from Constantinople. He was a protégé of one of the richest Armenian bankers. Some banking and other enemies to his patron, secured the exile of the protégé. He was sent to the interior of the country, with some of his friends. His journey to his place of exile was attended by every act of cruelty. The second day out, his sufferings were so great that he was obliged to bribe his attendants; this procured but a short release from misery. The next day he was obliged to bribe higher still. This system was carried on, on his arrival at his place of exile. He has been imprisoned one or two years, for the sake of Truth. This gentleman is staying with Mr. Agger, and assists in translations. . . .

7th. At six o'clock this morning took a walk to the Castle. Saw the head of Smyrna the Amazon; it is placed in the wall beside the entrance. The view from the Castle is very fine, taking in the bay, the city and the plain. Intensely warm; thermometer, 90. Went to a Catholic Church on our return home, attracted by a fine, pealing organ.

8th. In the morning, Mr. Calhoun took us to their book shop and gave us permission to select whatever books might please us. Their publications are all well got up. They publish a periodical in Greek, very similar to the Penny Magazine, of which they circulate from 1000 to 1500 copies. Last evening we took tea with Mr. Agger; met all the Missionaries; had quite an agreeable time. At three o'clock, we went on board the Austrian steamer, which we found overflowing with third-class passengers of all nations, who monopolized the whole decks. They were really of every nation, for we had on board Indians, Nubians, Arabs, Turks, Greeks, Portuguese, Italians, Poles and Americans. Our captain we like; he appears a good sailor, and gentlemanly in his manners. The breeze was a little fresh; threatened by a thunder and lightning storm. Arrived at Mitylene at two o'clock.

9th. Weather rather disagreeable. At twelve o'clock passed the plains of Troy; saw in the distance the mounds which they individualize as the tombs of Achilles and Patroclus! Soon afterward entered the canal; a fort is seen on either side ; at short intervals you pass six chateaus, two being always opposite each other. After dinner, passed Sestos and Abydos. Saw the place where Byron swam across. A young Englishman attempted the same feat lately, and entirely failed, losing his life. We find our captain a noble hearted fellow, and consequently our time passes pleasantly.

10th. At Gallipolis last night we saw part of the Turkish fleet—they are lying there to get in their stores —the Sultan being anxious to reduce his rebellious subject, Mahomet Ali, to obedience. Early this morning came in sight of a part of the Turkish fleet under sail, with two steamers. At 12 o'clock, passed around the point of Seraglio, and waited in the Golden Horn some time for the health officers. Constantinople with its domes and minarets equalled our expectations. The Porte had quite a lively appearance with its shipping and its graceful caiques which resemble somewhat a canoe in appearance but are more beautifully carved. We found, to our great delight, that there would be no quarantine, but that we must submit to a smoking. We thought we could escape this disagreeable ceremony by taking a caique, and rowing for the shore; this was " no go," for we had hardly left the vessel, before the health officer came after us, and in a great passion ordered us to the smoking apparatus. This was nothing but a miserable shanty, in the middle of which was a pan of coals, salt-petre, etc.; we were compelled to go round and round the fire, until our eyes were pretty well filled with dust. They did not consider it necessary to touch our clothes, so that we escaped without much vexation. Mad. Ro-boly's brother, who is attached to the health department, said that there were rooms to be had at her house, and accordingly we posted off there. We landed at Galata, a part of the town just below Pera, a most dirty filthy place. We crawled up the hill as well as we could, and soon arrived in Frank St., in which you see men promenading in every costume. We turned off from this street, and descending a steep hill, arrived at a small house which they pointed out as Mad. Roboly's. It was too late to get our letters.

11th. Obtained letters from our banker, Mr. Churchill. They were extremely satisfactory, and I don't know when I've been so happy. Mr. Churchill called for us at two o'clock, to take us to the opening of a Turkish theatre. A square was formed by wooden fences; on one side were boxes for men, on another for women screened from view by lattice work, on another side were rising benches for οἱ πολλοί. On the farther side was the orchestra, sit-ting on a small platform; their instruments, short pipes and noisy tambourines. The play was " The Opium Eater." In the beginning, dancing boys made their appearance dressed up as girls. Nothing can equal the low vulgarity of the piece throughout, as translated to us by Mr. Churchill. The audience seemed much amused with the low jokes.

Mr. C. made a large fortune by shooting a boy instead of a partridge; he was seized, beaten and imprisoned by the Turkish officers, for the offence, and afterwards recovered £5000 for the injury done. Called on Dr. Robertson who was formerly at Scyra, now stationed here as Missionary to the Greeks. He is exceedingly agreeable, as well as his wife and daughter. Called on Mr. Goodell to whom we had a letter from Mr. Calhoun.

12th. Made our first visit to Constantinople. We were much pleased with the immense extent of the bazaars, and the beauty of the articles which they contain. We became very much fascinated with the ladies' shoes, and made considerable purchases. We very much admired a pair which they offered us for 1000 piasters or $50. We lounged through a considerable part of the bazaars, and being somewhat fatigued refreshed ourselves with a dish of Kabobs, the elements of which are minced mutton broiled on a spit, sour milk and bread. After we had recruited ourselves, we went to the Hippodrome or At-Meidan. Here is an obelisk 60 feet high—erected during the reign of Theodosius—the remains of a serpentine column which was brought from the temple of Delphi, where it had supported the holy tripod. There are also remains of a brick obelisk or pyramid, which had been covered with bronze by Constantine Porphyrogennetus. We entered the " cistern of 1001 columns," which is in the neighborhood. It is a large reservoir, or was so intended by its builder Constantine. Instead of 1001 columns it has 224. This reservoir is now used as a weaving shop. By engagement, we met Mr. Brown an American, who was unfortunate in business in America, and now is endeavoring to support himself honorably here. By appointment we met at the tower, from which they watch for fires. The tower is high, but you are well repaid with a splendid view of the Bosphorus, the Porte, the Sea of Marmora, Galata, Pera, etc., and regaled with a capital cup of coffee and a chibouque. From the tower, we went to the bazaars, accompanied by Mr. Brown, who assisted us in our purchases. We were much amused in seeing the attempts of the Turks towards civilization. Their poor attempts reminded me of the passage in Shakespeare, where we read:

> As patches set upon a little breach
> Discredit more in hiding of the fault,
> Than did the fault before it was so patched.

Square-toed shoes, embroidered suspenders, badly made coats!—The Turks are in as bad a state as the Indians on the borders. Cairo is the city for oriental manners and customs. The shopkeeper generally takes half his original price.

Tea-fight at Dr. Robertson's. Took a walk with Mr. Goodell, the little Goodells and Robertsons, before tea, on the large burial ground. A singular fashion this in Turkey, to use a burial ground as a fashionable promenade! Gloom is banished from the abode of the dead; the deceased friend is not shunned; his tomb is made the resting place for his attached friend. Death instead of separating from a departed relative as a loathsome creature attracts by its silent repose.

13th. Took a boat and crossed over to Scutari; here we took horses and galloped up Mount Boulgourlou. The view could not be equalled. You see Constantinople in the distance, with its domes and minarets; rolling below you, the Bosphorus, its shores marked with numerous villages. At three o'clock, we went to see the " howling dervishes " in the town of Scutari. We were admitted into a small room, with a gallery running round two sides, one all screened, for women, like similar precautions in a Catholic Church for nuns. The walls were ornamented with tambourines, flags, and instruments of torture by means of which they formerly persecuted themselves; the Sultan at present prohibits their use. A railing runs round the room, leaving a way and place for the spectators; within the railing, mats of colored wool and

skins of various kinds, were strewed on the ground. In
a short time, they made their appearance, wearing their
usual dress—a tall, white conical hat and a loose gown.
They all engaged in prayer, and afterwards in turn kissed
the hand of the head dervish. The chorister then struck
up a dismal howl, and the rest joined in, in chorus. Their
music was accompanied by motions of the body, the
rapidity of motion increasing with the rapidity of the
music, till some poor fellows almost fell from exhaustion.
There was something horrible in their motions and atti-
tudes; the mind fairly sickened to witness it. The howling was carried on in fine style. It sounded much like
enthusiastic chanting in the Greek Church; the leader kept
time with his hands. It was not therefore an individual
howling, but a grand chorus. Before they parted, a child
was brought in. This is always done when strangers are
present, in order to prove their power of performing
miracles; they wish the people to understand that the
infant is sick and is cured. They are something of a set
of jugglers. I could not but think, that these poor fellows were working extremely hard for their living, and
all perhaps for naught.

14th. Rowed up the Bosphorus about six miles to see
the Sultan go to mosque. Soldiers were on duty at the
mosque, with a splendid band of music. At twelve
o'clock, his Serene Highness approached with his six
boats or caiques of state. These were very long and
beautifully painted and gilded, two of them being provided
with splendid canopies, with velvet and damask, also
mahogany sofas. Twenty oars! The Sultan arrived in
the third boat, attended by two Pachas, who escorted him
up the stairs to the mosque, the stairs being covered with
carpet. He looks like a man of decision, but not of much
energy; as he was quite unwell, complaining of a bleeding
from the lungs, I could not judge. He was dressed somewhat like a European, his breast being ornamented with
a splendid decoration. He returned in a carriage and six;
the carriage was a miserable old hack. As he entered and

left the church, there were crowds of people with peti-
tions, which the Sultan ordered his officer to collect. He
pointed out several poor creatures, and sent for their pe- .
titions. There were many distinguished people present,
Prince George of Cambridge and others. After this lion
was killed, we rowed up to the " Sweet Waters," which
is only two miles above. We were obliged to be pulled
through a very severe current before reaching the " Sweet
Waters." It is a beautiful place and was crowded with
Armenian ladies, who made their appearance on the
ground in " Arabans "—a long vehicle richly carved, with
cushions on the floor instead of seats, on which six or
seven women place themselves. This vehicle is drawn by
oxen, which are dressed off in grand style with looking-
glasses on their heads; from the pole, two sticks rise in
the air and project over the oxen, and to these sticks are
attached small tufts of different colors. Many women
were collected together, listening to some musicians and
story tellers. We were anxious to know what was going
on and approached them, but were soon stopped by several Turks, who from fear of their wives got into a great
excitement. I'm sure, we meant them no harm.

15th. Mr. Rhodes, Jr., called on us yesterday and invited us to the launch of a steamer and cutter, which took
place today. We had the pleasure of being launched on
board the steamer, which is a beautiful model. After the
launch, sixty persons dined at Mr. Rhodes'. Before the
launch, instead of breaking a bottle of champagne over
the deck and thus naming her, they sacrificed five or six
sheep, and sprinkled blood over the bow. The Astrologer
and Mufti were present, to mark the happy hour, and to
pray for the vessel's safety. The Sultan was too sick to
be present. At dinner, Mrs. R. wore a ring—which is a
present to Mr. R. from the Emperor of Russia, for a
model which he built for him—valued at $5000—being
an enormous emerald surrounded with diamonds. After
dinner we went on board the steamer; it is a beautiful
model and beautifully fitted up. In the steamer's pantry

was an abundance of champagne glasses, the Sultan finding that this wine is not forbidden in the Koran.

16th.   Went to the English Chapel.

17th.   We were delighted to hear this morning, that Prince George of Cambridge intended to visit the mosques today, with a firman.   When a firman is granted, all can go who wish.   We accordingly availed ourselves of the privilege of the rabble, and joined the crowd.   We picked up recruits as we went along; a motley group we were, our friend Prince George at the head, with his red cravat, green vest, blue coat and light pantaloons.   We were all obliged to wear slippers, or to pull off our boots on entering the mosques; this is for the sake of cleanliness.   They say that some years ago any one could enter St. Sophia, but an unfortunate Russian gave great offence by spitting on the carpet, and thenceforth a firman was necessary to procure entrance.   Many contented themselves by pulling their slippers partly over their boots, but many poor fellows in this way were left slipperless.   St. Sophia pleases by its immense dome, its open grandeur and historical association.   Achmet pleases by its great extent, its gayness of appearance, and beauty of its ornaments; Solymania from its extreme chasteness and symmetry.   St. Sophia has a gallery, as also Achmet, running in the first around the church.

Our friend Fleming arrived today, and is unfortunately put in quarantine for the same cases of plague which were reported at Smyrna when we left.

19th.   Called at the Lazaretto; saw Fleming and poor Mr. Hatfield.   They are as comfortable and happy as any one could be similarly situated.

20th—23rd.   Our time is filled up in rowing up the Bosphorus, visiting the pretty villages that line its banks, and in wandering through the bazaars.   Looking out of our window the other day while at dinner, being aroused by human cries, we saw a poor fellow who had been employed in dragging stone for the French palace, placed with his feet before the fire of a small furnace.   On enquiry, we found that the unfortunate fellow had pushed off a drunken soldier who had rubbed against him, and had been bastinadoed for the offence; his feet were much lacerated, and he was consequently placed before a fire to make the parts unite. 23d. Went to English chapel; afraid to visit Brusa, fearing a quarantine on our arrival.

28th. This week, visited New Palace, in company with Mr. Rhodes and all the Americans in town; had the pleasure of passing through a harem. Some of the rooms are large, and fitted up with much taste. Thence went to the Gun Factory; from this to Mr. Rhodes' and took a family dinner. Afterwards took a sail in his cutter. After tea we took a walk across the hills, and saw the place where the Mussulmans pray for rain. On one occasion the Mohammedans prayed in vain, and the prayers of the Christians alone availed to prevail with the Deity. The Turks got over the affair by saying that God was so tired of the Christian prayers, that He gave them rain immediately to put an end to their supplications. On the 27th there was a rumor that the Sultan was extremely ill; on the 28th that he was dead, and that a regency had been appointed.

July 1st. Left Constantinople in Ferdinand Primo, Captain Everson. Head wind; bad sea.

2nd. Arrived at Varna at two o'clock. Went ashore with the Captain. Visited the Pacha.—Well fortified by nature and art.

The unusual extent of the tour, and the enterprise of the travellers, are indicated by the route here set down. Even nowadays, when European trips are common, not many Americans will sail up the Grecian Archipelago, making an excursion into the classic regions of Asia Minor, then through the Dardanelles, familiar to schoolboys as the Hellespont, so reaching Constantinople; thence

again by steamer on the Black Sea, so as to enter
the river Danube by its mouths, well up on the
Russian border. The journal continues:

3rd. Arrived off mouth of the Danube, 3 o'clock.
Ten feet of water upon the bar. Vessels cannot take in
all their freight before clearing the bar. The banks of
the river are edged with rushes; occasionally you see a
house on props, surrounded by water on all sides: these
are the stations of the Russian guards. Passed two or
three gun-boats of the Russians.

4th of July. This day we celebrated in grand style last
year, in London. I am afraid it must glide by neglected
on this occasion, as our friends, our Captain and all
around us, are those who could with little pleasure enter
into our feelings. Arrived at Galatz at ten o'clock; cannot land without being subjected to quarantine. We lose
one of our companions here, *n Israelite, who has afforded
us much pleasure in discussion. He is well informed and
liberal. He was anxious to make an appointment with
us to have a public discussion at London.

Here, again, let a fact be noted. The writer of
the journal is yet a youth. Fresh from college, he
is interested in the site of classic story. Yet more,
he is mindful of the lessons learned at Flushing, as
also at his mother's knee. Religion is always an
attractive subject for him. He desires to visit the
seven churches, and he likes to enter into long
debate, upon the side of Christianity. It will be
remembered that he is not yet in holy orders or
even a student of theology; so far as may be known,
he has no definite plan of life; he is a young man,
very young, just entering upon a brilliant career
of fashion. Nevertheless, he is strongly interested

in the old-fashioned Bible.   The journalist continues his entry for the fourth of July:

We passed the day very agreeably. The dinner was merrified by a few bottles of wine, so that the day did not pass by entirely unobserved. At five o'clock we left for I——, two hours' sail from Galatz. Here we stayed all the evening, and were almost devoured by mosquitoes. They have almost realized our expectations; rumor said that they were as large as donkeys—I think that they approximate more to the snipe species. All were obliged to leave the cabin and to go on deck.

5th. It is extremely provoking, this detention! Here we remain at this dirty, overflooded town until four o'clock, when we leave in the Galatæa, which takes us to Orsova. We all were sorry to take leave of our good friend Captain Jack Everson; we bade him good-bye several times, and as we left gave him three cheers. This steamer, as well as the Ferdinand, was obliged to go up the river to make a turn; as we passed each other in the turn cannons were fired from either vessel. Proceeded on our way until dark; then lay by for the night. We are all provided with mosquito nets—still, I was sadly bit. We have no berths, but German spring-sofas.

6th. At twelve o'clock at Hirdsova; the river very broad. The banks begin to show some signs of life; they are prettily covered with foliage. 7th. In the morning at Silistria; lost three or four hours, taking in coals.

8th. At seven o'clock arrived at Rustchuk; went ashore and bought some pipe-bowls peculiar to the place—quite a pretty Turkish town! The news is here confirmed of the death of the Sultan. Who can tell the effects that this infliction of Providence will bring upon Turkey? Perhaps its day is over. The Janissaries may arise and take vengeance on the Franks; there are no troops in Constantinople, all are in Syria. Russia may come down and seize the city. We saw the Sultan go to mosque for the last time; he then appeared extremely ill. His decision of character, overcame all his opponents. A regency, at least a Turkish regency, is unfit to cope with the enemies of reform.

9th. Last evening anchored at 8 o'clock; this morning we arrived at Nikopoli—we were unfortunately all asleep. The river varies little; devoid of beauty and interest. We are amused by the immense droves of cattle that are seen on the banks; see an abundance of wild fowl, pelicans, etc. Stopped at Sistor—dinner time.

10th. Arrived at Widdin at ten o'clock. Paid a visit to the Pacha, one of the wealthiest in the kingdom; his salary is estimated at $3,000,000. Nearly all the passengers were presented to his Pachaship. We had in our company, our two French fellow passengers, the Armenian and his wife and a young German woman. The palace was nothing extraordinary in appearance. In the court-yard a number of beggarly soldiers were hanging about, sufficiently miserable in appearance to touch the feelings of a sensitive man. The palace formed a square; on one side the reception room of the Pacha, on another his harem, and on another the stable. After passing through a crowd of attendants, we were ushered into the reception room. The room was large; it showed signs of better days as the eye wandered around the walls. It had been once gaily gilded according to the Turkish fashion. A divan ran partly round the room; on the un-occupied sides were French satin bottomed chairs. The Pacha was seated in the farther corner. Nothing was visible but the trunk of his body; his feet were wrapped up so well under his body, that they were to the eye as good as none. The gentleman wears spectacles, and is possessed of a fine, grey beard.

We made our *salams*, and then were seated. The servants retired. A short conversation was kept up by the Armenian gentleman. A eunuch appeared, and the ladies were requested to follow him, and they repaired to the harem—something of a compliment to the young German chambermaid! The Pacha then gave a gentle tap of the

hands, and servants came in from a door on either side
of the room, bringing some jelly in beautiful French
china, some iced water in a similar vessel, and a silver
spoon for each of the company. Each spoon was filled
with the sweetmeats. The spoon was taken, its contents
devoured in two mouthfuls, and then a sip of cold water
was taken. This done, the Pacha again clapped his hands,
and a crowd of servants rushed in, each bearing a chibouque with a small brass pan to put the bottom of the
pipe on. These chibouques, about 16 in number, were as
splendid as any I ever saw, the amber exceedingly clear
and costly. My mouthpiece had a ring of diamonds
around it; I suppose the chibouque was worth $1000.
There were others equally beautiful. The Pacha smoked
a hookah of silver. Then coffee was served; the chibouques were removed, and the attendants made their
appearance again, bringing pipes whose jewels made the
room actually brilliant. These pipes have been valued
at £400 to £600. There were as many of these, as persons
to use them. We smoked our pipes and then retired,
highly delighted with our visit. We met the ladies without, who had just left the harem, where they had seen
three lovely women, one 50, another 20 and the other 35.

We saw a little Nubian who had come with us from
Galatz, destined for the harem of the Pacha, presented
to him. He first kissed his feet, and afterwards went
through other servile offices and retired.

We left Widdin at five o'clock; the batteries were firing
a salute in honor of the new Sultan. 11th. Proceeded
on our way only for a few hours, having been detained
for some time at Widdin. 12th. Thursday. Landed at
five o'clock. We here leave the Galatæa, and proceed to
Orsova by means of a small boat drawn by oxen, the current being too strong and the channel too narrow for a
steamer of 60 horse power. The river hourly increases
in beauty; from where we are now lying, a beautiful pass
is seen. The river seems to be suddenly changed into a
lake, whose surface is graced with two or three pretty

islands. The mountains that hem it in, in the distance, rise up one behind the other, forming seats in a mighty amphitheatre.

13th. Left the Galatæa. The Captain and the Engineer (Leay, a Scotchman) have made themselves as agreeable as they could. The fare however was execrable. We started off at five o'clock in a long boat, a cabin running the whole length, very roughly constructed of unplaned boards. We brought seats from the steamer. It was possible to sit on the roof of the cabin, and in this way enjoy the scenery. Going through the Iron-gate (a rapid falls) we were permitted to walk under the charge of a Servian soldier. The distance to Orsova is about fifteen miles, which we accomplished in nine hours, by the aid of oxen, sometimes 10, sometimes 22. We passed New Orsova, a beautiful town not far from Orsova, where was seen flying the Turkish flag; it is an island, I believe, and well fortified by nature and art. The river for these fifteen miles has been exceedingly grand; from its sides rise mountains richly coated with foliage, and occasionally decked with a golden crop of wheat.

Orsova is a smaller place than I expected to find. Ox-carts were in readiness to receive our luggage; neither the cattle nor their drivers were in quarantine—to keep the animals from becoming infected by contact, their tails were tied to a rope attached to the horns. Not much liking a half hour's walk, we jumped in the carts—the Armenian lady and all—and marched off with a guard in advance, and in our rear. The Lazaretto is about half a mile from Orsova, prettily situated in a small valley, hemmed in by high hills richly foliaged. The Lazaretto is a small village in itself. There are many houses, capable of accommodating from six to seven persons, with a large court surrounded by four high walls; to promenade around these houses, a road passes; a gate doubly barred and locked opens on this road, and through or at this door your friends disinfected converse with you.

On arriving, the director being absent the doctor presented himself, demanded our passports and desired us to follow him and receive our rooms. The doctor is a small man with a black beard, a hyena-ish grin, and a fencing master's air in flourishing his stick. He seemed inclined to pen us up, either like so many criminals or so many wild animals. Finally, all were lodged except Captain Bennett of the British Navy, my friend Bob Fleming and myself. They took us to a house where three of our friends were lodged. The doctor said that the house must contain seven persons. Three persons already occupied two rooms decently furnished; the other was to be our quarters. He opened the door; it was a miserable, dark, gloomy den, with nothing to conceal its earthy or brick floor but a platform which was intended for our bedstead. We told the doctor that it was a barracks, scarcely fit for a horse; that he ought to be aware that he was not dealing with malefactors or beggars but with gentlemen, one an officer in the English Navy; that we were here against our will for their convenience. He was insolent, as far as he was able with his meagre collection of French words and his menacing gestures with his cane. We told him that we would not occupy the room, but find another for ourselves. Presently one of my friends came in with the Armenian family; they desired to occupy the room to be near our party. They consequently took the den, but being only three, they wanted one more to fill up the number; for the doctor said that the room could hold four persons, and one of us must be one of the required four. We let him understand that his beastliness would not be countenanced by us, and turning our backs, looked until we found the best room left and occupied it. This was poor enough—the same sleeping accommodations; the room was larger, more light, and having a large yard. Our luggage we carried in ourselves and took forcible possession. A black rascal and a beggarly old Greek moved in their bedding, and took possession by order of the doctor. This was a little too much for a

Captain in the British Navy, and for Americans, especially a Southerner. We sent for Monsieur Doctor. "Que voulez vous?" We told him our complaint; his acquaintance with French was just sufficient, with the assistance of his own conscience, to understand the reason of it. He said that the room could hold seven persons. We let him know that we had and would keep the room, and that the black man and Greek should not be our room mates.

The doctor had taken charge of our passports. C—— in going about our room picked up his passport; he was exceedingly provoked and demanded the presence of the doctor. He appeared, and in a warm discussion told C—— that he lied. This was exceedingly gentlemanly! Before dinner a man came to all the rooms and wished to know what we had in our possession; this is required, they say, so that property can be sent to friends in case of death. The real reason appears to me to be, to entice people to tell what they have, expecting—for the reason they assign—that travellers for their own protection will openly disclose all that they have, contraband or otherwise. Notice is then perhaps sent on to Vienna, and the unwary traveller taken in. They asked if we were married, of what religion, etc., which impertinent questions we answered as we chose. Our dinner was infamous; however, we were in capital spirits after dinner, and were enjoying ourselves in spite of our misfortunes, when the jailer came, and ordered us all to our respective rooms. We were just getting in tune, and were completely struck down to hear the order. Immediately we struck up "We won't go home till morning," and so we intended, for the Armenian and his lady could be well provided for, and the gentlemen could also pass a very comfortable night in our commodious habitation. It was no go however. They were marched off.

14th. We all dined together; the Armenian and all the party spent the day with us, not intending it; but the gates were locked at twelve o'clock, and kept so until two. The dinner was somewhat better—indeed, much better—but was in some respects not clean. The Captain, who is one of the best-natured men in the world, unfortunately caught sight of a wandering hair. This exceedingly vexed him, and he told Nicholas one of the guardians that the dish was exceedingly dirty, and that he must never bring such a dinner on table again. He was insolent. The Captain told him to retire and conducted him to the door. A few minutes afterward, the doctor appeared. "Que voulez vous?" was his interrogatory as usual. We told him our complaint. He pretended to understand, and departed in a violent passion.

After dinner as on the preceding day, we clustered around the tree in the middle of the yard, and amused ourselves with a few songs. In the midst of our hilarity, we saw a number of ladies and gentlemen, counts and countesses, in front of our gate, looking at us like so many wild animals or malefactors. We were not at all abashed by their impudence, and accordingly advanced toward them and interrogated them—who and from whence they came and for what? They said they were from the Baths in the neighborhood, and had come to see all the sights. We asked them to enter; they said it was far easier to enter than to go out, and besides, that they thought we could not have everything we wished. No doubt they had seen the doctor.

The bell rang to retire to our rooms. A short time afterwards the doctor appeared with two or three soldiers, and demanded Francesco, a man who had left the steamer which had brought us from Galatz. We had employed this man as our servant, inasmuch as he spoke German and Italian, and we were subjected to every kind of imposition from the beggarly Austrians, they giving us no tariff but one in German.

The record sets forth the further tribulation in quarantine, where the surly medical official tries to injure the party, as he endeavors to arrest their attendant on the ground of his non-possession of a passport. On the next day, the

15th. The doctor made his appearance with his suite of soldiers and demanded Francesco, but on showing another paper which he had purposely withheld, he escaped imprisonment. When we got up, we found the gates of our court-yard shut, and orders issued that there should be no communication between us—that we should not even dine together, nor visit with a guardian. This was a little too bad! He had already deprived us of many privileges, which we had a right to demand, and now he was disposed to treat us rather as thieves than gentlemen. We had as yet done nothing; we had merely defended our servant, whose assistance as an interpreter was indispensable. The idea of not seeing our friends, made us quite melancholy; but this was soon cast off when it was proposed that we should obey the orders of the doctor " to air our clothes," by filling them with straw, and amusing our friends by sticking them up high, so that every one could see them. This was soon done. Fleming had an old blue coat, I an old pair of black pantaloons, and Mr. Vieuxville a new hat. Unfortunately, this coincided exactly with the dress of the doctor. We elevated the stuffed clothes, which soon produced a considerable excitement, affording amusement to all around us. We and our friends were quite contented with the effect produced.

Presently to our astonishment, when we were reading in our rooms, the jailer came and locked us in. This was a little too severe! The doctor soon followed, attended by a corporal and three soldiers, and stationed them before the stuffed clothes. Finding we could not get out of the door, we thought we would enter the next house through a flue, ascending the chimney by means of a rope ladder, which we had made the night before to scale the wall which separated us from our friends.

We had returned, and all were tranquil, when the gate

opened, and the doctor entered accompanied by a suite
of officials. They came to the window, and put some
questions to us. We respond: "Who are you who inter-
rogate us?" "Sir, do you know whom you are speaking
to—the major of the quarantine?" We approached the
window, apologized; said that it was necessary to know
who addressed, as it could not be expected that we would
answer any impudent rascal, like the doctor, whenever he
thought fit to question us. The Captain said that it gave
him great pleasure to address a brother officer. We then
made our obeisance, in the most polite way. They asked
us if we meant to insult the Austrian government. We
told them that the idea never entered our mind; that if
the doctor insisted it was an effigy of him, it was a personal affair. We then told the major our grievances, the
total want of politeness on the part of the doctor. The
doctor cried out all the time "I shall have satisfaction."
We told the major that we should say no more; that
we had informed them of our reason for elevating our
clothes; that if the doctor still persisted it was an image
of his person, the Captain offered him any satisfaction he
sought, and kindly offered him his choice of any one of us
three, when out of quarantine. Fortunately for himself
and perhaps for us, he refused such satisfaction, insisting
that we must be conducted to prison, or he would leave
the quarantine. All this time he was most violent, in
menacing gestures and words in a language which I could
not understand. We asked the major if that was gentlemanly; he shrugged his shoulders, as much as to say
"don't mind him." The secretary of the quarantine who
was the interpreter of the party, said that he hoped we
would remain tranquil, and that if we wished anything, to
write to him. Francesco not having any passport, was
obliged to go to prison. We apologized to the major, for
having indirectly troubled him.

The major desired us to remove the offending object.
A soldier was left—for what purpose, we knew not; we
asked the doctor; he could not tell us. One of us

attempted to remove it, when the soldier presented his gun and cocked it.

They had taken away our servant, and consequently, unless we suffered ourselves to be cheated, we could not obtain any dinner. Very fortunately, we had brought a ham into quarantine, and Bennett had a small heating apparatus. We cut the ham in slices, and put them on a plate, and the latter article over the heater. We enjoyed our dinner much.

16th. The servant asked us if we wished dinner, we told him we would have nothing until we had a Tariff, and made our dinner on our ham. The restaurateur would not give us any forks or knives, so that we were obliged to cut our ham with a razor, and eat it with forks made of wood and our penknives. This afternoon the agent of the steamer called; he was very civil, heard our grievances, and said that he would call on the major himself.

17th. Ham dinner again. Our friends met us in the afternoon. Delighted to see them. The Armenian lady has acted with much spirit; she said that she did not care about her liberty, when we were slaves or prisoners; and that if she was compelled to visit the German chambermaid and not us, she would prefer to remain in her room. When we were all together, the agent of steamers came to see us; he had drawn up a protest against the doctor to be handed to the major. He said that he called on the major; that the major and many other persons, some of considerable influence in Europe, had made complaints against the doctor already, and that a courier had been despatched the previous evening to bring here a Commissioner, to examine into the complaints. It is a fortunate thing for us that the major and the agent have personal complaints against the doctor. We were granted permission to go around the wall, but the agent advised us not to avail ourselves of it.

18th. While we were washing, the doctor came to the door of our house, and requested to see us; we told him

to wait until we were dressed. He came into where we
were washing, most politely asked us how we were, and
whether we had received a Tariff in Italian (we had); that
if there was anything we wished that was not on the Tariff,
to mention it the day before, and we should have it. We
dined together today; passed it pleasantly; took a walk
in the evening before the gates were shut. We have at .
last obtained our washerwoman, a nice looking, German
damsel.

When the gates were closed for the evening, Joseppi our
Italian interpreter came to us and said that he would come
again in the evening, and tell us something important. We
watched out for him and at dark saw him at the door. He
gave us the intelligence that tomorrow morning at five
o'clock two of us would be in irons in prison. We could
not do otherwise than believe it, inasmuch as we had seen
what free use they made of their chains; for poor Joseppi
was put in chains this morning, and kept there for three
hours, because he had introduced into our rooms a washerwoman, without consulting the doctor who wished to
employ another. We arranged all our things; vowed to
defend and stick by each other to the last. As we had
the expectation of a pallet of straw, the court dress of
Austria with its bracelets, etc., we thought we would enjoy
our bed for the last time for some period—stretch out our
limbs and play the gentleman, for tomorrow we were to
be state prisoners; and for what? What have we done to
bring ourselves to an equality with malefactors? Had we
disobeyed the laws of quarantine? Here we were to be
confined and chained, without the power of saying a word
in our defence! I had a disturbed rest; my imagination
brought before me strange and disagreeable scenes. I
awoke just at five; the doctor had not yet appeared. Perhaps the servant was wrong, or had deceived us.

Later in the morning the doctor came, bringing
word from the Commander-in-Chief, that the party

should be held as prisoners until the arrival of the Commissioner. By advice of the major, the afflicted ones themselves wrote to the Commander-in-Chief asking that the commission be sent at once. They wrote also to the English Consul and to Mr. Muhlenberg, the American Minister at Vienna.

Four soldiers were marched into the premises occupied by our travellers. Afterward the English Consul called and rendered some welcome service. He joined his offer of parole to that of the major, on the strength of which the ones held in detention might leave the place. Again :

20th. Wrote according to the request of Col. Hodges, British Consul, our grievances in detail. The Director of Lazaret who has just returned from an excursion against some robbers in the neighborhood, called on us early this morning; he is an exceedingly polite and gentlemanly man, advanced in years. He expressed his regret that he had been absent; apologized for the doctor, saying that his conduct had been disgraceful, but that he was a man "sans education." On leaving us he told the guardians that if any of them were guilty of the least incivility towards us, they should be immediately discharged. After breakfast we had a visit from the Secretary of Lazaret, who kindly sympathizes with us, and says that he thinks the doctor will be discharged.

The others have been allowed to walk about the quarantine, and dine together. We are prisoners.

This afternoon we were aroused by some noise, and on enquiry, heard that the doctor had ordered Sam [Mr. Whitlock,] Thring and Cram to their rooms, saying that they must remain there, prisoners, until the Commission arrives, which he says will probably be on Wednesday next. This is bad news! I am dreadfully enervated and worried. I can't see how the word or parole of a Major and British Consul can be cancelled by the *ipse dixit* of a physician.

21st. News received from Director that the Commission will arrive tonight, and we be out of this hole tomorrow.

It was a serious and unfortunate experience for our travellers, else so much space would not have been devoted to it in the journal. That it was keenly felt by the participants is further shown in the entry made on the same day as the last:

Read the English service in company with Bennett and Fleming. The Psalm of the Day (the 105th) was extremely appropriate to our situation.

There are other reasons for the insertion here of the records of the time, despite their lengthened dimension. The occurrence needs telling as a vivid part of the life that was lived, an experience unusual in any biography. Again, the story will show the possibilities of existence in quarantine at the date referred to and under the rule of an officious health officer puffed up by his petty authority.

The frequent mention of quarantine throughout the journal will call attention to the universal dread of the plague, which a few years before had wrought havoc in the older lands, and about the near approach of which there were reports at the time.

At last, deliverance is at hand.

22nd. This evening, the long expected Commission arrived. They were twelve or fifteen in number; they received us with much civility, and desired us to make our complaints in writing.

The doctor called on us this morning at eight o'clock; made us show our bodies to see that we were not affected with the plague; then shook hands, saying in French that our probation was finished. We supposed, from this, that we were free, and would soon be at liberty and join again our friends; but on inquiry, we found that his cordial shake of hands was only a piece of cold formality.

23rd.   The Commission commenced their sitting at seven o'clock. At ten o'clock, Capt. Bennett, Fleming and myself, were waited upon by the aide-de-camp of the Colonel and our friend the Steamer Agent, and desired to appear before the Commission. The Secretary read the complaints of the doctor against us, which we proved to be entirely unfounded in every instance. Bennett then, on the request of the Colonel, read our complaints against the doctor, which were interpreted by the agent. All present were astounded at the base behavior of the doctor. We were kept in attendance three hours, the time being occupied in translating our complaints, which the Colonel desired us to retain to be sent to his government. On retiring, they said that we were free, but must wait the examination of the other gentlemen, in order to make the whole affair as clear as possible against the doctor. After dinner, the rest were called in, in order. Rhinelander and Rawnsley had been detained, when the doctor had told the English Consul that they had been guilty of nothing. At seven o'clock, we were all summoned. They received us standing. The Colonel then addressed us; said that we were acquitted, apologized for our detention; that he should inform our government of our innocence, and of the course his government should take in the punishment of the doctor for our uncalled-for treatment. He closed his address by saying that we were free to leave when we might choose, and advising the Captain when he should again receive ill treatment from the doctor of a Lazaretto, not to hang him up until he was clear of the quarantine. The agent stayed with the Commission until twelve o'clock, making charges against the doctor. We left the quarantine at eight o'clock for Orsova.

24th. Detained until five o'clock, P.M. in obtaining our passport. We had been kept too late in quarantine to meet the steamer, or to send a special messenger to detain her for us. Went off to Mehadiah, a beautiful watering place, situated between mountains with a torrent running between them. We entered the town at nine o'clock. A gay scene was presented to us; all the fashionables were promenading, and a fine band of music playing in the streets. The only sleeping apartment to be had was the ball-room. We were great lions, being recognized as the rioters at the quarantine.

25th. Took a beautiful walk through this lovely place; took a bath, called on Col. Hodges and lounged through the day.

26th. This morning at three o'clock, left for Pest, by post. Sam, Fleming and Capt. Bennett preferred to remain, rather than make the disagreeable land travel; we wished to save time. Our vehicle was nothing more than a country wagon, without seats even; we were obliged to use our luggage and hay, for this purpose.

27th—29th. We found the road extremely dusty; I was fortunate enough to have a veil. Our wagons broke down constantly, and sometimes detained us for hours. We travelled all night, and after much inconvenience and fatigue, reached Pest at eleven o'clock. I have never passed through a country that can compare with Hungary, in richness of soil and cultivation; you see fields of grain ten miles square. The men are lazy, the women the principal agriculturists. The women are extremely amiable and pretty. We met with much roguery from the postmasters, such as showing false tariffs; withholding change, a very common habit, as far as I've seen in Hungary. We had on one occasion as our postboy, a lad who spoke Latin as fluently as his own tongue, and as correctly—

according to our Englishman who took the first honors at Cambridge—as the best scholars in England.

30th. Roamed through Pest, a beautifully built town, with broad streets well paved, and prettily finished houses. It is celebrated for its fine baths. I was struck with the beauty of the signs before all the shops. I purchased some brushes from a man who had a coronet on his ring. At dinner we saw some of our quarantine associates; after dinner, called on our Armenian friends. Went to the opera—Belisarius.

31st. Intended to have left this evening by the peasant post, and so arrive at Vienna before the steamer and gain a day at Pest; but by some rascality, after we had left and got about a mile on our way, we were informed that our carriage was unfit to proceed, and that we must consequently return to Pest. The valet de place who made our arrangements was to be blamed. In an hour's time he would procure another vehicle; we waited until ten o'clock, when he arrived and said that he had a carriage, but must walk a mile or two out of town to meet the conveyance. We had lost much time, and were unwilling to make concessions; therefore we desired him to return the money we had advanced, which he did.

August 1st. This morning, found Thring exceedingly, in fact dangerously ill of bilious colic. At five o'clock, he was pronounced out of danger, and we thought of leaving him—taking the Eilwagen—but again we were frustrated by the rascality and deception of the Hungarians.

2nd. Thring is much better, but extremely weak. Great news from the East: Mahomet Ali has vanquished, in a masterly manner, the forces of the Sultan; it is even rumored that the Turkish fleet has surrendered to the Egyptian, that the English and French fleet are in the Dardanelles, and that Russia meditates an attack upon Constantinople or that as an ally she will defend the Dardanelles against the English and French and Egyptians.

My attention was drawn today to a strange object, at the corner of the principal street; it resembled the trunk of a tree covered with iron. On examination and inquiry, we found that a locksmith had made a lock and placed it in this public situation, offering a large reward to any that could open it, and demanding that all that failed should affix a nail to the trunk of the tree. It is now actually sheeted with iron nails.—It is a delightful custom of the country to have music all the time you are at dinner, and at supper also. The Casino is a delightful place—news-papers from every part of Europe—splendid ballrooms.

3rd. Left in the steamer for Vienna; boat very small (The Nador), 40 horse power. The river, in point of scenery, much finer than the part of the Danube we have already seen; the view is occasionally relieved by an old ruined castle. Many passengers, consisting principally of Hungarian nobility—rather a tough set in spite of their gentle blood! Passed the night horribly—no regular sleeping accommodations.

4th. Much amused and disgusted by Hungarian man-ners. They use no soap to wash their hands, but fill their mouth with water, and then spit it out on their hands; they wash or clean their teeth with the forefinger. When they sit down to table, they take off their coats, and proceed to the tedious and arduous duty of wading through a German meal, which consists of a series of sweets, sour salads and grease.—At two o'clock, arrived at Presburg, where the Diet now sits. We intended to leave immediately for Vienna, but to our disappointment no carriage was to be taken without the vilest imposition; so we determined to remain with the steamer which leaves in the morning. Very disagreeable! Obliged to leave the boat, and go to the hotel. Poor Francesco, extremely ill with the bilious colic, removed to the hospital.

Presburg is a beautiful place. Some excitement in the Diet. The King demands soldiers, and the Diet demands the release of some of their nobility. I don't feel well; severe headache, no appetite.

5th. At five o'clock, with few passengers, left for Vi-enna; wind strong; the boat found it extremely difficult to make way against the current, sometimes it was stationary. We arrived, three hours after time, at Vienna, or at the place where carriages are in readiness to take you to Vienna. The Custom-house officers, whom I had so much dreaded, treated us remarkably well. No difficulty, in the least! Vienna seemed, in the distance, situated on a plain, with mountains rising in the rear. Our ride for an hour was through the Prater, a large park, a fashionable place for driving and a lively scene of gayety on Sundays and holydays; it abounds with deer. We stopt at "The Lamb" in the Faubourg—all full; thence went to the Kaiserinn von Oestreich, where we found good accommodations.

6th. Went to our Bankers, the Police Office—to obtain our *Carte du Sejour*, and to the Custom-house to obtain some books. Our minister, Mr. Muhlenberg, is out of town—in Italy with his family. He had received my letter and had spoken to Prince Metternich, who said that we would be liberated before a letter could reach us. The Viennese dine between one and two, so that two or more hours are lost each day. Took a walk on the Glacis, in the Volksgarten, and went to the Church of St. Augustine, where there is a beautiful monument to Maria Christina, wife of Albert. It is by Canova; the design reminds you of his own tomb at Venice; youth and age are beautifully contrasted. It is considered one of his finest efforts. In the Volksgarten is a statue of Theseus by Canova; it is a bold, spirited thing, placed in a miniature temple of Theseus. Spent the evening at the Opera. A Ballet " The Revolt of the Harem " well got up; the last act admirable. The women of the Harem appear as soldiers fortified in a recess of the mountains. They were as well drilled as so many Austrian soldiers; were provided with real guns and fired a volley. It was admirably done. The house is splendid, tastefully decorated and large.

7th. Went to the Arsenal, one of the finest in the world, beautifully arranged. It was crowded. A guide accompanied us, giving a minute description of the various objects of curiosity, in German—which made it extremely irksome. There are arms for 300,000 men. Among the curious things is the coat of Gustavus Adolphus—with a hole in it—which was perforated by the bullet which caused his death.

Paid a second visit to the Church of St. Augustine and the Volksgarten. Our friend Thring arrived today; we had left him at Pest recovering from his illness. Today, after dinner, I had a severe chill, and am somewhat alarmed; my headache still remains. Rhinelander, for the last few days, has kept his room, complaining of a severe headache also.

8th. Visited the Imperial Gallery at the Belvedere; a large collection of paintings of the Italian School. Much trash, and but few fine paintings.

Here follows a list of canvases. After a reference to Ruisdael, Rubens, Gerhard, Dow, Teniers, Albrecht Dürer and other artists, our traveller records his impression:

Although these paintings are of such a remote date, they please by brilliancy and freshness; but are indeed too vitreous in appearance. Some modern paintings quite beautiful. A vile collection of statues, four or five in number; one, a reclining figure, is quite pretty.

Another chill today, and as Rhinelander called in a physician yesterday, I thought it advisable to call in one myself—Dr. Vivenot, who sent me to bed this evening.

9th. This morning quite sick; raging headache; much pleased with the kindness of the physician. The servants extremely kind; the chambermaid, in the absence of a nurse, sat up with me all night, and applied ice to my head every five minutes.

10th. Passed a bad night; the fever very severe, also the chill. I feel no better, and lose confidence in my physician. Rhinelander remains as he was.

11th.   Rhinelander at nine o'clock was much better; at two o'clock he was much altered for the worse; he became extremely enervated and ill.   The physician was sent for. He was much astonished when he saw his patient, and hurrying into my room, with his face flushed, asked " Is he a Catholic? "   At first, I did not perceive his meaning, but afterwards I soon perceived that my poor friend was just hovering between life and death.   At four o'clock, he was still much more enervated; another physician was called in.   The disease had changed to cholera, and poor Phil's life was despaired of.   We inquired for a Protestant clergyman: in this gay city, not one was to be found, who spoke English.   One of our English friends, Thring, kindly volunteered to read the " Service for the Visitation of the Sick," in which my poor friend entered with much interest.   I was anxious to leave my bed, and visit my sick friend, but it was forbidden.   He sent me messages to his friends, which I was obliged to commit to Cram, in consequence of my inability to write.   He lingered until nine o'clock, in great agony and anxious for death.   He said " he was happy " and that " he loved his sister."   At nine o'clock, he calmly died away.   What an affliction of Providence!   I scarcely can realize it—that one who yesterday, who this very morning was so strong and spirited, was cut down and removed from all things living!—one just in the prime of life, just entering upon his estate; one just arriving home, after an absence of nearly two years; taken sick in a strange land, and carried off without the privilege of saying adieu to beloved relations and friends. How gloomy are now the once pleasant associations!   The retrospect is now all saddened.   I cannot think of one pleasant hour, but that I recall to mind the friend who has been taken from us.   But he died happy: this should be to all sufficient consolation, and it should be always remembered that " God moves in a mysterious way."   'Tis certainly a great blow.   With what pleasure we had all looked forward to Vienna!   The amusements we had set apart to add to our pleasure—what are they now to us?

It is so unexpected! In Egypt we looked for sickness and danger, but at Vienna we expected to find nothing but amusement. We have been so intimately associated since we left America, that I feel as if I had lost a near relative —it makes such ravage in our little party!

12th. Passed a horrible night. Yesterday I obtained a nurse. She can't speak a word of any language intelligible to me; and is not clean, as she wipes the spoons on the sheets, in the absence of anything more suitable. The body of my friend is exposed today in the Cathedral—a custom of the country to prevent burying alive.—I don't feel as well today. The doctor proposed a consultation; Baron Turkheim was accordingly called in. My thoughts were all gloomy, and I could think of nothing but the pleasure of dying at home, among your friends.

13th. My friend was buried at three o'clock. Several English gentlemen staying at the house, attended the funeral. A Protestant German clergyman had been engaged to officiate, when it was afterwards ascertained that there was an English clergyman in town, who kindly promised to officiate. At the grave, however, the German minister said that the government would not allow the English service to be read, without special permission. An Englishman called on me this morning, and said that anything he could do for me, or his friends in town (for he had several)—that he or they would do it with pleasure; that I must consider him my servant. Others offered to assist us in any way, *financial* or otherwise. Since I've travelled, I have received nothing but kindness from the English. Our two travelling companions, Thring and Rawnsley, left today for England. It is a melancholy day, but I feel better.

14th. Permitted to take a short ride to Prince Schwarzenberg's garden, accompanied by Cram who is exceedingly kind and attentive.

15th. Our friends Fleming and Sam arrived from Pest; delighted to see them. They were much shocked by the dreadful news. I took another drive today.

6

16th. I begin to feel quite strong. Another drive to Prince S.'s garden. I walk out a little.

17th. Accompanied Mr. Hatfield and my friends to Hitzing and Schönbrunn, about three miles from Vienna. We left at two o'clock, in the carriage of Mr. Hatfield. Strauss was to play at the Casino at Hitzing. The palace and gardens pretty—quite Frenchified in appearance. The place is called from a pretty fountain (schön Brunnen); said to be the best water in the world. Saw the Emperor in the garden; looks like a benevolent, good man, but of little mind or decision of character.

18th. Walked out in the morning with Vivenot. I feel almost well, only a little weak.—Heard the opera of Somnambula sung by Mad. Lutgar, the favorite singer at Vienna. She has much sweetness of tone, not much compass and moderate force. She sings very pleasantly. I should not call her a great singer by any means, not so great as Mad. A. whom we heard at Florence.

19th. Visited the Archduke Charles' palace; prettily furnished. At twelve o'clock we heard as we supposed a fine band of music, but on investigation we discovered that it was nothing but a clock. It played an overture, and can play at least fifty other pieces of music. It is an astonishing piece of mechanism by Maelzel. The collection of drawings belonging to the Archduke is very extensive: 180,000 engravings—some exceedingly interesting —sketches and drawings by old masters; Raphael's sketch of the Transfiguration; many figures of The Last Judgment, by Michael Angelo himself; 122 sketches by Raphael; 20 by Andrea del Sarto and others.

Paid a second visit to the Belvedere palace. Spent the evening by invitation, at the house of Mr. Swartz, our Consul. We met a family of Fishers from Baltimore, Mr. and Mrs. Clay, *Chargé d'Affaires* in the absence of Mr. Muhlenberg, an American Missionary and wife, an English Captain, etc. Left early. Swartz, a good meaning man perhaps, but extremely coarse and disagreeable in manners. On my recovery, he told me he was extremely glad to see me up, in fact that there was no one in Vienna more so; that he was glad for my sake and for his own, because if I died I should give him so much trouble.

Since I have been here, I have heard Lanner the rival of Strauss; he is perhaps not so brilliant, but certainly plays with more taste, more beautiful finish and science.

On the 20th a visit is paid to the Ambras Museum.

After referring to various antiquities and curiosities, the journalist adds the remark:

Among the jewels which are more brilliant than curious, is a " splendid "—at least so its maker Benvenuto Cellini thought—salt-cellar; after reading his own description, I was somewhat disappointed with it.

21st. Anxious to make an excursion to Baden and Laxenburg, but the weather is too unfavorable. The cabinets, of antiquities and gems, closed for the present.—I must not forget to mention the noble Cathedral of St. Stephen's. It is Gothic, and as far as concerns the interior is perfect. Its tower however is its chief beauty; nothing can exceed its graceful majesty. It rises gradually tapering to the skies. Its height is 465 feet. Unfortunately it is now three feet out of the perpendicular, and they are compelled to remove it for reconstruction; they commenced the operation of removal yesterday. It is something of an undertaking, and many persons were assembled to witness it.

22nd. Rains very hard. Paid a visit to our Armenian friends who are recovering from their illness, with the exception of poor Thomas who has left for Constantinople in consequence of ill health.

24th. Today at one o'clock, we leave in the "Eilwagen" for Linz. Our friends Messrs. Morrot and Vieuxville go with us. I am sorry that circumstances have interfered so much with my seeing Vienna properly. It certainly is the most delightful place for travellers. Rather, no city can equal or surpass it in amusement: a good opera, theatres, the best instrumental· music, balls, fêtes—in fact the people seem to do nothing but amuse themselves. Upon us, rather a melancholy impression is left.

Vienna is one of the cleanest cities I've seen; the pavement the best. Each stone a few inches in diameter costs 20 sous. The houses are large, and occupied by several families. . . . The streets all radiate from the Cathedral. No very conspicuous public buildings; the Church of San Carlo is unique in its exterior. The shops are prettily arranged; no sidewalks—constant danger of having the toes taken off, unless care is observed in turning corners.

We left the city at one o'clock. Our road lay toward Schönbrunn, so that I've seen the palace three times. The Eil- or Speed Wagon is not such a rapid manner of travelling as its name would indicate. Horses are changed at each post, every two German miles (10 English). Some of the vehicles are intended for four, others for eight persons. There is no reason for slow travelling, but the repugnance of Germans to hurry themselves; they look upon dignified inaction as the height of luxury. The first town we passed through was Hütteldorf, a place much resorted to by the Viennese in summer; you see here some beautiful villas, and the country is cultivated and picturesque by nature. We met crowds of men and women walking along the road, on their way to some pilgrimage Church; they are generally preceded by a priest carrying a cross. Near Purkersdorf, you pass along the Wien, a torrent which gives the name to the Austrian capital. At nine o'clock, at St. Polten, we had a German supper, consisting of meats and beer in abundance.

Travelled all night—a thing to me by no means agreeable. The Germans travel by night, to allow themselves more time to eat and drink during the day.

25th. At six o'clock, breakfasted at Strengberg. It being Sunday, we have an opportunity of seeing the

picturesque costumes which you find in every section of
this part of the country. Two German miles farther on,
we found Enns, a town of 2000 inhabitants; its old walls
were built out of the money which was paid for Richard
Coeur de Lion's ransom. All along the road from this
town to Linz, you see representations of St. Florian, who
is much esteemed by the Austrians and Bavarians—he
being principally engaged as chief engineer on all occasions of fire.

Three or four miles from Linz is Ebersberg, at the extremity of a long wooden bridge. The town was the
scene of a severe engagement between the French and the
Austrians in 1809. The passage was disputed with much
spirit. In this town the battle was kept up, and 12000 men
fell. A mile or two further on you pass a tower, a part of
the series of towers, forming the new fortifications just
finished at Linz.

We reached Linz about twelve o'clock, and took up our
quarters at the house opposite the Post, the Golden Cannon. After dinner, we took a valet de place and a fiacre.
A young Swiss gentleman, on understanding our intention of making a *petit tour* through the village and immediate environs, came to us and in a polite way requested
permission to join our party, saying as an apology for
making the request, that he believed there was no one of
the party who could speak German, which was the only
language with which our guide or valet was conversant.
We gladly accepted his offer, and endeavored to pack our
party as well as possible in a small vehicle, and hastened
to visit the curiosities of the place. The city is surrounded
by a series of forts, 32 in number, about a mile or two
apart; they occupy a circuit of nine miles. Having obtained permission from the Governor, we examined one
of the forts. Each tower is 30 feet high, and 80 in diameter; they are however so sunk in the ground that only
the roof projects. Around each tower is a ditch, and a
glacis toward the town. On viewing the inside arrangements, you are immediately reminded of a man-of-war.

Each tower consists of three stories: the lowest for provisions, and supplied with a pump; the middle for the quarters of the troops; the highest is a platform which is mounted with ten guns, ingeniously arranged so as to be made to bear on any single spot. There are many advantages in this system of fortification, but its success is to be tested. There is much economy in this series of forts over a long continuous fortification, there being 32 points of attack. Each two contiguous forts have a secret communication under the earth.

From the fort we went up to the Jagermeyer Garden, to obtain a view of the environs. Near the Garden is a beautiful Church almost finished; it is small but perfect in its way; it abounds in painted glass, whose varied tints play fantastically throughout the sacred place. Next to the Church is a Convent; this building has all the appearance of a tower; it was originally a fortification. Here we found some young priests, one of whom kindly took us to a platform on the top, which gave us a splendid view of the scenery. On the South, the view is bounded by snowy chains of the Styrian and Salzburg Alps; the Danube below you and as far as the eye can reach is seen meandering through the valley which lies before you in all its beauty, richly ornamented with picturesque chateaus and graceful looking cottages.

The girls of Linz are distinguished in guide books for their beauty. Perhaps it is ironical flattery; perhaps one unfortunate, or rather fortunate fellow, may have met with a charming damsel, and have become enamoured. They all wear on their heads, a kind of helmet of gold gauze, which gives them the appearance of so many Minervas, rather than Venuses. They seem too martial and masculine, to please my taste; and their costume is rather curious than pretty. How different the tasteful way of arranging the hair which you find in Hungary and about Vienna!—that is all simplicity and beauty.

Our Swiss friend we found all gentlemanly in his manners; but two bottles of beer made him rather gay, and in the Volksgarten he was far too lively. In all German towns you find public gardens which on Sundays are enlivened by a fine band of music, the fashionable part of the community and happy peasantry.—In honor of a royal personage who was staying at the same hotel, we were gratified in the evening by a fine band of military music, composed of about 50 performers. It was decidedly the best military music we have yet heard. These things are well managed in Germany. The musicians have their stands for music, and are provided with lights, so that they can play the most difficult pieces.

26th. At six o'clock left for Salzburg by Ischil. We engaged a separate wagon on the railroad, and were conducted by means of horses to Gmunden. On our way we visited the Falls of the Traun. I was somewhat disappointed after what I had heard of these celebrated falls. There was an abundance of water, but I think this is all that can be said. The height is about 42 feet. Along the falls runs a curious aqueduct, by means of which the salt barges ascend and descend the river. At two o'clock we arrived at Gmunden, a town beautifully situated on Lake Traunsee. Here we found a steamer in readiness to take us across the lake. It was quite a miniature concern, but amply sufficient for the purpose intended. The lake is small, but exceedingly beautiful. Its pure green waters are frowned upon by the majestic Dachstein and the gloomy Trauenstein. On one side and in the distance, the view is terminated by retiring hills, lively and picturesque with houses and villages. An Englishman is the proprietor and captain of the steamer. Carriages are in readiness to take passengers to Ischil. They, on the present occasion, were soon filled; we were advised to wait until the arrival of the steamer at four o'clock. In the meanwhile, we visited a salt establishment. The process is by evaporation, the brinish water being brought from Ischil by means of aqueducts—it being much cheaper to manufacture the salt here than at Ischil in consequence of the abundance of fuel at this place. In the next steamer,

the Duchess of Parma arrived, in consequence of which
the palace was illuminated, and music was playing as we
entered Ischil. There was difficulty in finding a hotel,
the Post being full; got at last taken in at a small but
comfortable house.

27th. Got out early. The public bath is in a fine house.
Over the door is seen in large letters " In sale et in sole
omnia consistunt." Took a walk around the town ;
crossed the river to obtain a better view. It is hemmed in
on every side by high mountains. We endeavored for a
long time to find Schwalmann's Garden, to obtain another
view of the town, and to see the beautiful Franzel, the
daughter of the host, who has received so many encomiums from guide-book writers. We were about giving
up the search, when we met a young man who spoke a
few words of French, who kindly accompanied us to the
garden—which I must allow is beautifully situated. A
hunt was made after Franzel, whom we found in the
kitchen among pots and dishes. Each had conjured up
some beautiful image, when, what was our disappointment to find nothing but an antique beauty, or rather an
antique who they say was a beauty!

At ten o'clock we started off in two posting establishments, to Salzburg. The road was extremely interesting,
passing by three or four lakes. One post from Salzburg,
we were overtaken by a severe storm of rain. Arrived at
Salzburg about ten. Hotel Schwarzmoor, which we preferred in consequence of recommendations we had received of it, in point of view.

28th. Horrible rainy day! No one would go out but
Mons. Morrot, who visited the salt-mines at Hallein,
which are exceedingly interesting. Vieuxville, Fleming
and myself were afraid of exposing ourselves to the
weather and to the dampness of a salt-mine.

29th. Indications of a clear day, and we determined to
visit the castle. We accordingly procured an order from
the Governor, and ascended at nine o'clock. It is situated on a high rock commanding the city, and during the

middle ages was occupied as the residence and retreat of the Archbishops, against their rebellious subjects, the peasants. These Archbishops were, during the middle ages, princes of the land. From the galleries of the castle, you have the finest view the eye could wish. The clouds were slowly and lazily wreathing their way up the mountain sides, and through a small opening, the sun was glancing his beams over a distant part of the valley. To the cloud effect was added the grandeur of the view. The mind and eye could play at random with the size and distance of the mountains; they appeared to reach the very skies. No limit could be placed to their height. Ridge rises on ridge, and mountain on mountain, in silent dignity, while below, the eye could pleasantly gaze on the rich valley, which, with its graceful, bending river, its green meadows and golden crops, its chateaus and villas, lay in beauty beneath us. I thought that it was the most pleasing view I had yet seen. The castle is a curious old place, containing some singular antique shields of the Archbishops, weapons of the peasants, and the stuffed skin of a famous horse which the leader of the rebels rode. The torture chamber still is to be seen. We returned by way of the Mönchsberg, a part of the ridge on which the castle stands, beautifully laid out in pleasant walks, and affording fine views of the valley. We stopped at the stables for the cavalry; the horses for the officers were splendid animals—a good menage. Near it is the tunnel which passes under the Mönchsberg, finished by an Archbishop, who gave his name to it—" Sigismund Thor."

In the afternoon, took a ride to a garden belonging to the Emperor. It certainly abounded in curious playthings in the shape of water-works, etc., but has little else to please; some of the curious things however are beautiful. Fountains are so arranged as to appear as glass vases over natural flowers. You are requested to sit down at a table of stone, on stools of stone with a hole in the middle; as soon as you are seated you find fountains springing up on every side so as to surround you with jets

of water, while you feel a little nervous when you see
water spouting up from the holes in the unoccupied seats.
There are large fish-ponds in which you see every kind of
fish, which are exceedingly fond of being fed by visitors.
There are some curious specimens of mechanism: in a
grotto, you find yourself surrounded by birds, which keep
up a most unmelodious chant; you see a large village—
all the villagers actively employed at their different trades,
some amusing themselves by looking at a dancing bear,
or waltzing to the music of a band. There are other
smaller pieces of mechanism, well adapted to childish
tastes.—Mr. Morrot left us today. Vieuxville preferred
to remain with us, and enjoy an excursion to the Königsee. Fleming, I am sorry to say, is again quite unwell.

30th. I forgot to mention the beautiful fountain which
we saw yesterday, as we passed near the Cathedral, on our
way to the castle. There is much grace and skill shown
in the management of the figures which support the upper
receptacle of the water; perhaps however the figures are
too large, and show too much exertion in sustaining a
basin too small for their united powers.—Today we made
an excursion to the Königsee and Berchtesgaden. The
ride is extremely agreeable, passing through a beautiful
valley and along the side of the Untersberg, which is interesting as being appropriated to the Emperor Barba-
rossa and his vassals, as a prison until the day of judgment.
Our guide here gave way to an excited imagination, and
told some curious stories: that this mountain was inhab-
ited by beautiful women, who occasionally allured the
poor peasants to their mountain recesses, and repaid their
eager embraces with a long period of sleep, which finished,
they returned them to the world which had undergone the
changes of a century. Entering the narrow defile of the
" overhanging rock," we soon approached Berchtesgaden,
which we left on our right and proceeded to the Royal
Lake. Here boats were in attendance, to convey us *partly*
across the lake, it being forbid to go to the farther extremity, as preparations were making for a royal chase.

We were rowed by women, something quite new in its way, and which would have been more agreeable had they been pretty and more effeminate in appearance. There is a melancholy grandeur which surrounds this lake. High mountains, some covered with snow, hem it in, rising perpendicularly from its margin so as to prevent the possibility of building. There is nothing to relieve its solemn majesty, but the tinkling bells of the Alpine herds, struggling in search of scanty herbage. Having traversed half the lake, we arrived at the King's Hunting-ground, where we made our dinner on delicious trout. In the hall are seen some paintings of fish, which at different times have astonished the natives by their immense size, some weighing 20, 30 or even 50 pounds. The manner of hunting here is to send out a large number of peasants, who ascend the mountain and collect together 40 or 50 chamois; these are hemmed in and driven into the lake. The King and his attendants are then ready, and while the peasants drive the chamois into the lake, and the poor creatures are struggling in the water, they fire upon them. —We returned and stopped at Berchtesgaden on our way home. The place is celebrated for its manufacture of toys, in wood, ivory, bone, etc. We paid a visit to the principal store, and were much amused with the ingenuity and skill shown in the manufacture of these little things. A female showed us about, and gallantry compelled us to purchase some toy or other. We arrived at the hotel at seven o'clock. Unable to procure seats in the Eilwagen for Munich.

31st. Procured a long coucher (vetturino establishment) to take us to Munich—to start at ten o'clock and arrive at six tomorrow. Before leaving Salzburg we visited a few things that still remained to be seen, such as the House of Mozart, of Paracelsus, the inventor of *Elixir vitæ* and the philosopher's stone. In the Church of St. Giles is a monument to the memory of Michael Haydn, brother of the composer of the " Creation."

At ten o'clock we left punctually. We were not agreeably impressed with the appearance of our coachman; he appeared sulky and disobliging, as he afterwards proved to be. Our route was not the most agreeable, not being the one through Reichenhall, but the shortest by way of Stein. We slept at F——, a post further on than Stein, a place distinguished by a castle, which was formerly tenanted by the robber knight Hans von Stein; the dungeons of his unfortunate captives are still to be seen.

Sept. 1st. One post from Munich, while we were refreshing the horses with brown bread, of which they are extremely fond, we encountered a peasant ball. They were all whirling about in grand style. Beer seemed to circulate freely, and even the police officers were yielding to its seductive influences.

The country presented a gay appearance, with its rich costumes. As we approached Munich, we noticed a head-dress quite peculiar. It is made of gilt gauze, and fastened far back on the head; it tapers off into two points like the tail of a fish. Since then, in Munich, we have seen many of them; some of these are beautiful and costly. The King is extremely anxious to keep up this part of the national costume. Some cost from 30 to 50 florins.—The approach to Munich is by no means agreeable, being by a flat plain. It rained hard as we entered the city.

Munich. "Cerf d'Or." At first refused at this hotel, the house being full; however, they managed to put us four in a room, with a promise of two rooms tomorrow. Saw again our friend Morrot, who had seen nearly all the lions.

2nd. Rain. Mr. Morrot accompanied us to the Pinakothek.—The streets seem very wide, the houses well and newly built. As we went along, we passed by the bronze obelisk, in the Carolinen-Platz, erected by the present King to the memory of 30,000 Bavarians, who fell in the Russian campaign. It is 100 feet high, and made of the cannon taken from the enemy by the Bavarians.

The Pinakothek was commenced in 1826; it was designed by Von Klenze. It is a beautiful building in itself,

.and combines all the conveniences indispensable for a picture gallery. The collection contains 1500 paintings, taken from the galleries of Düsseldorf, Mannheim, Deux Ponts and others. The paintings are arranged in halls according to the schools, with cabinets at the sides, for smaller paintings, communicating with the larger rooms. A splendid corridor is now being finished, by Cornelius, Zimmermann, etc. It is divided in 25 loggie; in each loggia, the paintings or frescoes illustrate some particular state of the arts. There is much taste shown in the designs, and much power and skill in the execution; still they want that lightness, that airiness, which pleases so much in the Vatican. There is here too much work, too much paint, gilding, etc., not enough delicacy in the arabesques.

The gems of the collection are certainly the Murillos, which are exquisite. In one, two ragged boys are seen eating melons, in another a little girl purchasing fruit, in the third an old woman examining a boy's head; these are all true to life, and exquisitely finished, with all the softness and effect of Murillo. Here are some fine efforts of Rubens. His "Fall of the Damned" is certainly a curious production, when the position of the figures, tumbling one on the other in grand confusion, is considered; in foreshortening, many of the prominent figures are complete studies. Then his "Judgment," a large painting in the centre of the Grand Hall, is considered one of his finest productions, as also his "Susannah." . . . I have now seen some of the finest efforts of Rubens, and I must say, with but little pleasure. He is too gross. There is something too fleshy in all his compositions, a want of delicacy, of harmony; too much coloring—something which disgusts me. His "Boar and Lion Hunt" please me, but I can't, with pleasure, consider either his "Grand Judgment" or the "Fallen Angels." Of the Vandycks the most admired are his "Susannah," "St. Sebastian" and several portraits of burgomasters.

"Susannah" by Domenichino did not strike me agreeably; the design is bad, the bath too public—she looks like a frightened white mouse.

Altogether the gallery pleased me much, and reflects much honor upon the royal founder who appears an ardent admirer of the fine arts. The building itself is a splendid palace.

Dined at two o'clock at the table d'hote. The keeper of the establishment was formerly cook to Prince Eugene, and accordingly understands his profession, although ignorant of other things as important in this his new situation. A great want of management is shown through the whole establishment, a multitude of servants running about, bells ringing, lodgers calling and no one appearing to answer. Still we had a good dinner, a profusion of game, in fact every luxury, and all nicely served. We were accordingly quite recruited at the end of the dinner, about four o'clock, and set out in the rain to go and visit the Leuchtenberg gallery, formed by Eugene Beauharnois, Viceroy of Italy.

Few collections of paintings have given me equal pleasure; it resembled much the famous collection in the Chiara Palace, Rome, in one particular—in not being numerous, but containing great gems. Nothing is more annoying than wading through a large gallery, only here and there finding a picture to please; it is like wandering over the mountains in quest of views, when you might with greater ease be conducted to a spot unfolding all the beauties the country afforded. This it was that pleased me so much in this gallery. There are only two rooms, but they are filled with gems. In the first room you find modern paintings, such as those by Girard, David, and others of the French school. Belisarius (by Girard) conducting, for a moment, his youthful guide, who by some accident is prevented from leading her aged sire, is a masterly production, and displays much power, as well as beauty in the finish.

In the 2nd room, at the farther extremity, is the famous

Magdalen by Canova. She is in deep anguish, sighing over a cross, which she holds in her hands. She is all lovely in her grief. You sympathize with the cold marble. Nothing in the moral world is more beautiful, more grati- fying to the mind of a rational being, than the sight of a person, melting in tears, over some fatal act. It shows that the icy heart is dissolved by the genial rays of light, of wisdom; it shows the better feelings springing into action. The frozen water dissolves, and when melted it still is as pure and clear, as before it assumed its icy na- ture. In the midst of the tears, you see the bow of heaven, promising good to come. Yes, I could linger for days about this embodied sentiment of the artist. Behind it is the gem of the collection, the " Madonna " of Murillo. In the other gallery, we have seen his representations of fa- miliar life, here the artist has essayed the higher fields of his profession, and with what success! The Virgin is all loveliness. Her face beams with purity. She looks as we imagine the Mother looked; her Infant, who lies in her arms, although an infant, bears on His face the impress of divinity. Few pictures have pleased me better. The one by Murillo in the Pitti palace, Florence, was recalled to my mind. A Madonna by Correggio reminded me of the Correggio in the Tribune. . . . In the middle of the room are the " Three Graces " by Canova—all beauty, grace and modesty. It is astonishing to see the flowing easiness of the limbs, which would seem impossible to be attained in stone.

3rd. Bibliothek—in extent, the second in the world; 540,000 volumes. The curiosities are: the orations of Demosthenes on cotton paper from Chios; the New Testa- ment in capital letters, of the VIII century; a splendid Bible and Missal, richly decorated with miniatures by a Byzantine artist, the exterior covered with curiously worked ivory and precious stones; Albert Dürer's Prayer- book, ornamented by him and Cranach with sketches; 3000 books, printed early, at a period anterior to the year 1500; 50 block books; Luther's Bible decorated with his and Melancthon's portraits; some manuscripts of Martin Luther; a letter of Charles I. to his sister.

From the Library, went to St. Michael's, the Jesuit Church, where is Thorwaldsen's monument of Eugene Beauharnois, erected by his wife. There is a whole-length statue of the Duke, attended by History, and the two Genii of life and death. It does not please me much. It is, I think, unworthy of its much admired artist—something tame. History is a beautiful figure; the main statue is perhaps faultless; still there is but a poor effect produced.

Glyptothek, or Sculpture Gallery, near the Pinakothek. Here, as on every occasion, the King has shown great liberality, taste and much good sense. Perhaps there is no building in the world, erected solely as a storehouse for statuary so splendid and so well adapted to the object, as this. It is of the Ionic order; designed by Von Klenze. An apartment is set apart for each stage of the art. In the first you find Egyptian; second, Etruscan; third, Æginetan; fourth, Hall of Apollo; fifth, Hall of Bacchus; sixth, Hall of the Sons of Niobe, etc.

In the first there is little to interest. An obelisk decorates the middle of the room; it is a miserable imitation, although many persons, even some who have been in Egypt, mistake it for a veritable antique; its four faces are ornamented with the same figures, some of the figures too are not polished. The Æginetan collection is extremely interesting. The sculptures were discovered in the island Ægina by Baron Haller, Messrs. Cockerell and Forster; they are supposed to have belonged to the temple of Jupiter Panhellenius, or to a temple dedicated to Minerva. They are supposed to represent some action of the Æacidæ: they have been rejuvenated by Thorwaldsen. There are two groups; one representing Hercules and Telamon (son of Æacus) fighting against the Trojans —the conflict between Greeks and Trojans.

Here the journal ends abruptly; according to appearance, it was never completed.

In the year 1839 Mr. Tucker was yet a youth, nineteen years of age. The juvenility of the writer comes to the front now and then, as when he sets down the age of the girls introduced to his party. But the future Doctor Tucker appears in many manifestations; the germs of characteristics, prominent and palpable in later days, are easily discernible. Certain features abide, running through the whole of his life. At Smyrna, wandering about the streets, the traveller drops into a church, " attracted by a fine pealing organ." He likes painting and sculpture; he has much to say about them. He is not afraid to adventure the performance of a critic's office; at Salzburg he makes judicious remarks about the size of the statues in a fountain: " perhaps the figures are too large, and show too much exertion in sustaining a basin too small for their united powers." He is not afraid to dissent from Rubens or Thorwaldsen. Religion has place in his daily living; her obligations are remembered as when we find him, almost a boy, a layman, reading Service within the unhappy precincts of quarantine. So the journal affords a preliminary glimpse and promise of the larger, adult existence.

V

SOCIETY—VOCATION

When the traveller returned from his two years of wandering, a leading impression produced upon his friends was that of commanding good looks. Once and again I have heard the matter referred to by the few yet surviving who knew him at the time. There was an air of distinction and culture, natural to him, which had developed; there were a graceful bearing, a gentleness embodied, also a winning smile and a clear, trustful eye which betokened an admirable example of humanity. His erect figure was always faultlessly attired in quiet, perfect taste; its every movement was unaffected but elegant.

As it had been at home, so it was his custom abroad—he fell naturally into the society of cultivated associates. Wherever he went, whether in Scotland, England or on the Continent, it was usual for him to meet with a cordial, at times an effusive, reception.

When he came back to his own land—" Yes, he was the idol of his family," said one closely related. But the admiration spread abroad throughout a larger circle. He possessed many characteristics which make captives of willing hearts. Is it any wonder, then, that the young man entered into the whirl of social living, that he became the centre of a sphere which in sober truth was adorned by his presence? Therein he shone, bright light of many a festive scene. A relative tells me that the young Mr. Tucker was the cynosure of many eyes; that he was "run after, the pet of social circles," that he "went everywhere, sang delightfully, and danced elegantly."

Soon after the day when the Church began to mourn the loss of Doctor Tucker, the writer had a conversation with Bishop Coxe, his early friend and comrade. The subject of our talk was this early section of the life recently completed. "Yes," said Bishop Coxe, "I remember what a regular spark in society Tucker was when a young man here in New York. He was in everything. When the Italian opera came to town he took advantage of the presence of the company and received lessons from a prominent artist-member. He sang delightfully." Here the Bishop uttered the words with enthusiasm, as if he enjoyed the very memory. "Tucker was in demand everywhere for his social qualities as well as his music, but wherever he went he was sure to be called upon to sing. And oh! how handsome he was, how handsome!"

The good Bishop confided to me a plan cherished by him for some time. He hoped to write a series of papers, under the general heading of "The Men that I Have Known." Dr. Tucker was one of these, about whom he intended to record his own complete reminiscence. He expected that the paper

would be ready in the autumn, and kindly offered
the use of it for the incorporation of its facts into
the present story. Unfortunately the grim messenger came soon to the Bishop himself, and interfered with the carrying out of his plan. Not long
before the date of present writing, the news came,
unexpected as sad, that the Bishop of Western New
York had been called away from earthly scene.
The Church will never know all that he had to tell
about his younger days, and about the lives of those
associated with him. All the more thankful are we
for the fact that the one short conversation upon
the topic now considered was set down at the time;
that we possess the testimony of the Bishop about
the junior days of his intimate companion.

So the young man passed happy hours among
his friends during a twelvemonth or so after
his return from abroad. Amid the whirl of daily
engagements, doubtless there were times when
he thought about the possibilities of the future,
when he wondered what he should take up as
his life-work. At first it would appear that he
cherished no especial inclination toward the ministry. He looked upon it as a distinct renunciation
of the world. If he entered into that, he must give
up this pleasant mode of life to which he had become accustomed. After a while, when he did
reach a decision, he adhered to the same view.
When he entered Holy Orders he gave up much,
and he renounced it of his own free will. The
familiar and attractive " fashion of this world " became unknown to him. His graceful form faded

away from the scene of the dance. Thereafter he
was never known even to sing a secular air, except
occasionally in a part-song when he revisited his
first home. In Troy it came to be an understood
thing that he would not accept invitations for a
Friday, not even to the harmless assemblage at a
family tea table. It was a serious business with
him; when he did come to a determination he took
up his cross with a full perception of the fact that it
was a burden. So far as he himself was concerned,
in some respects, he became an ascetic, although no
one was more considerate in behalf of the worldly
happiness of other people.

But I anticipate. As yet he thought little of
these things. Then it happened that friends inter-
vened, bringing a message, a call.

Said Bishop Coxe, upon the occasion referred
to: " One day Hobart (son of Bishop Hobart) said
to me, ' We must get that young man to study for
the ministry.' We agreed to broach the subject
to him. In the meantime we would, each one,
make it a subject of prayer. We did so. To
Tucker we gave Newman's sermons to read; you
know we young men were all enthusiastic about
Newman in those days."

After a while the mother's prayers were recalled,
the grandmother's hopes prevailed. The way of
the Cross seemed more sweet and alluring. The
fashionable young man, whom to look upon was
to admire, turned toward his Saviour and said,
" Send me."

Two letters are at hand which will indicate the

course of events.   In the first the subject of our memoir writes to his friend:

New York, Nov. 25th, 1841.

Dear Hobart:

I intended to have got the start of you by sending two letters for your one, when quite unexpectedly I received your welcome letter. I cannot give you a better idea of my mode of life, feelings, etc., than by describing my situation when your letter found its way upstairs to my snug little retreat in the third story, which may now be called either my study or bedroom, as I study more than I used to do and sleep less, being up at 6 o'c. every morning, reaping all or rather some of the advantages promised to those who are "early to bed and early to rise." If you had been nicely smuggled in the folds of your letter and had as suddenly come down upon me, I think you would have been startled.

I was *standing up* (another improvement by the way) with a grammar, Chrestomathy, Hebrew Bible and Lexicon before me, and was deeply engaged in translating the 5th chap. of Genesis.

The fact is, dear Hobart, I have at last arisen from my state of apathy, and begin to feel and act like a man. The chaos of the little world within begins to assume form, and I trust will soon produce. The clouds which so long have been brooding over my mind, mystifying it, tormenting it with doubts, depressing it, leaving me in that horrid state of uncertainty where the feelings either stagnate, or rudely burst forth making a channel for themselves— these clouds have been graciously dispelled. I at last see my proper course. I have accordingly notified the Bishop of my intention of becoming a Candidate for Holy Orders. To you, dear Hobart, mediately as a human agent, will I feel for ever indebted for the benefits and honors, temporal and spiritual, which prospectively I view as a faithful minister of Christ. Never can I forget your unwearied endeavors on my behalf; nor can I remember them without a feeling of mortification that they did not operate more actively upon me. Again, when I call to mind how often I was cold and dead, drawing into myself, repulsive by my vague indifference and indecision, it is to regret my carelessness and to admire your perseverance in well-doing. But, my dear friend, you must not for a moment imagine that I was ever in reality so indifferent and spiritless, as I appeared to be. No one, except those similarly situated, can appreciate the state of feeling I have been in for the last year. As I have said before, my mind was in a state of chaos; my feelings did not run in any one current, and I could not hear any allusion to the life I was leading without exciting regrets, and at that time painful reminiscences. How one's thoughts and feeling color things around us! those reminiscences which *then* gnawed the heart, *now* wreathe themselves like clouds of sweet-smelling incense around that image of my affections, whose fondest wishes I now hope to fulfil.

I do not regret, that I did not immediately on my return home select my profession. Many things urged me to that course. I utterly detest an inactive life, and was then anxious to devote myself to some pursuit. I was willing to do anything rather than nothing. If I had then selected a profession, I could have connected myself with no pursuit, except as a means of doing something. With such views I could not have studied theology, not being so unpolitic as to purchase damnation at the miserable price the devil might offer in the shape of a minister's paltry salary. As it is, I trust that my motives are pure. All that remains to be done, is to devote the rest of my life solely to the active duties of my profession. I can't now say anything more of myself, but must tell you something about our mutual friends.

Mr. William J. has taken Mr. Gibson's house for the winter; it is a small two-story house nearly opposite Mr. Fields'. The family have not yet come in town, but Miss M—— and L—— are here making the necessary preparations for their arrival. Miss E—— was in town two or three weeks since; she had two beaux in the shape of two friends of Mr. Balch. Don't be agitated: she is as sensible as pretty, and she will be very careful to whom she commits her heart. She will demand nothing short of perfection, will be very deliberate, in the end be governed by her good reason and sound judgment, and decide as she ought. This she ought to do, but we cannot philosophize on anything connected with woman or love, but are forced to make every allowance for woman's caprice and love's blindness. John has just given birth to an essay on money, full of clever bits of satire, but a little too foppish in classical quotations; he has managed to smuggle in that contraband article, slavery, with much adroitness.

We intended to have gone out last Thursday to pay Coxe a visit. We had given him a hint of our intentions. By agreement, James Constable and myself met at Mr. Fields' at one o'clock, when we were informed that Coxe and his wife had got the start of us, and in person had informed Mrs. J., that we must postpone our visit because they had neither cook nor waiter—they, like most young housekeepers imagining that their guests intended their visit for the domestics rather than the lord and lady. As yet we have had no little " reunions " at Mr. Fields'; we may have no more of those pleasant little gatherings, which we all so heartily enjoyed. Whether we do or not, they are bright spots to look back upon.

Miss Elizabeth O'Key is now Mrs. G. W. Costar. Miss A—— hopes to be Mrs. P—— on the 1st of December; your brother Dayton is to be one of the groomsmen— there are 5 others, Stephen Williams, Benjamin Silliman, etc. The Prince de Joinville is to be entertained on Friday night by Mrs. Dr. Mott. The people are crazy about lectures. The lecturers at present in the field are: " The Learned Blacksmith," " Sparks, the Biographer " and " The Notorious Dr. Lardner." I may add that the Dr. Ned Spring Sparks' course is the best attended, but I believe the majority of his audience are disappointed in him as a lecturer—his manner is decidedly bad.

John Jay is preparing an attack upon you for the *uncivil* manner in which you speak of the godly Calvinists who dealt harshly with poor Servetus.

N. B. Your letters generally go the round of your intimate friends.

Write soon and believe me ever

Yr attached friend.

John Ireland Tucker.

In this bright letter certain parts come into prominence, offering corroboration of statements already made. One of these refers to the unfailing influence of the loved mother, gone before, who is still the monitress of her boy; another to the busy routine of social affairs in which the young student is interested, and which demand time and attention. For his voluntary renunciation the hour has not yet come.

Fifteen days were required—to say nothing of a postal charge of twenty-five cents—for the transmission of the letter, first to Milwaukee and thence by forwarding to Prairie Village, where it found the Rev. Mr. Hobart.

The way that Mr. Hobart happened to be in Wisconsin was this. About the year 1840 Bishop Kemper had returned to New York from the mysterious wilderness—the Western Territory—and preached about it to the students at the Seminary. Their enthusiasm was aroused. Some offered themselves for the untried duty. They were ready for a crusade or any other service. Eventually three young deacons, under the leadership of James Lloyd Breck, started out to establish an associate mission having monastic characteristics.

Mr. Hobart was one of the three who commenced work at Prairieville. It was during the period of his short residence in the place that he wrote the letter now quoted. As he pens the name of the locality it has not yet attained to the dignity of a " ville."

The friend's reply was sent without delay:

Prairie Village, W. T.
10th Dec. 1841.

My Dear Jack:

Tho' this is Saturday night, and I have yet some labor before me in preparation for the morrow, I cannot refrain from immediately writing an answer, tho' only a few hasty words, to your letter dated 25 Nov. I read it, walking up from the Post Office hither, with emotions of most sincere gratitude to GOD, and heartfelt joy for you. You will never know the nearness to my heart, of my wish that you and I might be brothers in the ministry; and my persuasion, that so far as I could judge, it was your duty, —and the strong certainty that it would be your unspeakable gain. So far as I properly could, I tried to influence you this way; and when I found how you seemed to hesitate, I began to fear that the end would be different from what I hoped. Looking back on what I had done, it appeared evident that I had relied too much on my own ability to urge reasons, suggest motives, etc. I had not enough remembered that a Christian's most powerful means of influencing his brother, was prayer, fervent and intercessory. It seemed to me I had thought too much of my own agency, and not enough of GOD'S. So when I found I was to be separated from you, so far and so long, and that but one mode was possible to be used in behalf, as I thought, of your best interests, I resolved to betake myself to *that*, and since I have been here have been continually praying GOD, that He would show you what was the right way. Pardon me if in any respect I had (unconsciously) dealt untruly with you.

You will understand now what has been the frame of mind which, when I read of your most blessed decision, made me exclaim at once and aloud, and most naturally " Thanks be to GOD who giveth *us* the victory." I looked to you as a conqueror who had overcome the enemy in the first struggle; and as we were brothers in Christ, and in affection, your cause was mine, so that the victory seemed ours. Then, how naturally, and as it seemed providentially, did the next words of the Apostle come to my mind, with express application to you: Therefore, my beloved brother, be thou steadfast, unmovable, always abounding in the work of the Lord, forasmuch as thou knowest that thy labour is not in vain in the Lord.

Is it indeed to be so, dear Jack? Is it possible then that you and I may yet stand side by side at the Altar, and *there*, have all the remembrances of our past friendship, all that mutual knowledge of each other which makes men in old age turn to their friends as parts of themselves, all our mutual relations, hallowed and strengthened, and deepened and made eternal, by communion with our eternal Lord in His Church, at His Altar, in His Ministry? From the ground of my heart,—GOD be thanked for it!—I do not realize it yet, but I begin to see what Christian fellowship is; and in view of that intense perception of it, as a thing more real than ties of blood, more tender than mere human affection, more close than anything we call the mingling of hearts and souls in sympathy, more ineffable than, in our unspiritual state, we can find any image to liken it to—in view of all this, as attainable by you and me, I could run on in what the world would call the ravings of mysticism and fanatic phrensy, were I not afraid it would be irreverent to use words so freely about a matter I as yet dimly see, but would ardently long for—and would be strong to attain.

It has strengthened me already to know that you will soon be sworn to pursue the same object, in the same way. Think of you, and me, and Cleve—friends on earth indeed, but better and more! friends taken out of the rest of men, to stand as it were in the very court and presence of the Great King, and be sacramental channels of His grace, His Spirit, His Flesh and Blood, Himself, to our fellowmen, to each other, to ourselves!

Things may so come round, perhaps, that we shall all be together, or in near neighborhood, before many years. How we will joy to give each other sensible marks of this glorious communion, by words and acts, of assistance, kindness and love! It will be more than mortal joy. What a putting of shoulder to shoulder there will be, and interlocking of arms when there is special need of standing fast for Christ and His Church! And we have a share in the struggle!

I long doubly now to see you again. I am dashing off my words, not writing them; and when I can calmly think over what is in prospect for you and me, and estimate the particulars of our gain by this step you have taken, I will send you a more sober epistle. But, believe me, you have given me the most joyful news, and sent a deeper satisfaction into my heart than I had thought of experiencing in my solitariness here. Jay is sure to me in the Church, you and Cleve doubly sure in the ministry. Now, all four of us have an object, Heaven; all four of us a position, *contra mundum!* Love and Christian greeting to my *brother*, and all blessing, and added grace and new strength day by day, be upon you—is the earnest prayer of your affec'te

J. H. H.

In a diocesan paper Bishop Coxe printed a brief note, in which he spoke thus of the young manhood of Dr. Tucker: "He was a noble youth in New York, reared in luxury and endowed with qualities of character and graces of person which made him an idol in the fashionable circle of New York society, while as yet the old Knickerbocker respectability and the predominance of Church influence were undiluted. 'Chancellor Livingston, Dr. Hosack, and Bishop Hobart,' said a contemporary, 'were the tripod on which "society" was based in New York.' It was the wonder of such a *monde* when Mr. Tucker, 'the favorite of all circles and the pride of his own,' deliberately threw aside his 'prospects in life' and entered the General Theological Seminary as a candidate for the diaconate. When he accepted the Rectorship in the parish at Troy, it was supposed that this was a mere stepping-stone to rapid and brilliant preferment. But he *took it for life*, and devoted himself to the most self-denying features of missionary work."

While yet a resident of New York the musical abilities possessed by Mr. Tucker came into use, in a way of which many know not. For a considerable period he was organist of St. Thomas' Church. It is as relating to this time that he used to tell a story. One Sunday morning the young organist had performed a "voluntary," probably at the offertory, which was more elaborate and showy than usual. After the service the venerable Rector called him into the rectory and made the suggestion that these *tours de force* would better be discontinued, as in that Church the clergyman intended that the pulpit should be the chief attraction.

The knowledge of the organ possessed by our student, as well as the cultivation of his fine bass voice, both fitted him the better for the peculiar and life-long service to religion which he was about to render.

In a catalogue of the General Theological Seminary of appropriate date, among the graduates of the year 1841, I read the names John H. Hobart and " Arthur C. Coxe."   The career of the latter is well known.

It may, however, be fitting to interject a remark about recent occurrences taking place at the Seminary Commencement of 1896—as it turned out the last attended by the late Bishop of Western New York.   Then Bishop Coxe presented the diplomas to the graduating class, some forty-five in number, and spoke touchingly of a period long gone, even fifty-five years before, when he, " in that very place, stood with Breck and others of his class to receive his diploma from the hands of the sainted De Lancey."

The son of Bishop Hobart took up labor in the Western Territory, in the jurisdiction of " the Missionary Bishop."   While yet a deacon he came back to New York, in July, 1844, to take charge of St. Paul's, Red Hook, in Dutchess County—doubtless in time to witness the ordination of his friend.

In the year 1842 J. Carpenter Smith graduated from the Seminary—whose recollection about the Brooklyn life has already been set down.   Arthur Carey, whose name became well known, was a classmate.

It was in the same year, 1842, that John I. Tucker entered the institution as a member of the middle class.   Robert B. Fairbairn was a Seminary mate during a part of the course, graduating in 1843.   He had further association with the Rector of the Holy Cross, and remained the close friend of the other, at times his companion, until death called one of the two.

According to the initials given in the Seminary Catalogue, " John I. Tucker " was graduated in the year 1844.   From the New York *Churchman* (Dr. Seabury's), bearing date July 6, 1844, we derive information, given after an explicit fashion:

The 21st Annual Commencement of the General Theological Seminary of the Protestant Episcopal Church in the United States was celebrated in St. John's Chapel in this city on Friday, June 28th.   Morning Prayer was read by the Rev. Wm. Shelton, D.D., of Western New York, assisted by the Rev'd. Robert W. Harris of N. Y. who read the lessons, alumni of the Seminary.   The Ante-Communion Service was read by the Right Rev. Benjamin T. Onderdonk, D.D., of New York (the Right Rev. Thomas C. Brownell, D.D., LL.D., of Connecticut the Senior Bishop present, being prevented by diseased eyes) assisted by the Right Rev. George W. Doane, D.D., LL.D., of New Jersey, who read the Epistle, and the Right Rev. John H. Hopkins, D.D., of Vermont, who read the Gospel.   The Commencement Sermon was preached by the Right Rev. Manton Eastburn, D.D., of Massachusetts.

The Reverend, the Dean of the Faculty [Dr. Samuel H. Turner] in the name and behalf of that body, then presented to the Bishop of Connecticut—for receiving the testimonials awarded by the Trustees and Professors to students who have acceptably prosecuted the full course of study, and faithfully discharged their duties—the following young gentlemen, composing the Senior Class:—

Henry B. Bartow of New York, . . . etc., including John I. Tucker of New York.

The testimonials were delivered accordingly, with a short but interesting and solemn address to the class by the Bishop of Connecticut.

The Bishop of New York then proceeded to the administration of the Lord's Supper, in which he was assisted by the Bishops of Connecticut, Vermont and New Jersey, the Missionary Bishop and the Bishop of Western New York. There were also present the Bishops of Maryland and Delaware. The Faculty and students of the Seminary, a large body of Alumni and other clergy, and many other Christians—all probably amounting to between three and four hundred—united with the Bishops in this very solemn and interesting Communion. The Blessing was pronounced by the Bishop of Connecticut.

It remains yet to be noted that within a few weeks after his graduation from the Seminary, that is, in July, 1844, our candidate was admitted to the order of deacons by the Rt. Rev. Benjamin T. Onderdonk, Bishop of New York.

JOHN IRELAND TUCKER

In his twenty-fifth year

VI

THE BEGINNINGS AT TROY

After the beneficent career had been finished, and after it had become evident to all that the recent incumbent had transformed a position—which most men would call obscure—into a shining centre of powerful influence, then the question was asked, "Who made this nomination? Who suggested the name of John I. Tucker to the patron at Troy?"

The late Bishop Coxe claimed the honor for himself. In the conversation already referred to, the Bishop of Western New York remarked: "I got him his place in Troy. They (the Troy people) said to me, ' Now we have this building, and everything prepared, what shall we do to get the most important part—to find the man to work in it?' I have the man for you," said the Bishop; and he told the story about his friend, enlarging upon his manifold virtues and capabilities.

"A few years later," continued Bishop Coxe, "I went up to Troy. There was the young man of society, the pet of fashion, the brilliant centre of its circles, recently devoted to its endless whirl of gaiety, now standing before a blackboard with a class of poor girls around him, drilling them in the rudiments, teaching this uninteresting matter, teaching hour after hour!"

In truth, it was a metamorphosis!

The mention of the name may have been made by "Mr. Coxe" to and through "Mr. Williams," then Rector at Schenectady, who was an enthusiastic supporter and forwarder of the project at Troy, and a constant adviser of the foundress. Dr. Warren writes: "I suggested to my mother that Dr. Williams should have charge of the Mission. His reply was that he could not leave St. George's, Schenectady, but that he knew a young man in the Theological Seminary who would be just the right man in the right place. That young man was secured, and how thoroughly correct was the estimation of Dr. Williams, the faithful and uninterrupted ministrations of the Rev. Dr. Tucker . . . are a living witness."

For the sake of those who are not Trojans, let me pause to give a brief recounting of local history.

Mrs. Phebe Warren was a benevolent Churchwoman, a native of Norwalk, Conn., who with her husband and family settled in the then village of Troy in the year 1798. The newcomer took large interest in the planting of the Church in her neighborhood. After the parish of St. Paul's was started, in 1804, she undertook the Catechetical instruction of the children—that is, she formed a class or school for instruction in the Catechism, and this before the day of either Sunday or Parish School.

The desolations of war, in the year 1812, brought about an increase in the number of neglected chil-

dren. Mrs. Phebe Warren met the fresh demand;
she gathered a company of little ones into a " Saturday Sewing-school," wherein they were to be
taught the " Catechism and plain sewing."

In 1835 the little school came down as a bequest
to the daughter-in-law, Mrs. Mary Warren, who
had promised the dying foundress to continue the
benefaction.

Four years after, the Saturday Sewing-school was
converted into a day school, which met in an apartment belonging to St. Paul's Church. From the beginning the singing of the children was made much
of; frequently do we read of visitors, that they were
taken " to hear the children sing." A competent
instructor, William Hopkins, had been engaged to
give music lessons to the school. A further and
more extended interest was awakened in view of
the fact that a son of the benefactress was himself
a musician, and that at special services he acted
as organist for the choir of children.

In St. Paul's Church, six or eight pews in the
gallery, next to the organ loft, had been set apart
for occupancy on Sunday mornings by the members of the school. As among them much attention
was given to music, they would be likely to take
part in the musical sections of the service. Their
participation, however, was not grateful to the professional members of the quartet choir, who desired
the exclusive right of performance. The story is
told by Dr. Nathan B. Warren, present patron of
the school:

" One Monday morning, in the summer, of 1843,

the patroness of the little school went in as usual, and found the children all in tears. On inquiring the cause of the disturbance, she was told by Miss Pierce, the teacher, that the Sunday-school Superintendent had just been in, and had lectured the children on the impropriety of uniting their voices with the regular choir. The choir were unwilling, the Superintendent said, that the children should assist in the music of the Church, and that unless he could stop them they would quit.

" This musical strike frightened the Superintendent, who was a benevolent man, and doubtless had no idea of the pain he was inflicting. The patroness said to the children: ' Dry your eyes, and like good children do as you are bid, and you soon shall have a Church of your own to sing in, and in which you can sing to your hearts' content.'

" The children had been a little exalted since their elevation to the organ loft on the Holydays occurring on week-days, and since a Sunday-school celebration at which they assisted at a Choral Service, on which occasion the venerable Superintendent expressed himself decidedly pleased, declaring that ' it was very solemn.' "

So good came out of evil. The churlishness of the quartet brought about the starting of a charity, which under accomplished and wise direction grew up to be a creation unique, poetic and Christian.

Mrs. Mary Warren had already made provision in her will for the establishment of a free Missionary Church in Troy. Now it appeared that the working out of her plan must be expedited. She decided at once, after the complaint about the children, to become her own executor. The charitable work was begun and carried on; her children uniting in the effort.

For information about the laying of the cornerstone, we are indebted to a diary kept by the pious foundress, and discovered the day after her death. On the date, Wednesday, the 23rd April, 1844, she writes:

I have been much engaged preparing for the reception of the Bishop who arrived this evening at 6 o'clock after a very refreshing thunderstorm. Dr. Potter of Albany accompanied him and they both remained with us until Friday morning. On Thursday the Bishop ordained Mr. Fairbairn in the morning; after service, we had the Bishop to dine with us. Among the company were Dr. Potter, Mr. Williams, Mr. Kip, Mr. Selkirk of Albany, Mr. Metcalf of Duanesburgh, Mr. Babbet of Hudson, Mr. Hecock of Western N. Y., Mr. Twing, Mr. Bissell, Mr. Van Kleeck, Mr. Cox, Mr. Fairbairn, Mr. Hubbard and Mr. Van Rensselaer.

½ past four. After driving we had service at St. Paul's, when the children formed the choir. Immediately after service, the Bishop and clergy attended by the vestry of the several churches and the laity formed a procession and went up to 8th street, to lay the cornerstone of the Free Mission Church of the Holy Cross. After the Bishop laid the stone, Mr. Van Kleeck our Rector delivered a most excellent and appropriate address: the children of the school chanted the Psalms and sang an Anthem, assisted by their teacher Mr. Hopkins and several others who accompanied them on instruments of music of different kinds. The music was very fine, and seemed to delight every one. After the services were over, the Bishop attended by the clergy and vestry, all came to our house and remained for a short time. We had a succession of visitors throughout the evening which seemed very gratifying to our Diocesan as well as to all of our family. The Rev. Mr. Ingersoll also came in town and passed a part of the evening with us. We had a bright and glorious day for our services, which I trust is an omen of the smile and approbation of an overruling Providence on our undertaking. We have had so much to discourage us ever since it has been known that we contemplated building and dedicating this Church to God. By some people it has been said that we were going to join the Romanists, and by others it was said we were going to build a Puseyite or Puseylite Church; and all sorts of ill-natured remarks have been made about it. I will remark that the corner-stone was laid on St. Mark's day, it being the birthday of my son Nathan B. Warren. This Church when completed is designed to have the daily service.

An inscription made on or in the corner-stone, announced: "The Church of the Holy Cross was founded in the year of grace, 1844, by Mary Warren, as a house of prayer for all people, without money and without price. Glory be to the Father and to the Son and to the Holy Ghost. Amen."

At the laying of the corner-stone two anthems were sung—"O send out Thy light and Thy truth" and "Great is the Lord and greatly to be praised." About the music our authority says: "If it was not artistic it was given with a hearty good will." There was an orchestral accompaniment, led by William Hopkins, who that day laid the foundation of the choir ere long famous throughout the land.

As yet Mr. Tucker has nothing to do with it. In New York on that day, the student in the Seminary very likely had no thought about the doings up the Hudson, in a locality with which his whole future was to be identified. Soon, however, he is nominated to the patron, and appears upon the scene. Mrs. Warren writes:

Oct. 26th. Saturday evening. My sons Nathan and George came up in the boat tonight with the Rev. Mr. Tucker. He stayed with us and we were much pleased with him.

Sunday. Mr. Tucker read prayers for Mr. Van Kleeck this morning, but declined preaching. The children sang between services, and Mr. Tucker seemed much gratified.

Monday. Mr. Fairbairn dined with us today with Mr. Tucker. We then went up to the school and heard the children go through the services for the Consecration. Mr. Tucker sang with them, and the music was never finer. Mr. Tucker then left us in the evening boat for New York.

Saturday, 30th. [November.] The Rev. Mr. Tucker arrived this evening, and has come up with an expectancy of having our Church consecrated next week on Thursday or Saturday. We shall however be disappointed as our Bishop has declined for the present attending to any official duties, and has not yet appointed any Bishop to act in his place.

December, Friday, 6th. Mr. Tucker left us this morning for New York, with the hope of making arrangements with Bishop Doane for the Consecration of our Church, after the trial of Bishop Onderdonk, which is to take place on Tuesday the 10th.

VII

THE DEACON IN CHARGE

At last the newly-fledged cleric goes to Troy, to stay. He settles down for his lifelong performance of duty.

The Church building, which is ready, includes at first only a square nave, with a little square tower in front. Nathan B. Warren was its designer, himself drawing the plans. Arrangements for the consecration were not completed; instead, there is an "opening service." Mrs. Mary Warren, in her diary, recounts the method of procedure; a few extracts are given:

December 24th, 1844. Mr. Tucker arrived today and has made arrangements for opening our little Church tomorrow, by permission of the Bishop.

Christmas Day. We were permitted to meet in the Church of the Holy Cross both morning and evening. After service in the morning we went to St. Paul's to receive the Holy Communion, and at four o'clock we assembled in our new Church again, when we had the full choral service both morning and evening: it was exceedingly fine, and Mr. Tucker gave us a beautiful sermon. After evening service we returned home; the children of the school 81 in number with their teachers all came to wish us a merry Christmas, and see their Christmas tree, and receive their presents which as usual consisted of

books, pocket knives, cakes, candies and fruit.   Dr. Potter
and family, Mr. Williams of Schenectady and several of our
friends came in to see the Christmas tree.

In Troy there is a tradition that the opening service took place on the eve of Christmas.   According to Mrs. Warren, however, the first office occurred on Christmas day in the morning.

The order started with a " Choral " office at the
Holy Cross, after which the Deacon in charge
preached his first sermon to his people.   The
congregation then removed in a body, going from
the Holy Cross to the mother Church (St. Paul's),
there to receive the Holy Communion.

The diary proceeds:

January 1st, 1845.   This day has been passed as all New
Years' are generally passed in receiving visits from our
friends.   Mr. Tucker dined with us, and we had not the
usual number of visitors.

6th.   *Feast of Epiphany*.   We had service in our Church
this morning, and had several of our clergy there, among
whom were Mr. Williams (who preached a most excellent sermon), Mr. Bissell, Van Kleeck, Fairbairn, Van
Rensselaer, and Dr. Potter came in time to dine with us.
We had Mr. Tucker and his father and sister, Mr. Williams and his mother, Mr. Fairbairn, Mr. Van Rensselaer.
After dinner we went over to Mr. Joseph Warren's to
attend a clerical party.

7th.   Visited the school with Mr. Tucker's family, and
heard the children sing.

Saturday, 11th.   Mr. Tucker and daughter and son dined
with us and Mary Cannon; we had a pleasant dinner.

Sunday, 12th.   Major Tucker and daughter went to
Church with us at St. Paul's in the morning, and in the
evening we all went up to the Holy Cross, where we

heard a most beautiful sermon from these words: "And all they that heard it wondered at those things which were told them by the shepherds. But Mary kept all these things, and pondered them in her heart."

Monday, 13th. This has been a very snowy day. I called to see Major Tucker's family this morning to say good bye to them, and visited the school.

Sunday, 19th. Commenced having service this morning at half past 10 o'clock. The day has been exceedingly cold, and the walking never was more slippery. We had another beautiful sermon from Mr. T——; in the evening he catechised the children.

Feb'y 2nd. Sunday Morning. Attended the Church of the Holy Cross, altho' it was exceedingly cold and slippery. Heard a sweet sermon from Mr. Tucker from I Corinthians 13 chap. and 13 verse: "And now abideth faith, hope, charity, these three; but the greatest of these is charity." It was the best sermon I ever heard from this text of Scripture, and intended as an introductory sermon to our Sunday offerings. A collection was taken up after, but our congregation was unusually small; there was but $3 received on the occasion. We had service again at 4 o'clock and a baptism; the first child that was baptized in our beautiful stone font.—It belongs to Mr. Roden, an Englishman, and the child's name was Robert Stephen.

5th. *Ash Wednesday.* Attended the Church of the Holy Cross in a tremendous snowstorm, and of course had a small congregation. From this day we commence our daily service.

6th. Attended Church this morning at 11 o'clock, altho' we have had a heavy fall of snow. Our congregation was small—the children of the school are having a vacation now, consequently but a part of the children are in Church.

7th and 8th. Attended Church both mornings; had a good attendance both of children and adults. The music very good; Nathan plays the organ for the daily service and plays very well too. Old Mr. Sheldon died this morning at 7 o'clock; he is the father of Miss Pierce. His funeral is to be attended tomorrow.

22nd. Saturday. At Church again; being a warm springlike morning 60 of the school present. After service went to see Mrs. Clarkson with Mr. Tucker, and he promised to give the old woman a load of wood. This evening Miss Sutherland and Miss Douglass took tea with us, also Mr. Tucker.

23rd. Sunday. Went to the Holy Cross this morning and heard another sweet sermon from Mr. T——. St. Luke, 11 chap. and 23rd v.: " He that is not with me is against me." Mr. T—— improves every Sunday, each sermon seems better than the last. How fortunate we have been in getting so good and excellent a man! A kind Providence has certainly smiled on us in giving us all that we could desire; he is truly a watchful shepherd, looking constantly and perseveringly after the lambs of his fold in the dear little children of our school—and seems to do it too with so much kindness and affection— and not only the children but their parents and all who attend the Church of the Holy Cross. This afternoon, went to St. Paul's to hear Mr. Van Kleeck—it being so rainy I have been prevented going up to the Holy Cross to the 4 o'clock service. This is the first time I have missed any service in our dear little Church, and I have been greatly disappointed in not being able to go, as my sons say I have lost much in the lecture and catechism as well as good music. Mr. Tucker dined with us to-day as he usually does on Sundays.

March 8th. Had a pleasant visit from the Rev. J. H. Hobart and Mr. Williams; they attended the services of the Holy Cross and dined with us.

21st. *Good Friday Morning.* Found Major Tucker and daughter at the Holy Cross this morning, when we went up to the service. Had a large congregation and a most excellent sermon. In the afternoon, had prayers and no sermon. Saturday went to service in the morning and to Church in the afternoon to hear the choir practice. The evening the Tuckers passed with us.

23rd. *Easter Sunday*. This morning is cold but pleasant; had a large congregation and a beautiful sermon. The whole school in attendance, 80 in number, all in their new dresses—blue plaid calico, bonnets fawn color trimmed with blue, white gloves and white capes. Our music was never finer, 6 gentlemen volunteered their services to sing with the choir—the two Mr. Concies, Mr. Brinkerhoof, Mr. Clark, Mr. Ilsley and Mr. Hopkins; Major T—— also accompanied them. We had the Holy Communion administered this morning, Mr. Fairbairn assisting Mr. T——. 33 communicants went forward to receive the consecrated elements, several of whom had never communed before. Major T—— and daughter and son dined with us, also their friend Mr. Whitlock from N. Y. and Mr. Fairbairn. Attended service again in the afternoon at 4 o'clock; had an overflowing congregation and delightful music; no sermon.

In her Easter entry, the loyal parishioner thinks naturally of her pastor as in charge of the service, which leads her to speak of Mr. Fairbairn as assisting at the office of the Holy Communion. Mr. Fairbairn, however, was Priest and Celebrant. Mr. Tucker was still in the Order of Deacons.

24th. Went to Church this morning and had Major T—— daughter and son with Mr. Whitlock to dine with us; the Major and Mr. W. left for N. Y. at 5 this afternoon and left Miss T. to pass a few days with us.

Monday, 31st. Attended Church to-day. After dinner Miss Tucker and her brother left us for New York. This evening Mr. Fairbairn took tea with us.

Another authoritative source of information is to be found in a " Book of Records " about ser-

vices, etc., started by the young Deacon in charge
and continued for a time. In general, the words
are quoted as he wrote them, without condensation
into the form of a summary.

We retrace our steps, going back to the commencement of services at the Holy Cross.

Upon the title-page of the book we read as follows:

A Record of the

CHURCH OF THE HOLY CROSS
Founded

by

MRS. NATHAN WARREN

as a

Church for the poor and all people.

JOHN IRELAND TUCKER,

Deacon—first Minister of the Parish.

1844-45.

The entries are made in the form of a Journal,
sometimes with explanations—interjected remarks
—which throw light upon the subject. They begin:

In consequence of the unfortunate position of this Diocese, owing to the trial of its Bishop, it was thought expedient to open the Church of the Holy Cross, without
waiting until it was consecrated. Accordingly the Church
was opened for Divine Service on Christmas-day (morning and afternoon). In the morning I offered the prayers
and preached, in the afternoon I was assisted at Evening
Prayer by the Rev. Dr. Potter of Albany, the Rev. Mr.

Williams of Schenectady, and the Rev. Messrs. Van Kleeck and Fairbairn of this city.

St. Stephen's Day. The Rev. Messrs. Williams, Van Kleeck and Fairbairn, assisted at the service; myself preached.

St. John the Evangelist, Dec. 27th. Assisted by the Rev. Messrs. Walter, Fairbairn and Van Kleeck.

The Festival of the Holy Innocents. Dec. 28th. Assisted by the Rev. Mr. Walter; myself preached.

Festival of the Circumcision. Morning Prayer at 9 o'clock.

Epiphany, Jan'y. 6th. The Rev. Mr. Williams preached.

Septuagesima, Jan'y. 19th. Introduced the regular Morning Service, previously to this having confined ourselves to the Evening Service on Sundays, and the full Morning Service on Festivals and Holydays. Now, we have on Sundays, Morning Prayer and Sermon at half past 10; Evening Prayer, followed by a Catechetical Lecture, at 4 o'clock. After the lecture, and before the congregation is dismissed, the children are assembled around the Chancel and catechized.

Conversion of St. Paul. Morning Prayer and Sermon.

Quinquagesima Sunday. Introduced "the Offertory" on Sunday mornings. In the afternoon of this day, baptized, after the second lesson, the first person at the Church of the Holy Cross.

Ash Wednesday, Feb. 4th. Very stormy—few at Church.

Feb. 5th. Introduced *Daily Morning Prayer* at 11 o'clock.

Feb. 10th. Assisted by the Rev. Messrs. Twing, Williams and Gibson.

Feb. 13th. Assisted by the Rev. Messrs. Twing and Bissell.

At divers times and occasions assisted by my kind and obliging friend, the Rev. Mr. Fairbairn, Rector of Christ Church, this city.

Feb. 22nd. The daily service is usually well attended;

including the children, we generally number between 60 and 70—considerably more than "the Church quorum."

Feb. 23rd. 100 persons at the Church attending Morning Prayer.

Feb. 24th. *Festival of St. Matthias.* Morning Prayer and Sermon. The Rev. Messrs. Bissell, Fairbairn and Gibson were present.

March 8th. The Rev. Messrs. Hobart and Williams officiated at Morning Prayer.

March 13th. The Rev. Messrs. Fairbairn, Bruce, Selkirk and Gibson were present at Morning Prayer.

March 23rd, *Easter Day.* The Holy Communion was on this day administered in this Church for the first time. Rev. Mr. Fairbairn officiated for me after attending to the services in his own Church.

Remark has often been made about the number of men, prominent in future years, who clustered about the beginnings of the work in Troy. Dr. Horatio Potter was then Rector of St. Peter's, Albany; later, Bishop of New York. Mr. Williams of Schenectady is now Primus or Presiding Bishop. Mr. Kip became Bishop of California; Mr. Bissell, Bishop of Vermont. Mr. Fairbairn has been for years the honored Warden of St. Stephen's College. Messrs. Van Kleeck and Twing served the whole Church in connection with her Missionary department. These and many others are found at the services of the Holy Cross—some frequently, some constantly. We see the entry day after day about Mr. Fairbairn or Mr. Van Kleeck. At dates not far removed we note other well-known names—Muhlenberg, De Koven, Wainwright, Bishop Doane of New Jersey, Buel, Mahan, Van Rensselaer, Stubbs and Haight.

The fact is to be explained not merely by the pleasant association with the patroness, who was a devoted daughter of the Church, and a friend of clergy, and who manifested an apostolic grace in that she was "given to hospitality." Not only this; nor was it only the attraction of the new pastor, who began at once to exert his wide-spreading influence. Rather was it that these and other acute minds were interested in the then new development of Church life. Here was the first American example of the Church revival, about which much had been heard. Here were daily prayers; the appropriate offices for holydays, even for Ascension, a day heretofore ignored in American religion. Here again were choral services, also the unknown and fearful mysteries of Gregorian tones—features identified with the awakening. What wonder that these Priests, whose pulses stirred with sympathy, should crowd round the standard freshly set up in Troy as a beacon for the entire land! What wonder that these earnest souls should lift up their eyes unto the hills, should climb often the hill of Mount Ida, to pray and worship there!

Once more, Mrs. Warren's diary:

Saturday, April 5th. Mr. Tucker returned from N. Y. this morning, and came to breakfast with us. He gives us favorable accounts of our Bishop. We went to Church this morning, and Mr. T—— took tea with us.

Ascension Day, May 1st. Attended Church and the Holy Communion was administered. We had the pleasure of Dr. Muhlenberg to assist in the services; he also preached a most excellent sermon. His sister Mrs.

Rogers and her daughter came up with him, also Major and Mrs. Tucker, and young Mr. Berryan; also we had Mr. De Koven, Berryan and Mr. Fairbairn to dine with us. Mrs. Rogers and daughter with Mrs. Tucker passed the evening with us. We took the party up to see the cottage in the afternoon.

Friday, 2nd. Went to the services of the Holy Cross this morning, and in the afternoon took Major and Mrs. Tucker with Mr. De Koven to drive to the snuff factory and around the hollow road.

Monday, 5th. Went to New York with my family this morning, all except Stephen. Stayed at the New York hotel. Went a shopping on Tuesday. Had several of our friends to see us.

Wednesday, 7th. Dined with my family at Major Tucker's; met Dr. and Mrs. Beck, Miss Sands and Miss McVicker. Had an elegant and delightful dinner.

Thursday, 8th. Went a shopping most of the day and returned home very tired.

9th. Went this morning with Mrs. Rogers to see the new Church she is building on 20th street. It is a very beautiful gothic building, in the form of a cross; it will be large enough to contain 7 or 800 people; to be finished the first of October. We went to see Dr. Pott's Church which is now erecting; it is also gothic with beautiful stained glass windows, and I spied two ornamental crosses in the top of the windows. After driving out with Mrs. Rogers, went with Harriet and the Capt. to return visits.

11th. *Whitsunday*. Attended the Church of the Holy Cross to-day, and we had a large congregation and two most excellent sermons, from Mr. Tucker, very appropriate for the day. He is truly a delightful preacher as well as a most devoted and faithful pastor; he seems to have gained the affections of all his little flock both old and young. How fortunate we have been in obtaining the services of so good a man! I feel that he has been sent us by the overruling hand of Providence, and I cannot feel sufficiently thankful to our great Creator for all the belongings he so bountifully bestows upon me and mine. I see *His* hand in everything that concerns me. I have for the last 10 years given myself up to His guidance, and all that belongs to me or that I am interested in, feeling assured that whatever befalls us would be for the best; with the assurance I go on my way rejoicing, and have the greatest reason in the world to feel happy in being so highly favored and blessed in my undertakings by my Heavenly Father. May He continue to smile on my humble endeavors until I reach my journey's end, which cannot be far distant; and when I have passed through this vale of tears, may that ever dear and blessed Saviour receive my soul; as it leaves my frail body, may it be attended by the bright company of Angels, and commended to the Almighty Father whose creature I am and who formed me out of dust. May I not be terrified at the approach of death. Let not Satan impede my journey, but may the adorable Saviour who suffered death upon the cross for me, deliver me from all torments and death eternal, and place me forever within Paradise; and may the Good Shepherd receive me among His sheep and pardon my many sins; may I behold my blessed Redeemer face to face, and be permitted to stand in His presence and to enjoy the sweetness of Divine Contemplation for ever and ever.

Tuesday, 13th. Moved up to the cottage to-day. It has been quite summer like, and the grounds around and about the cottage are looking beautiful. I attended morning prayers at the Holy Cross before we moved up.

27th. Tuesday. Five clergymen present at a weekday service.

Friday, May 30th. At the Holy Cross at prayers this morning, Messrs. Walter and Fairbairn assisted Mr. T. with the services. Visited the school in the afternoon. Heard the children sing a beautiful anthem, taken from the 27th Psalm: "I will wash my hands in innocency." The Solo was sung by Margaret Hauer and Alice Rockingham. It was one of the most touching things I ever heard and melted me into a flood of tears.

Saturday, 31st. Was at St. Cross again this morning with my family. Five clergymen present and quite a full attendance. We have had at least three of the clergy at our daily service every day this week.

Parallel entries in the " Record of Services " may yet be quoted:

May 1st, *Ascension Day*. The Rev. Dr. Muhlenberg preached and officiated at the Holy Communion assisted by the Rev. Mr. De Koven.

May 18th, *Trinity Sunday*. The Rev. Mr. Van Kleeck administered the Holy Communion.

June 15th, *4th Sunday after Trinity*. The Rev. Mr. Walter preached and administered the Holy Communion. The Rev. Dr. Wainwright preached in the afternoon.

July 20th, 1845, *9th Sunday after Trinity*. The Bishop of New Jersey officiated in the Church of the Holy Cross, preaching in the morning and in the evening.

July 21st, Monday. The Bishop of New Jersey offici-ated at Morning Prayer, with the Rev. Messrs. Tucker and Fairbairn.

July 23rd, Wednesday. The Rev. Dr. Wainwright and the Rev. Mr. Tucker read Morning Prayer, and the Bishop of New Jersey catechized the children.

The three foregoing entries are made in a hand-writing different from that observed throughout the book; hence the variation in terminology about the pastor. The ordinary handwriting is resumed on

July 24th. The Rev. Mr. Van Kleeck officiated at Morn-ing Prayer, I being obliged to go to Saratoga to baptize the daughter of the Rev. Mr. Hobart.

August 4th. The Church closed for the purpose of painting.

August 31st. *15th Sunday after Trinity.* The Church was reopened for divine service. Assisted in the morning by Rev. Mr. Bissell; in the afternoon, assisted in the service by Rev. Mr. Twing. The Rev. J. P. F. Clark of Long Island preached.

September 7th. *16th Sunday after Trinity.* At 5 o'clock (Evening Service) assisted by Rev. Mr. Gibson, Cohoes. For some months past, I have lectured in Church at ½ past 3 (Sundays) to a Bible Class. Subject: "The Acts of the Holy Apostles."

14th. *17th Sunday after Trinity.* In consequence of indisposition, was compelled to break off the service at the Litany. At 5 o'clock there was the usual service, when the Rev. Messrs. Van Kleeck and Fairbairn assisted, and the Rev. Mr. French of Washington preached.

21st. Rev. Mr. Fairbairn, after service in his own Church, administered the Holy Communion.

28th. Rev. Mr. Spooner, Rector of Zion Church, Sandy Hill, preached.

October 12th. *21st Sunday after Trinity.* I was ill. The Rev. Mr. Parks, Chaplain at West Point, officiated for me.

October 19th. *22nd Sunday after Trinity.* The Rev. Mr. Samuel Buel, preached and officiated at the Holy Communion. The hour for Evening Service now changed to 4 o'clock.

From 20th to 25th. The daily service was attended to by the Rev. Mr. Fairbairn, assisted by the Rev. Messrs. Saml. and Hillhouse Buel and Weaver; I being absent from the city on a visit to my friends. During the week, the children without the aid of the organ or any one to lead them, chanted the canticles to the Gregorian tones.

October 26th. *23rd Sunday after Trinity.* Officiated all day. In the afternoon, instead of lecturing on Catechism, catechized the children openly in the Church, before dismissing the congregation.

Succeeding entries—not quoted—make frequent mention of the names Samuel Buel, Hillhouse Buel, and Fairbairn.

November 2nd. The Rev. Hillhouse Buel preached at Morning Service. I lectured in the afternoon—an Introduction to the Ten Commandments. The Anthem: "The Lord is King" by Chappell.

30th. *Advent Sunday ; St. Andrew.* J. I. T. officiated and preached in the morning. In the afternoon, the Right Rev. L. S. Ives, Bishop of North Carolina, preached. The Rev. Mr. Fairbairn assisted me in the service. Anthem: "Come unto Me."

December 7th. *1st Sunday in Advent.* J. I. T. officiated morning and evening. Anthem: "I was glad when they said unto Me," Callcott.

In many of the daily entries, not quoted here, there is a reference either to Mr. Fairbairn or Mr. Van Kleeck. On the 10th of December, the Rev. Mr. Hallam of New London is noted as present. On the 14th (3rd Sunday in Advent) the Anthem is "Hear my prayer," Kent. On Christmas Eve there is service at half past 6, the Rev. Mr. Van Rensselaer assisting.

25th. *Christmas Day.* The Rev. Mr. Van Rensselaer of Albany kindly officiated for me and preached. The alms collected at the Offertory were appropriated to the relief of the Nashotah Mission.

On the evening of the 28th, there is a sermon by the Rev. J. Williams. Anthem: " Behold, a Virgin shall conceive," from the " Messiah."

January 1st, 1846. *Festival of the Circumcision.* [In another handwriting.] The minister being absent from the city, the Rev. Mr. Fairbairn officiated for him.

The same note is made having reference to the morning of the 4th. But "The Minister" officiated and lectured in the afternoon. Anthem: "There were Shepherds," from the "Messiah."

6th. *Festival of Epiphany.* Assisted by the Rev. Mr. Van Kleeck, Messrs. Twing, Van Rensselaer and Fairbairn. The Sunday-school of Trinity Church, Lansingburgh, the Parish-school of St. Paul's (this city) were present, with the girls of our Parish-school, about 200 in all. The Rev. Mr. Van Kleeck addressed this youthful congregation.

February 2nd. *The Festival of the Presentation of Christ in the Temple.* A full Choral Service. The Rev. Messrs. Van Kleeck and Fairbairn. Anthem: "I waited patiently." The Christmas decorations taken down this day,

The last note will supply indication of an advance in Church intelligence. The "general Church" in America had not yet awakened to the fitness of things. As late as one of the "sixties," the writer remembers a case in Jersey where the sexton had neglected to take down the "greens" in time (not for the Purification, but) for the office of Ash Wednesday morning. A few officials demolished things immediately before the hour of service. When the congregation arrived they found floors and seats still covered with the pine needles which had fallen everywhere.

On the 4th of February, Rev. Mr. Hobart assists at Morning Prayer, and five other visiting clergy are named as present.

8th. *Septuagesima Sunday.* In afternoon, lecture again on the holy rite of Confirmation; qualifications &c.

of candidates; benefits of the rite. Anthem: "I will wash my hands."

In the evening, the Rt. Rev. Samuel A. McCoskry, Bishop of Michigan, administered the rite of Confirmation at St. Paul's Church; about 86 candidates, 30 presented by myself.

9th. I assisted at Morning Prayers, the Rt. Rev. Bp. McCoskry. The Rev. Messrs. Van Kleeck, Weaver, Potter, Fairbairn, and Van Rensselaer, were also present.

15th. *Sexagesima Sunday.* Exchanged with Dr. Potter of Albany. A very stormy day! There were few at Church. The Holy Communion was administered to 21 persons.

25th. *Ash Wednesday.* The Rev. Dr. Jarvis took part in the service and also preached. The Canticles and Proper Psalms for the day, were chanted, without the organ, to Gregorian tones.

March 1st. *1st Sunday in Lent.* In the morning preached on the necessity of fasting, as a means of self-discipline. In afternoon, lectured on Catechism. Anthem: "Turn Thy face from my sins," Attwood.

8th. *2nd Sunday in Lent.* In the afternoon, the Rev. Mr. Gibson assisted in the service, and the Rev. Dr. Jarvis preached; the subject of his discourse—"The Presence of the Holy Ghost in the Church." Anthem: "Teach me, O Lord, the way of Thy statutes," Dr. Rogers.

April 10th. *Good Friday.* Morning Service and Sermon at ½ past 10. Evening Prayer at 3 o'clock. A good congregation at both services. A bright, clear day. No chanting or singing at the Evening Prayer. The children learned a portion of the 53rd chap. of Isaiah, and recited it to me in the afternoon. No singing lesson or other studies.

12th. *Easter Day.* We could not begin the service in the morning before 11 o'clock. We waited until this hour to obtain the services of Mr. Hopkins as Organist. The service was through at about 2 o'clock. The Psalms for the day, Litany &c. chanted. The Rev. Mr. Fairbairn administered the Holy Communion; about 43 communicants. Two girls of the school received the Holy Eucharist. The offerings, appropriated for Domestic Missions, amounted to $41.29.

The girls put on today their new uniform—a straw colored bonnet with pink lining, and a lilac calico dress, with white cape. [The variation from Mrs. Warren's record, is attributable to the point of view—the way the woman looks at it compared with that of a man.]

Service without sermon in the afternoon at 5 o'clock. The Anthem: "Now is Christ risen from the dead," written for the Church of the Holy Cross by Mr. Hopkins. The weather cold and cloudy; rained a little at times during the day.

13th. *Monday in Easter Week*. Psalms and versicles chanted. Anthem: "Hallelujah," Jackson.

14th. *Tuesday in Easter Week*. I *chanted* the Morning Prayer, the choir responding, as it is given in Tallis' service, and performed in English Cathedrals.

Three girls of the school baptized after 2nd lesson. Anthem: "Hosannah," and after Gospel, "Hallelujah," Jackson.

19th. *Low Sunday*. In the afternoon, lectured on "Forms of Prayer," introductory to the Lord's Prayer which next comes before us in the Catechism. Anthem: "Christ our Passover is sacrificed for us," Chappell.

25th. *St. Mark's Day*. The whole service chanted, prayers read on a monotone, &c.

26th. *2nd Sunday after Easter*. In the afternoon, lectured again on "Forms of Prayer." Anthem: "Hosannah." I meet the children in the schoolroom at 4 o'clock. They say the Collect; are questioned on the lessons in the Morning Service, and on the Sermon (the text and what I was preaching about). The principal exercise is the examination of their "proofs," texts of Scripture, written out, to prove certain truths or facts of our religion.

May 4th. Assisted by the Rev. Beach Carter who is now officiating at St. John's in this city.

10th. *4th Sunday after Easter*. It has been my rule since the Church has been opened for divine service, always to preach on Sunday mornings from the Epistle or Gospel.

The weather today not pleasant; in the afternoon it rained furiously about the time of service. Lectured for the fourth time on " Forms of Prayer "—the usage of the Church in respect of Liturgies. Text I Cor. xi., 16, " But if any man seem to be contentious, we have no such custom, neither the Churches of God." Anthem: " Hosannah."

15th. Mr. Greene (a candidate for orders) read service. The Rev. Messrs. Van Kleeck, Carter and myself, and the clergy in the neighborhood, went to Albany, to meet the remains of the Rev. Mr. Walter, Rector of St. John's Church, this city.

17th. Exchanged with Rev. Jno. Williams of Schenectady.

21st. *Ascension Day*. The Rev. Mr. Carter officiated for me. The rest of the clergy were absent from the city, as this was the day set apart for the consecration of Trinity Church, New York.

31st. *Whitsunday*. Assisted in the morning and afternoon service by the Rev. Mr. Greene, deacon of New Jersey, ordained last week.

June 7th. *Trinity Sunday*. The Rev. Mr. Greene preached in the afternoon. Anthem: " O praise God in His holiness."

21st. *2nd Sunday after Trinity*. (Communion Sunday.) The Rev. Mr. Weaver of West Troy officiated for me. In the evening service, assisted by Rev. Mr. Greene. This is the first instance when we have *not* had the *full* choral service in afternoon. By " full " I mean here the Versicles and Psalms for the day. Mr. Hopkins, the Organist, was late, and I was forced to commence without the voluntary.

24th. *Festival of St. John the Baptist*. Versicles, Psalms for the day, Litany &c. chanted.

The titles of Anthems are noted in many entries. As a rule, one occurs on each Sunday and Holy-day. Upon the 12th of July the choir sings a new Anthem, " The Lord is my Shepherd," composed by Mr. Hopkins. The record for the 19th of July states:

In the afternoon at Evening Prayer, the Rev. Mr. Greene read prayers and I lectured. The Rev. Mr. Greene, not having received a formal license to preach from the Bishop of New Jersey, does not feel at liberty to preach. The Anthem: " Teach me, O Lord, the way of Thy statutes," Rogers.

At ¼ of 4, I married a couple from Albany; the marriage to be kept from the public for 3 months. The man was introduced to me by Mr. David Thompson, a respectable person in this city; it was on his assurance that all was right, that I consented to officiate under such suspicious circumstances.

26th. *7th Sunday after Trinity.* At Evening Service, the Rev. Mr. Weaver pronounced the Absolution, and the Rev. Mr. Stubbs of New Jersey preached:—the Character of Cornelius, particularly his devotion. The Anthem: " Blessed is the man that hath set his hope in the Lord," Chappell.

August 2nd. *8th Sunday after Trinity.* I was pre-vented by illness from attending to my duties. The Rev. Mr. Mahan of St. Paul's College officiated for me in the morning; he also preached in the afternoon. The Rev. Messrs. Fairbairn and Carter assisted in the service. The Anthem: " Teach me, O Lord," Rogers.

August 3rd—30th. The Church closed.

August 30th. *12th Sunday after Trinity.* The Church reopened for divine service. Officiated myself morning and afternoon. Anthem: " The Lord is King," Chappell.

During the vacation 17 of the children have had the measles; by the care and mercy of God, they have all now recovered, and not one was prevented by illness from attending the services this day.

September 2nd. Assisted by Rev. Mr. Stokes, a clergyman of Rhode Island, a gentleman of color in charge of a colored congregation at Providence. He is travelling to raise money to pay off a debt on his Church building.

4th. I was alone; my friend Mr. F. is officiating at St. Paul's in Rev. Van Kleeck's absence.

13th. Anthem: "Sanctus" from Mozart. Rev. Mr. Arnold of Canada in church.

20th. *15th Sunday after Trinity*. The Rev. Hillhouse Buel officiated, preached and celebrated the Holy Communion. I preached at St. John's. The Rev. Mr. Pike, Canada, present at morning service, and preached in the evening. After 2nd lesson (Evening Prayer) baptized 7 children (infants and children). The service being longer than usual, we were obliged to introduce lights. Anthem: " From the Rising of the Sun," arranged from Mozart.

27th. *16th Sunday after Trinity*. I officiated at Morning and Evening Prayer. In the morning, preached from the Epistle; in evening, lectured the third time on the Sacraments. The Minister's part in the Versicles (Evening Prayer) was *intoned*.

Two splendidly bound copies of " The Daily Service " with the musical notation, a book compiled and edited by N. B. Warren, Esq., were placed upon the Altar today.

From 28th to October 4th, I was in New York attending the Convention; the Rev. Messrs. Carter and H. Buel kindly officiated for me.

October 4th. *17th Sunday after Trinity*. I could not leave New York before Saturday night; unfortunately detained on the river by fog, and did not reach Troy before 11 o'clock. When I arrived at the Church, they were singing the *Te Deum*. Capt. Schriver had officiated, reading the service outside the chancel rails. I relieved him at 2nd lesson.

In afternoon, I did not lecture: the service is so late, or

rather the days so short, that it is almost dark before we get through service.

11th. *18th Sunday after Trinity.* Rev. Mr. Fairbairn preached. At Evening Service, the Rev. Dr. Haight pronounced the Absolution and offered concluding prayers, and the Rev. Mr. Baker of Baltimore read the lessons. Anthem: "The Lord is my Shepherd."

14th. Assisted by the Rev. Messrs. Haight and Van Kleeck. Rev. Messrs. Bronson of Ohio, Buel, Weaver and Fairbairn present.

18th. *19th Sunday after Trinity ; St. Luke the Evangelist.* Snow, hail and rain. The Rev. Mr. Buel preached and officiated at the Holy Communion. He also assisted at Evening Service when I *intoned* the service. *My* object in intoning is to prevent the inconsistency of reading half a verse (as in the Versicles) and singing the other half; another reason is to get rid of the organ accompaniment in the Versicles and Amens. They cannot "keep the key" unless I intone, and thus keep it for them. I am now convinced that the whole must stand or fall together. The singing the Versicles or Responses merely, is an imperfect, a half-way sort of thing, defective in a musical as well as ecclesiastical point of view. If the Choral Service is to be maintained, it must be the *whole service and not in part.* However, I do not like to intone, because I am conscious that as yet, until the novelty wears off, I am but *exhibiting* myself, when I would like them to regard me simply as *praying*, not thinking of the mode. Anthem: "Blessed is the man."

November 1st. *21st Sunday after Trinity ; All Saints' Day.* Preached in the morning on the text "This honor have all His saints."

The hour for Evening Service changed to four. I think I shall not resume my lectures, because after a Sunday or two, if I lectured, before I got half through I should not be able to *see my congregation*—and this is *dull* and unprofitable business. I am sorry that I was compelled to break off just where I did; 5 lectures more (4 on the

Sacraments) would have completed the course on the Catechism. But I suppose the people (I can't say *my* people) are just as wise. Anthem: Mozart's " Sanctus."

2nd. Assisted by no one.

3rd. Assisted by the Rev. Mr. Fairbairn.

On 4th and 5th. Rev. Mr. Cox of Zion Church, N. Y., present at service.

6th. In the absence of Mr. Warren, Mary Cole (who has been entirely educated at our school) acted as organist. The chanting went as smoothly as ever it did.

26th. *Thanksgiving Day.* Assisted in the service by the Rev. Mr. Lewin of Maryland, who is on a visit to our city to collect funds for a " Religious House " to be established at Georgetown, D. C., under the supervision of the Bishop of Maryland.

I was pained to find so small an attendance of my parishioners. The worshippers and servants of mammon cannot find time to serve God, except on a Sunday. The ingratitude and irreverence of the mass of our countrymen are enough to bring a curse upon the nation. There were about 15 persons present beside the children of the school.

29th. *Advent Sunday.* The Rev. Mr. Lewin preached in the morning, on the parable of The Laborers in the Vineyard, and assisted at the Evening Service. He catechized the children in the school-room.

December 2nd—5th. Assisted by the Rev. Mr. Fairbairn. Since last Sunday we have used on every day of the week, the *Benedictus* instead of the *Jubilate*, as more suitable for the Advent season.

13th. *3rd Sunday in Advent.* Preached on the Christian Ministry. The Rev. Mr. Geer took part in the Evening Service.

20th. *4th Sunday in Advent.* Sermon: Preparation for Christ's Coming or the Necessity of Repentance. Anthem: " Prepare ye the way of the Lord."

23rd and 24th. Church closed for the purpose of adorning it for the Festival.

No service on Christmas Eve, because I think it interferes with the service on Christmas Day, many persons satisfying themselves with keeping Christmas by coming to Church on the Eve. Besides our experience last year convinced us that the children were worn out by the exertion and excitement of the Christmas Eve service, and thereby unfitted for a proper celebration of the Festival itself.

I assisted the Rev. Mr. Van Kleeck at St. Paul's Church.

December 25th. *Christmas Day.* Service at ½ past 11. The Responses, Prayers, Litany, chanted or intoned. After the Gospel, the Nicene Creed (music by Jackson) was sung as an Anthem. Boyce in A was the Service used. Tallis' "Sanctus." After the Sermon, the Anthem "Glory to God" with the Recitative "There were shepherds" from the "Messiah."

The Rev. Mr. Fairbairn consecrated the elements in the Holy Eucharist.

It was five minutes past one, when I concluded my sermon.

After service, the children of the school, and some of their parents, partook of a sumptuous dinner provided for them by the kindness of Mr. Warren. The children amused themselves until half past four o'clock, and then went to Mrs. Warren's to receive their Christmas presents.

There was the usual Christmas tree, only more beautiful than I had ever seen it: the table was covered with books, handkerchiefs, cakes, apples, candies, &c. The girls sang "While shepherds watched their flocks" (Antioch) and the Carol in Horn's Christmas Bells "How grand and how bright." The weather mild; rained in the afternoon. . . .

27th. *Sunday after Christmas; St. John the Evangelist.* Exchanged in the morning with the Rev. Mr. Fairbairn. Anthem: "Behold, a Virgin shall conceive," and "O Thou that bringest good tidings" from the "Messiah."

28th. *Holy Innocents' Day.* Assisted by the Rev. Mr. Fairbairn.

So the Record ends, with a statement which occurs many more times in the original than in the sections here reproduced. It will be noticed that the Diary of Services conducts to the close of the year 1846, through the first two years of the long and happy pastorate.

VIII

THE CHORAL SERVICE

Wholesome usages, or those of any other kind, must have their beginnings somewhere. The little ecclesiastical structure upon the hill of Mount Ida has been called a " Church of First Things," for the reason that many of our customs—reverent methods and fitting ornaments of service now firmly established—made their first start, and had their American introduction, at the Church of the Holy Cross in Troy. Here was settled the due observance of the Holydays of our Lord and of Saints' days. Here was started, for all America, the preaching in the surplice; the introduction of flowers as an adornment for the sanctuary; the turning toward the East in Gloria and Creed, and the use of colored stoles. Trifles they may be—at least so somebody has styled them—but they are the outward signs of an inward moving.

At this late day it may be difficult to realize the amount of agitation which accompanied the effort to bring about a simple restoration of that which belonged to this branch of the ancient Church of Christ. Prejudice, when once it has hold, dies hard. Witness an extract from a newspaper—published about the time whereof we write, in 1846—wherein the request that clergy shall appear in surplices at a Church consecration, is denounced as an " unwarrantable liberty," calling for protest and resistance.

Consecration of Trinity Church. [New York.]—This new edifice, erected by the Corporation of Trinity Church, will be consecrated on Thursday next, 21st instant (Ascension Day). We have not received any information to enable us to answer the inquiry of one of our clerical correspondents, " H. G.," whether the " clergy are to be invited to appear in their surplices, and if so, by what authority? " We are not willing to suppose that our worthy acting bishop is prepared to recommend or sanction such an innovation, believing that " as our own bishops have heretofore contented themselves with requesting the clergy to appear in their gowns, one officiating temporarily will be satisfied to do the same." By whatever person or persons such a request may be made, we question whether it is the duty of the clergy to submit to it, because, to give no other reason, it is clearly an innovation upon the established order of the diocese.

The misunderstandings concerning the disuse of the black gown have gone down into history, as is further betokened by an illustration in one of Thackeray's novels, where a stout and irate woman parishioner trounces out of the church, slamming the pew-door behind her, as the parson pops up in the wine-glass pulpit, arrayed in a full-blown white surplice.

Dr. Fairbairn calls attention to the prompt decision and action on the part of the young incumbent of the Holy Cross, when he asserts that Mr. Tucker

10

preached at once, at the beginning of his pastorate, in the surplice. " He never used the black gown."

Among other features of restoration, distinctly traceable to the work at Troy, was the use of the Choral Service.

In this connection, the credit of a founder—far-seeing and wise—must be attributed to Nathan B. Warren, Mus. Doc. The son of the patroness, while yet young in years, was devoted to the idea of a sung service long before the thought was carried out among us. Far back, even before the day of the building of the Holy Cross, he played chants, and had them sung to the ordinary Canticles—a proceeding then pronounced not pious by many good people.

At one time he made a tour of England, largely for the purpose of the study of the Cathedrals and the Cathedral service. In the parish of St. Paul's Church, Troy, when the children belonging to his mother's industrial school were formed into a choir, trained to sing at special services, and when upon occasion Mr. Warren used to act as organist, it will be remembered that, at a children's Easter service, he introduced portions of the old choral use.

What wonder that when the " Holy Cross " was erected and services started there the choral method should come into rapid and permanent adoption! About this speedy development, we are certified by records, made at the time, by Mrs. Warren and by the Deacon in charge. The latter was himself a musician and a solid Churchman. He

was ready and happy to work along the lines desired by the foundress and her sons.

The term " full choral " covers many variations
of meaning. Mrs. Warren makes use of it in her
Christmas entry, applying it to a service in which
there was no intoning at all; the latter feature—the
chanting of the prayers—is mentioned in the Journal of Services as a new thing, just introduced, in
the year 1846. Mr. Tucker himself gives his own
definition of the phrase " full choral ": " by ' full ' I
mean here the Versicles and Psalms for the day."
Even so, as it turned out, he meant only the choir
responses to the Versicles, for he writes, 27th
September: " The minister's part in the Versicles
(Evening Prayer) was intoned," *i.e.*, the minister's
part was first sung or chanted on this date.

Nowadays by the phrase " full choral " we understand a rendering in which everything is sung or
chanted—everything except the lessons. To that
sort of completeness the Church of the Holy Cross
soon attained. Witness the entry made on the 14th
of April: " I *chanted* the Morning Prayer, the choir
responding as it is given in Tallis' service." That
was indeed an achievement, a thing unknown in
America before. It was a restoration of primitive
usage as emphatic as any occurring in the later
history of the Church. The tones, the vocal harmonies then sounded out in Troy, were in very
truth " first things," also great things for the people
of God in the new land. After this they sang as
they journeyed on their way; their lips were opened
to show forth His praise. Gradually they are

coming, to claim their right and heritage, to make complete use of the powerful agency of music in their efforts to pay worship to the Most High.

While the method is yet a novelty to himself, we find Mr. Tucker debating in his own mind the question whether he can intone and avoid the feeling that he will make an exhibition of himself. But he soon discovers the value of the " praying tone," and adheres to it for the remainder of his earthly career. He is intellectual and at the same time artistic; on both grounds he is sensitive to the inconsistency of a proceeding in which half of a verse is read and the remaining response is sung.

Would that he had many followers in our own day! The fitness of things is sometimes lost sight of. Not long since a cleric from the region of New York was a visitor in Troy. He met there a Rector of a Church in that city. The conversation turned upon " choral services," with which both are familiar. The visitor remarked upon the strange fashion which had come up in certain parishes, in accordance with which an officiant would read a Versicle and the choir sing the Response; also read a Collect and the choir sing the Amen. The Troy Rector was incredulous; at first he doubted the accuracy of the report. He said: " Do you expect me to believe this? " Later, however, he rehearsed the story to another, speaking of it as an unheard-of " half-hitch " arrangement, as an abomination in the æsthetics of religion.

The fine artistic sense, the Church poise and musical training, were efficient guides for the inex-

perienced deacon. He would not be likely to
violate the proprieties. For the same causes he
kept himself separate from any and all modern fads
about the vesting of his women choristers in cotta
or surplice. Good taste was ever the law with him.
He could not be induced to dress up his girls in
boys' clothes, and this too as a public spectacle before men! Naturally, he tended toward the side of
refined culture.

The Choral Service has had much to fight against
in the course of its American development. Not
only has there been an invidious distinction depre-
ciating the musical participation of the priest or
the chanting of a prayer, but in many cases the
examples of the function as heard by the people
have been against it. Surpliced choirs and Choral
Services used to go together; the one implied the
other. But that day has passed. " Boy choirs "
have been multiplied beyond their natural proportion—even in localities where singing boys are not
to be had or made, and where no suitable trainer
is at hand. As a consequence, it is not unusual
now to hear a choir in which the treble voices are
strained or nasal, strident or squalling, in which
the whole body sings out of tune and the cultivation of tone is manifestly at a discount. Naturally,
when this sort of a choir essays a choral office, the
effort does not recommend itself; there is little possibility that it shall work for the edification of man
or the glory of God. Again, faulty training and
conducting will come to the front. It may happen
that the words of the Psalter will be taken at such

a rapid pace or so indistinctly that the people can take no part, and the backbone of a sung service will be broken; or the Responses may be sung so languidly, to such a quartet-like dying strain, that worshippers will have naught to do with it. They are left out in the cold. That which ought to be warming, inspiring and arousing, becomes a source of frigidity.

So it will appear that sufficient reason may be found to explain the apparent fact that the choral use is not as popular now as it was ten or twenty years ago.

But to return to our Mission. Another of the "first things" there introduced was the adoption of the Gregorian tones, sometimes as settings for the Canticles, eventually for the Psalter. For the last-named portion of the service the Gregorian setting came to be the invariable rule. In what may be called the middle age of the Holy Cross choir, when they used the Helmore pointing, where each word is printed under its appropriate note in the "black notation," the method of pointing, and the way in which it was read by the singers, seemed to affect their delivery. They were deliberate; they bestowed well-considered emphasis. They were free from the feeling, almost unavoidable when the words of a *recitative* are accumulated under a single note, that these must be got through with after an expeditious fashion, in a glib, "let-her-go" style, which is ruinous to congregational participation. I have been told by a worshipper who had in large part lost his sense of hearing, that when the choir sang

from the Helmore pointing he was able to detect
the words and to follow with ease. When other
pointing was employed he was not able. So it
was, during a large part of its career, that the choir
of the Holy Cross recommended the Choral Service, by its careful and reverent rendering of the
Psalter—the chief feature of the entire function.

Of course the clamor of opposition was not
wanting. Tongues did wag for a time. Hard
things were said about the institution and its clerical head. But both lived through it and outlived
it all.

Early in the history of the choir—two or three
years after the opening—there began to be doubts
within, among those most interested, about the
advisability of the continuance of the Choral Service. The thing was yet an experiment. It was a
novelty even to the Pastor, and he was willing to
let it go; at one time he pronounced it a failure.
Others agreed with him. But Nathan B. Warren
held to it and carried it through; he was sure of its
ultimate success. So he it was who began and who
continued the traditionary use.

In fact, as the Rector says in a sermon preached
not long before the " Jubilee," almost all the " novelties " introduced at the Holy Cross were the results of lay effort. It was not a case of priestly
autocracy, not that of a clergyman crowding down
his whims upon an unwilling congregation. There
was no " aggrieved parishioner." The parishioners
themselves planned and suggested that which was
carried out.

Perchance it may be said that the Church revival as set forth at the Holy Cross represented the æsthetic rather than the sacramental side. There would be a certain amount of truth in the remark, in so far as the one phase was made more prominent, more in evidence, than the other.

True it is that the congregation did not attain to the degree of " advancement " manifested by many at the present time. Eucharistic vestments did not come into use; there was only one silk chalice veil —a white one—and many prayer books were scattered about, or set in divers locations, upon the covering of the altar slab.

Yet the strong obligation of the highest service was recognized and acted upon; and this in a day of " the careful and niggardly economy of the Holy Communion which omitted the Celebration on the first Sunday of the month, if Easter or Whitsunday came just before or after it." The Rector of the Holy Cross acknowledged the purpose of the Church, to make the Eucharist a frequent or a constant offering. He saw in the Prayer Book a plain requirement, demanding a Celebration whenever a Collect, Epistle, and Gospel were provided.

So the weekly Eucharist was established, together with a " pure offering " upon each Holyday. Therefore was it that attacks and abuse, railing and contumely were multiplied.

. At the Holy Cross most of the Sunday Celebrations were early; the late ones occurred only on the festival of the " first Sunday of the month " or other chief feasts. Soon this later Celebration came to be completely choral, even as to the part taken by the Priest.

The Rector refers to this in the sermon just quoted: " We had in this Church a Choral Celebration of the Holy Communion, when there was not a Cathedral in Great Britain which dignified and honored the Celebration of the blessed Eucharist with the accompaniment of music—that is, with the *Trisagion* and *Gloria in Excelsis.*" As says the Bishop of Albany: " With the marvellous impressiveness of many a service in the English Cathedrals ringing in my ears—from St. Paul's in London, where the most majestic offering of worship on this earth is rendered to Almighty God, to the Cathedral of some small English town, where daily the beautiful harmony of choral matins and evensong makes the outgoings of the morning and evening to praise God—with these ringing in my ears, I have a sense of reverent pride, when I remember that here in the Holy Cross, in its day of small things, the Holy Eucharist was offered with its full musical accessories, when there was not a choral Celebration of the Holy Communion in any English Cathedral."

The leaven began to work. There was a slow waking up throughout the American Church, a growing perception of the power of music in religion; along with this, people began to talk about the Choral Service. The fame of the " Holy Cross " had already gone abroad.

The old New York Ecclesiological Society took up the subject. We read about a certain evening, early in the " fifties," when Mr. Edward M. Pecke —then a layman—read a paper, " On the Choral Service of the Church." Thereafter there is a discussion, but it is all on one side. Doctors Vinton and Haight, Mr. Pecke, and the Rev. Mr. Hopkins are the participants. The principal talk is about the singing of the Psalter—the legal and rubrical right of the method.

A " Church Choral Society " is organized in New York city, in order that the members may have the satisfaction of taking part in offices so conducteu, and that examples of the use may be given to the people. Nathan B. Warren is elected Vice-President. John I. Tucker is an officiant. A first public service is held at Trinity Church; a second at the Church of the Annunciation. Upon the latter occasion the clergy in the chancel comprised Drs. Berrian and Vinton, the Rev. Messrs. Mahan, Weaver, Tucker, Hopkins, and others. Mr. Tucker intoned the opening part of the office, John Henry Hopkins the Creed and prayers.

Dr. Hodges, first organist of the Society, presided at the instrument. As yet nothing more elaborate is attempted than double chants for the Psalter and Canticles. It was reported in the papers that the service was " decidedly better done than the first at Trinity "; also that " the Choral Service with its chastened fervor, its sweet simplicity, dignity, and solemn devotion, is winning its way more and more deeply into the hearts of the people."

But the question was still mooted for and against

the musical style of service at the Holy Cross. Dr.
Warren tells us that he asked a prominent divine
from a chief city what he thought of it. The wise
divine answered that the Choral Service would
never " go " in America, " because here we have
no aristocracy."

Dr. Croswell came on from Boston to hear it.
He was impressed and was persuaded of its " success." He went back, intending to introduce it in
the New England capital. He then started Dr.
Cutler along the same line.

Trinity Church, New York, sent on a delegation
to Troy, expressly to hear this service and study its
effect. They went back, and the parish authorities introduced it on Saints' days only. It was
soon noticed how remarkably the attendance
picked up on those Holydays which had musical
observance; as a consequence the officials decided
to try it there on Sundays.

In the city of New York the "Voice of the Ages"
encountered a stronger opposition than at Troy.
Jerome Hopkins in a recent article, speaking about
American composers of opera, writes as follows:
" The hostility they encountered reminded one of
dear old Dr. Ed. Hodges's first attempts to introduce that ' awful Popish ritual ' now known as ' the
Choral Service ' in the Episcopal Church, and now
as common as boy choirs. The first trial thereof
[in New York] was at St. John's Chapel of Trinity
Parish, and stones were thrown at the windows by
outsiders, while insiders giggled and snizzled because ' the intoning was so funny.' "

If the Holy Cross had been built and worked for nothing else than the establishment and perpetuation of the old choral use as a prime accessory of divine service, it would yet be a thing worth while.

Sir F. A. Gore Ouseley was a man of fortune, a Priest and a musician. Whilst he was engaged in the active duties of his professorship of music, at Oxford University, he was with a liberal hand pouring out his private means for the founding and building of a new college and Church. He had selected a lovely and picturesque location; there he erected a Church building noted for its surpassing beauty. But when utilitarians look on it, they ask, " What is the use of St. Michael's College?" The establishment trains young men in music, first of all in order that they may sing or play in the constant Choral Services of St. Michael's Church. The Church was built for that. The place has been styled a sort of cross between a monastery and a music school. Its use will be comprehended when we read the words of a reviewer: " We do sincerely sympathize with its founder in his desire to raise ' a thing of beauty ' as an offering to God, not for the admiration of men; and to gather within its walls efficient musicians to carry on a daily full Choral Service, not for the pleasure of a large congregation (the Church was often empty), but as offering his and their special gifts to God's glory." So Sir Gore Ouseley founded and equipped a Church, that in it the Choral Service might be offered regularly and at its best estate.

It has been asserted, as proven by undoubted

history, that no great religious movement—quickening and uplifting human life—has ever taken place apart from the use of music as a prominent agency. Reformers have worked that way. Politicians recognize its value in another connection. Music and life are indissolubly associated, especially in religion. Were the Holy Cross to exist then—like St. Michael's College—solely to teach and emphasize this feature of service, it would be well; especially in view of the further fact that the method of art employment, to which she has devoted all these years, is that which is identified with the history and usage of the Church of God from the first beginning on. Whether in the older or newer dispensation, the divine society has ever been a " singing Church." It is a good thing when she is taught to sing now.

However, let it be remarked, that the Church of the Holy Cross has existed for more and higher ends than the maintenance even of the Choral Service, as those who know her best can testify.

IX

CONSECRATION—THE ORDERING OF PRIESTS

In the year 1848 the fabric of the " Holy Cross " began to enlarge its borders.   To the nave and tower, built four years previously, a square chancel was added.   In the new planning, different levels were arranged for choir and Sacrarium; three steps led up to the first, and other three to the second.

At the beginning of the work the consecration of the Church had been deferred, on account of the complications about the Episcopate of New York. Now the services of Bishop Whittingham were secured, and the consecration was fixed for St. Nicholas' day, the 6th of December, 1848.   The Warrens always had a partiality for good old St. Nicholas.

Upon the Wednesday morning appointed, the Bishop and clergy, members of vestries belonging to neighboring Churches and other Churchmen— a goodly company—assembled in the school build- ing, thence marching in procession to the Church.

The Instrument of Donation was presented to the Bishop by Stephen E. Warren and read by Mr. Tucker.

The sentence of consecration was recited by

Dr. Benjamin I. Haight, Professor in the General Theological Seminary.

As during the years just passed, outside interest was manifested; there was a rallying of clergy deeply concerned in the work. The participating officiants were many. After the completion of the act of consecration, Dr. Van Kleeck of St. Paul's started the Morning Prayer. The first lesson was read by the Rev. Samuel I. Southard, Rector of Calvary Church, New York; the second by the Rev. Richard Cox, Rector of Zion Church in the same city.

Mr. Tucker commenced the intoning of the service at the Versicles after the Lord's Prayer, " according to the use of Westminster Abbey," as a journalist of the day expresses it. The Proper Psalms were chanted antiphonally. The Litany was sung by two Cantors, the Rev. Messrs. Tucker and Shackelford, the responses being given by choir and organ.

In the Eucharistic office the Rev. Reuben Hubbard, Rector of St. Stephen's, Schuylerville, was the Epistler. The Bishop was Celebrant and Gospeller, also the Preacher of the day.

After the Benediction the Bishop came down to the choir steps, and there made an informal address congratulating the congregation upon the completion of the work and upon the fact of dedication. The speaker reviewed the past history of the enterprise from the day when Mrs. Phebe Warren gathered a band of children about her to receive instruction from her mouth. The Bishop referred to the different steps of development, emphasizing the value of the training received by these pupils in vocal music. He showed how the design expanded into an edifice erected to the glory of God, in which the " sweet and well-trained voices of these little ones " were to take an important part.

The result was before the congregation: an edifice of singular beauty and much cost, free for all who choose to enter within its hallowed doors, erected and endowed by an individual member of the fold of Christ, with a large school of children in constant preparation for the duties of this life and the blessings of heaven in regular attendance on the *daily* services of the Church, and adding to the beauty and it may be efficacy of devotion, by the skilful harmony with which they share the choral parts.

A newspaper report published at the time speaks of the " great additional interest and solemnity " which were " imparted to the service by the very admirable and appropriate selection of music, and by the accurate and spirited manner in which it was performed." From the Order of Service we discover that one chant, Lord Mornington in E, was sung to the *Venite* and the Proper Psalms. The setting of the *Te Deum* and *Jubilate* was that by Mendelssohn in A. The anthem after sermon was by Naumann; the words from the 122nd Psalm.

The *Kyrie, Trisagion*, and *Gloria in Excelsis* were by Dr. Hodges; the first of these was written expressly for the occasion.

The printed account refers to a picture in oil

which " almost covered the east end " of the Sanctuary. The canvas had been painted by the artist Weir of West Point, and presented by him to the " Holy Cross." The scene was in keeping with the title of the Church. It represented the Cross, on the evening of the Crucifixion, at the moment when pious hands, dimly discerned in the fading light, are bearing the sacred body to its tomb in the garden. One who used to see the picture writes: " The whole air of the piece is of the deepest solemnity and pathos."

On the day following—the 7th of December—a service of equal importance was held in the newly consecrated Church. Then the Bishop of Maryland admitted to the Priesthood the Rev. John Ireland Tucker and the Rev. John W. Shackelford, Missionary at Cohoes.

The candidates were presented by the faithful friend, the Rev. R. B. Fairbairn. The Rev. Samuel Buel, Rector of Christ Church, Poughkeepsie, began the " Morning Service." The Rev. Joshua Weaver of West Troy read the first lesson, the Rev. A. T. Twing of Lansingburgh the second. The prayers were intoned by Geo. Jarvis Geer, a Seminary mate of the minister of St. Cross.

Again the Bishop preached an appropriate sermon. The selection of music was the same as that sung on the day before, except that a chant-tune by Aldrich was substituted for that by Lord Mornington.

Other clergy not officiating were present at the one or other of these two important services; among

11

them the Rev. Wm. Payne, Rector of St. George's Church, Schenectady.

Now the work of school and Church goes on with added completeness: a Priest is at the head. The Pastor had never been found wanting even through the years of his diaconate; the teacher had labored uninterruptedly. Moreover, the young Rector was making friends, firm and fast, whose friendship has never changed, and never will change in all the years to come.

One of his earliest companions was Robert B. Fairbairn, whose name appears so often in the Journal of Services. For a time the two dwelt together in the same house. During that period Mr. Fairbairn took sick; Mr. Tucker went off and got a nurse and paid for it himself. This was at a boarding-house kept by a Mrs. Roberts.

Another first friend was Henry C. Lockwood. After the period of " boarding," the Rector had hired a house on Fourth Street; there he took up his residence, and he begged his friend to come live with him. For a while the two kept house together, until the marriage of Mr. Lockwood.

X

THE SECOND JOURNAL

For our worker in Troy vacations were rare. For a few years the minister of the Holy Cross was absent during two or three weeks in the summer. Before long he gave this up, and remained all through. In later life he was appealed to by all denominations as the one " summer parson," as the cleric who was always at home. At that time the extent of his rustication would be measured by the few days which he would spend with Dr. Ferguson at the latter's place out of town.

Once again, however, he made a trip to Europe. This time the tour was undertaken for the sake of his sister, whose lack of health called for the rest and change of travel.

As before, the traveller kept a Journal. A portion of this has been found among his papers.

Part of the entries, made in his own hand, are here transcribed. They show the man; they grant an insight into his methods of thinking and doing.

Oct. 8th, 1850. We left New York in the Packet Ship Gallia, Captain Addison Richardson, for Havre. We had a bright day to commence our voyage, and were all as cheerful and happy as we could be under the circumstances.

Many of the sailors, as is usually the case, were under the influence of liquor, and of those who were not too drunk three or four were disposed to be very fractious and quarrelsome. The consequence was that shortly after the pilot left us, there was a scuffle between the mate and one of the crew; others came to the rescue of their messmate. The mate, Mr. Crocker, was too much for them, and he succeeded in putting one of them in irons, and in setting the rest to work.

I am now writing at Nice, from notes taken on board the vessel. Things do not now seem as important as they did when they actually occurred. I shall therefore not be very particular in recording what took place during the 22 days we were at sea. We were fortunate enough to see whales more than once. Besides we were favored with a fine view of dolphins, and were delighted with the beautiful sight of porpoises playing around the ship at night when the sea was highly phosphorescent. The fish through the waves looked like fiery serpents. They seemed to leave a track of fire behind them.

On Sunday, 13th, I read service and preached, as I did on the 20th. On the 20th I read Divine Service only, in consequence of a gale blowing, and much motion. On the 15th at about six o'clock in the evening, came up to a wreck. It turned out to be a deserted vessel, but from her appearance the Captain judged that it could not have been long since she had been wrecked.

Many of the passengers were most indefatigable in their efforts to acquire some knowledge, or more perfect acquaintance, of the French language before arriving at Havre. Among the amusements on board the Gallia were shuffle-board on the deck, working out puzzles, and occasionally a divertissement in the cabin, such as mesmerizing by Mr. Lefourcade, a story or imitations and songs by others of the company, and, the night before landing, the reading of a Journal. As one of the contributions to the Journal, I must particularly mention " Lines Addressed to the Captain " by Mr. Storrow.

October 30th. About 12 o'clock a sailor aloft cried "land ahead," and the mate acting under the Captain's orders told him to keep quiet. After dinner, with the naked eye, we could see the land. About seven o'clock we were off Havre, and lay by—unable at that hour to enter the docks—until five o'clock next morning.

31st. Mr. Punnett and also Mr. Whitlock came on board, and kindly offered to do what they could in assisting us at the Custom House, etc.

Havre, to a person who has never seen a French town, offers many sights in the streets to amuse. In general there are no sidewalks. Where there are, the pedestrians seem to prefer the middle of the street. The majority of the women are without bonnets, and the ladies take precious good care to keep their frocks from dangling in the mud, and to show their petticoats.

. November 1st. Left by railroad for Rouen. Excellent arrangements and accommodations. There was a lamp burning in the centre of the roof of the car, the use of which we did not discover until we entered a " gallery." We were all particularly struck with the appearance of the old Churches. They are plain, almost destitute of ornament, except in some cases there is a spire with some pretensions to a display of architectural skill. In all cases the spires are surmounted with a cock.

Arrived at Rouen at one o'clock. After luncheon, went to the Cathedral. It being All-Saints' day, we found the Cathedral crowded, and an immense congregation attending the Vesper service. The Archbishop of Rouen was present. We passed through and around the building just glancing at its beauties, and obtaining but a vague idea of the skill and zeal necessary to rear such a grand and magnificent edifice. On visiting these sacred places, these palaces on earth of the great King, I have a more lofty, a larger idea of God. My feelings to God are stretched out. On this very occasion, I should have been much more gratified, my wants have been more really met, could I have fallen on my knees and prayed with the multitude, than in following a *valet de place* in company with a half dozen inquisitive persons, in search of something to satiate an excited spirit of curiosity. I was as curious perhaps as they; I had perhaps other feelings which they were not conscious of, at least to that degree, that they could, as I did, receive as much pleasure from seeing so many persons at their devotions, as in examining the curious stone tracery, the beautiful rose windows, and *in noting the peculiarities of the costume of the motley assemblage*. And perhaps if my own feelings were more closely analyzed it would appear that my fondness for Church music is greater than for Church architecture; that may be the reason why I take chief pleasure in visiting the Cathedrals when they are wreathed with incense and ringing with the notes of praise.

The Cathedral of Notre Dame is sometimes severely criticized for its elaborate and profuse decorations. It is probable that the richness and multiplicity of the vast Cathedrals of the thirteenth century is but a type of the efflorescence of the ritual and ceremonial magnificence of the Church at this period. The variety and profusion of the ornaments with which the ecclesiastical buildings of this century are embellished may also be an indication of the diffusion and earnestness of the religious feeling that then prevailed. We can scarcely conceive of the possibility at the present day of erecting such vast and magnificent edifices for the worship of Almighty God. Our *secular* tastes do not tend to such lavish expenditure on buildings reared for religious purposes, where regard is to be had to God's honor and glory and not merely to human pride and individual vanity. That these Cathedrals do indicate a spirituality as generally prevalent at the period in which they were built, we may learn from historical testimony. In a letter written by the Abbé of Saint Pierre sur Dives, to the Religious of the Abbey of Tutberry, in England, we read: "It is an unheard of prodigy to see powerful men, men proud of their birth and wealth, accustomed to a soft and luxurious life, attaching themselves by ropes to carts and haling stone, lime and other materials for the sacred edifice. Sometimes a thousand persons, men and women harnessed to the same cart (so heavy is the load) and still so great the silence that not a murmur is to be heard."

We passed some minutes in examining curious figures carved on the South Portal. These are called "Marmozets." They were in many instances figures of animals mimicking the acts of men. Pigs and apes were in the greatest number. What is the symbolical meaning of this strange kind of ornament on the portal of a sacred building it is not easy to conjecture, except it portrays the animal propensities of man's fleshy nature. I suppose this to be a rational explanation. . . . Immediately over the south door is a large representation in stone of the Last Judgment; in this, devils are seen plunging the damned into a huge kettle. As in many, if not the majority of instances the architects were of the sacred order, they endeavored to impress the people as they entered the House of God with an awful idea of the Judgment of the Almighty which awaits the impenitent; thus endeavoring to hallow their thoughts and stir up their hearts to repentance, and induce them with feelings of greater earnestness to confess their sins, and to engage with greater intenseness of devotion in the sacred services.

We next visited the Church of St. Ouen, which is even larger than the Cathedral, and is generally considered more beautiful and chaste in its ornaments. "It is beyond doubt one of the most perfect Gothic edifices in the world." One of its most striking features is the largeness of its clere-story, which increases the effect of lightness. The "windows seem to have absorbed the solid wall."

We were conducted to the Place de la Pucelle, where a statue without any inscription marks the spot where Jeanne d'Arc was burned alive as a sorcerer in 1431.

On all the public buildings, churches as well as on edifices designated as national property, *Liberté*, *Fraternité et Egalité* are painted in most conspicuous letters, so that one is almost tempted to believe that all the Liberty, Fraternity and Equality in France, is just so much as one sees on the walls. And the thought has often passed through my mind—What a pity the French politicians would not scribble on their walls in *chalk!* It could be easily rubbed off at each ebullition of the national feeling, names, party words etc. be exchanged for new ones without injuring the appearance of their public buildings. Over each of the three front doors of St. Roch, Paris (probably the same is the case of every other Church in France) are the three cant words, Liberté, etc.

In our rambling through the streets of Rouen, we saw many old Norman buildings. A row of houses was pointed out to us, remarkably curious from their antiquity. Many of the women we met in the streets, in their curious headgear and otherwise quaint costume, seemed to belong to the houses, and to be the lineal descendants of the illustrious individuals who reared and once occupied them. These houses being unprovided with yards, large tin gutters run from each story on the outside to carry off nuisances, dirty water, etc., which in more cleanly places pass off in other directions. Perhaps the necessity of looking out for heads, in passing by these houses, compelled the Norman French to take to the street; and the custom, even when there may not be the same necessity for its observance, has been perpetuated to the present day.

Opposite to Notre Dame is a flower market where beautiful bouquets may be procured for a few sous. As the next day was All Souls', the flower women were exposing for sale chaplets of *eternelles*, to be laid on the tombs of friends. The yellow and black flowers were so arranged that they formed inscriptions, touchingly affecting, such as "à ma chere mère," "à amitié," etc. From the number of these chaplets, I infer that they must be in great demand, and conclude that in the French character, in spite of the apparent gaiety which distinguishes it, there is underneath a current of pure affection and love.

In the evening we visited the fair. We found on the

Boulevards a crowd of persons, men, women and children and on either side of the broad street, booths, tables and stalls where articles of every description were for sale. Beside these, were shanties where there were wonderful shows—exhibition of jugglery, slack rope dancing, feats of strength and agility, etc. On platforms in front of these shanties or tents were men and women in curious costumes beating drums and blowing trumpets, to "attirer le monde," as our young friend Adolphus, the son of our landlady, said. We were induced to enter some of the saloons of *divertissement*, and went first to see a talking fish, which turned out to be a seal. It actually did say "pa" and "ma," but we were not as much surprised by its powers of conversation as by the wonderful intelligence and docility it displayed in promptly obeying the commands of its master. We went next into a place where the young of either sex, by looking into a miraculous mirror, could see their future husband or wife. I can only say for myself that if I thought there was no chance of getting into matrimony without giving my hand and heart to the female individual whose charms were displayed to me in the magic mirror, I would be willing on the spot to make a vow of celibacy.

Next the travellers were astonished by the performance of a mesmerized girl. After that, "the most beautiful exhibition which we witnessed was a diorama of the accident that befell a regiment of French troops in crossing a suspension bridge." Still later, a menagerie in which "the man who showed off the rhinoceros was decidedly the lion of the evening." Concluding:

With the exception of the menagerie, each entertainment did not cost over one or two sous; so that we had this at least to console us, that we got the worth of our money. In answer to certain questions which we proposed as we went along, we were informed that not much was sold. There were plenty of lookers on, but few purchasers. One poor old woman who was selling roasted chestnuts, said that "the commerce" went badly, that nearly all the merchants were complaining, that it was enough to make one almost weep, so little was doing in the way of trade.

Pleasantly domiciled at the Hotel d'Albion.

November 3rd. At ten o'clock went to the Cathedral, where I stayed until it was time to start for the Protestant place of worship. Accompanied by my friend Mr. Degen, went to St. Eloi—in the interior, a shabby looking building. A man, from a reading desk, read prayers from a book, and after the singing of a Psalm, the minister in a black gown and bands, from the pulpit just over the desk, read—as we thought—a sermon printed in pamphlet form. The congregation were not very punctual in their attendance, and we observed that as each took his place or seat, he engaged on his knees in silent prayer. The Liturgy, or form of prayer, except that there were no responses, reminded us of our own. The Commandments were read after the singing of the Psalm and before the sermon. Each Psalm book had the music proper for the Psalm, and the music from its *unsecular* character, and from the fact of its being familiar to the congregation—they all taking part in it—had a charm about it, though in a scientific point of view anything but pleasing. The sermon, so far as I could follow it, seemed to be an apology for Christianity, setting forth its adaptiveness to man's moral nature.

From the circumstance of having just come from the Cathedral, I had an opportunity of contrasting Roman Catholic with Protestant. One seemed to be an imaginative, the other a rational religion; one addressing the feelings, the other the intellect. The heart, soul, mind and body ought to be united in Christian worship, and any form of worship therefore is so far defective as it exclusively affects the heart, soul, mind or body. I must allow, however, that, although not familiar with the service of the Mass, the idea of Christ's atonement, the great fact of Christ's sacrifice, was more vividly impressed on my mind by the pomp and magnificence of the Roman ritual at Notre Dame, than by the meagre, shabby, spiritual exercises at St. Eloi. There was more to bring my whole being into communion with my Saviour at the Cathedral, than at the Protestant place of worship. If asked in which assembly Christ crucified seemed most clearly set forth, I should unhesitatingly answer—Among the 2000 or more persons engaged in worship at the Cathedral.

In the afternoon, I went again to the Cathedral, and I found two Catechists, in front of the choir, catechising about 200 boys, from 5 to 10 years of age. The boys were questioned on the Incarnation. The answers were given promptly and correctly. In other parts of the Cathedral, other children were at the same time receiving similar instruction. Probably no less than a thousand young persons were thus employed in learning the doc-. trines of Christianity as held by the Church of Rome. And from what I have since witnessed at Dijon, I am inclined to believe that great efforts are now making in France by the R. C. clergy, to imbue the young minds of the present generation with the doctrines and principles of their faith and practice.

The music at the Vespers pleased me much. A greater part of it was in *unison*. The antiphonal chanting was very spirited, the effect being heightened by the full, rich toned voices of the 100 priests, who in two choirs were engaged in singing the Psalms. As an instrumental accompaniment, the voices were occasionally assisted by the organ, trombones and violoncellos. But, except at the beginning of each Psalm, and if I remember correctly at the *Gloria Patri*, in the chanting nothing was heard but the human voice. The chanting was very rapid, but not so rapid that I could not follow them in the book. The assistants and the congregation were seated during the

chanting of the Psalms, and did not always rise at the
Gloria Patri. All who were present appeared to be engaged with much devotion in this Vesper service. There
seemed to be but few listeners; the crowd were worshippers, if external acts are any indication of the soul's intentions and operations. I think I have never attended a
sacred service where the music so fully realized my idea
as to the province and uses of this art in connection with
the rites and ceremonies of the Church.

In the evening, in company with Messrs. Degen and
Eckford, started out for the Cathedral. It was, however,
closed, and we continued our walk up to the Boulevards,
and found ourselves on the fair ground where there was
even greater noise and fun than on the preceding evening.
It seemed strange to us, this folly and gaiety on Sunday
evening, and excited some conversation between Mr. D.
and myself. We agreed that our mode of observing the
day hallowed to God's service, seemed most in conform-
ity with the positive institutions of Christianity. However, it must be admitted that the nature of the people
must always be taken into consideration when examining
this and kindred questions. I mean that even when the
same amount of religious faith and holiness prevailed
both in France and America, national habits, from national
prejudices and temperament, would be different. We cannot infer that we are decidedly a more religious people
than the French, because we never desecrate the Lord's
day by raree shows and vulgar amusements, because without respect to any religious principle we would never
seek pleasure in any such kinds of diversion. We must
also remember that of the multitudes whom we met in
the streets, the large majority of them, perhaps, had been
in the Churches once or twice in the course of the day;
and in connection with this, we must consider how many
individuals among us who although they may never take
part in any street or public amusements on Sunday, still
never in any one respect, hallow the day, even so much
as to go to Church or read a chapter in the Bible. With-

out wishing to apologize for the frivolous diversions of the Continental R. Catholics on the Lord's day, it is but fair to them to suggest the probability, that taking the whole week into the question there is much more Church going and praying than prevails even amongst our most rigid and devout countrymen, even when we admit they attend Church three times on the Sabbath and a prayer meeting twice a week.

We had to walk about two miles through the fair to get to our hotel; and although I never saw a more orderly, well behaved crowd, and notwithstanding what I have written now, and then felt, I must confess that my religious feelings were shocked, and that I felt mortified in having, even though unintentionally, witnessed what I did on Sunday evening. Still I have this to console me, when my conscience disturbs me with the thought of my Sunday evening's sauntering at Rouen, that I have had an opportunity of seeing how the French people keep the closing hours of that holy day.

November 2nd. I find that I have skipped over Saturday. . . . Went to the Cathedral, and had a better opportunity of examining its objects of historical interest. . . . Our *laquais de place* pointed out a tomb and effigy in the wall, and said that a Bishop who murdered his servant in a passion, was buried there. He confessed and died penitent, but on his deathbed he requested that he might not be buried in a sacred place, so they placed his body in the wall.

We were persuaded to mount one of the towers, in order to take a view of the surrounding country. But the ascent was not quite so easy as we imagined; the staircase gradually diminished in its width, until fears were entertained by the stoutest man of the company that possibly he might be wedging himself between two walls, from which he would not be able to extricate himself without the assistance of others. But such fears were unfounded, as we had reached the stairway's minimum, and in safety we got as high as the central spire, which is of iron, with as much architectural beauty as a cork-screw or ramrod. The view was beautiful. It was strange to see how crowded the city was, how closely packed together the houses, and how neighborly the inhabitants of Rouen seemed to live.

One of the towers is called *Tour de Beurre*, because it was built, between 1485 and 1507, with the money paid for indulgences for eating butter in Lent.

November 4th. Went to the Church of St. Gervais, which is on the outskirts of the town. The Church itself is considered one of the oldest in France, but it is chiefly interesting from its crypt which you enter through a trap door in the body of the Church. Here you find a Church about 50 by 15 feet, which from historical evidence and from the construction of the building itself—the presence of Roman tiles between the layers of masonry—is supposed to have been constructed in the fourth century. It is apsidal. At the end of the apse is a stone altar, on pedestals; it is not solid, and is marked with five crosses. The altar is on a raised floor. Stone seats attached to the wall are on either side of the nave; and there are two low-arched recesses in the wall, which are said to be the graves of two former Archbishops of Rouen.

The arrangements of this primitive Church reminded me of the Holy Cross. It has been conjectured that there is a subterranean passage of considerable extent communicating with this crypt, and they had commenced exploring it a few years since, when the search was discontinued by reason of the Revolution.

I cannot in journalizing about Rouen omit speaking of the strong, powerful horses that are seen in this part of France. They are able to draw 16 or 18 bags of cotton. It has been a matter of surprise to some of us, that some clever Yankee has not attempted a speculation by taking a few of them to America. We have been informed, however, since leaving Paris, that the French government does not allow their exportation.

In the Church of St. Ouen, I read a notice in English,

as if chiefly or exclusively intended for English and
American travellers, requesting all who should come to
visit this Church to remember that it was the House of
God, and to conduct themselves accordingly, abstaining
from loud talking, etc. At St. Ouen, and in fact in all
the Churches, attached to the pillars are charity boxes,
labelled " pour les pauvres," " pour les malades," " pour
les prisonniers." Wherever you turn, you meet with
silent and speaking appeals upon your charity.

This is the second time I have visited Rouen, and I
leave it now with regret.

At half past one left for Paris, where we arrived about
half past five. A few trunks—none belonging to our
family—were opened, and we hurried off to the Hotel de
Lille et d'Albion, which had been strongly recommended
to us by our landlady at Rouen. We secured for our
party, consisting of eight persons, magnificent apartments
for 50 francs a day.

November 5th. It being our intention to leave Paris
as soon as possible, we devoted ourselves to making the
necessary arrangements for our journey to Italy, and
therefore found little time for sight-seeing.

Nevertheless, the travellers find opportunity to
inspect the Gobelins Tapestry Works, the *Jardin
des Plantes*, the *Palais de Justice*, several Churches,
the House of the Protestant Sisters of Charity, also
one of the largest *crèches* in Paris. At the *Con-
ciergerie*, then occupied as a tribunal of justice:

The different halls were handsomely furnished, and in
every case were sanctified, if I may so speak, with a picture of the Crucifixion. Christian mercy is ever to be associated with Christian justice.

St. Gervais is remarkable for its modern decorations.
I have not yet entered a Church in France without finding several persons engaged in their devotions. Here

in this Church I was forcibly impressed by the apparent devotion of a man in a blouse, who while I was in the building—about half an hour—was absorbed, as he seemed, in meditation and prayer. If our Churches were opened, would there be any among our working people, any of our mechanics and laborers, who would enter them and spend thirty minutes or more in silent devotion?

The Roman Catholics on the Continent seem to use their Churches as places of prayer, and not merely to resort to them as lecture halls. They appear at home in Church, without any restraint or foolish bashfulness; indifferent to others they fall on their knees, say their prayers, and go out again perhaps to pursue their ordinary avocations.

At St. Eustache, a strange mélange of Gothic and Roman architecture, I read a notice which said it was *indecent* for persons to pass through the Church (to make by it a short cut, in passing from street to street) without stopping for a few moments to offer a short prayer to God. Persons visiting the Church were also requested not to talk loud, and not to spit on the floor or walls, but if compelled to expectorate to use their handkerchiefs for that purpose. This notice reminded me of one, in a meeting-house at Canandaigua, N. Y.: "The ladies of the congregation would request the gentlemen to take the quids out of their mouths before going in, or to bring spitboxes with them."

I heard part of a Mass at St. Roch. As an artistic performance, it was the best music I have heard. There was a delightful tenor voice. The singer wore a moustache, and standing in front of the choir organ, surrounded by a number of men and boys in clerical costume, presented rather a droll appearance. It looked as if the priests at St. Roch had been forced to go to the opera, to get some one to help them out with their service. But, the music was exquisite, and I confess it required no little effort to forego the pleasure of listening to it, in order to attend the English service in the Rue

d'Aguesseau. Here we found the Church well filled.
Three priests officiated. The sermon was only fair, suggested as I thought by "the recent papal aggressions,"
as the English papers style it, on England. The music,
most execrable, more like mummery than anything I have
yet heard in a Romish Church. It was vile to listen to,
and so indistinctly and badly given, that it was almost
impossible to take part in it. I cannot conceive how
any good can be derived from such a musical performance, either as a tribute of praise, or a mode of expressing
religious emotions. It was too shabby to offer to God,
and was so repulsive to the ear as to repress rather than
excite feelings of devotion. The whole service, although
conducted with decency and order, was cold, that is thoroughly English. We paid a franc each for our seat. In
the afternoon, as I was a clergyman, my mother and myself were conducted to seats on the ground floor, and not
taxed for our accommodations.

Institution of the Deaconesses of the Evangelical
Churches of France. I had read of this institution in
one of the English reviews, had referred to it in a sermon, and of course was very anxious to see this Catholic
phase of Protestantism. It is situated in the Faubourg
St. Antoine, one of the worst quarters of Paris. During
the revolution of '48, in the very street where it is located,
there were no less than nine or ten barricades, to raise
which, even women, girls and little children of five or six
years of age, had worked together. I obtained without
any difficulty, permission to go through the establishment,
and was put under the charge of one of the sisters.

Various are the departments in which this admirable
institution performs its work of mercy and of Christian
love. It has its " Refuge," in which females who have led
a dissolute life can retire from the contagion of vicious
associates. . . . There is also a place of detention
called *Retenue* in which are received young girls confided
to the institution by their parents or the civil authority.
In the *Disciplinaire*, young persons from 7 to 14 years of

age, are confided by their parents or protector, for moral training and discipline. The most common vices of the children when they enter the " disciplinaire " are " dishonesty, trickery (*la ruse*) and lying."—The *Maison de Santé* has two departments, one for sick men, the other for women.

An important branch of the " Maison de Service des Diaconesses," is that which has for its object the education of the young. This branch includes the *Crèche*, the *Salle d'Asile*, the School for Mutual Instruction and the School of Apprenticeship.

The *Crèche* (manger, taking its name from the manger of Bethlehem) is a nursery, where poor women leave their infants for the day, to be taken care of, whilst they themselves are engaged in working for the support of their families. Each infant costs the institution about 7 sous; the parent pays perhaps 4 sous. The *Salle d'Asile* is an infant school, attended by about 200 children.

As an evidence of the appreciation of the *Crèche* and *Salle d'Asile* by the poor people in the neighborhood, it is stated that on the 24th of February, when in this quarter of the city and in the immediate vicinity of the House, a number of barricades were erected, in the midst of the tumult, through groups of armed men, mothers full of courage and pious confidence, followed their accustomed way, and brought their infants to the *Crèche* and their children to the school.

In the Journal seven quarto pages are filled with descriptions of this institution of benevolence. Nine more are crowded with detailed information about another " La Crèche Saint Louis d'Antin," which is under the charge of a Roman Catholic sisterhood. The explanation of so large a devotion to the subject may be found in an entry: " Something like the *Crèche* might be established at home, which apart from its charitable provisions for poor children, would be an excellent school for nurses." The object of this *Crèche Saint Louis* is like the other:

They receive in this Asylum, every morning, except on fête days, children under two years of age, whose mothers are poor and obliged to do work away from their own homes. They come to nurse them at the hours of repast, and return for them again at evening.

Here follows an exact and full account of the three rooms filled with cradles, the kitchen, linen room, balcony garden, the nurses, the infants and their uniform, the hygienic regulations, and many other matters. Among the rules given in the " Manuel," under the head of Hygiene, the following is quoted:

Advice to the Mothers. Rock the child but little, let it take the air often. Scold it but seldom, beat it never. Gentleness always. When lying down, place it sometimes on one side, sometimes on the other, the head being always a little raised. Never take it up by one arm. Feet warm, the stomach unconfined, the head cool. Let it have no painted playthings. Caress it, but seldom embrace it. Do not wake the child out of a sleep. Never fret it and make it cry. Let the children amuse themselves, and place them near those they love. Much attention; little medicine.

There are special rules for the direction of the nurses; such as, they are never to carry about their persons, pins, needles, scissors or knives. . . . They are to abstain from every vulgar expression and improper word, and interdicted all gossiping.

Amusement. Sleep.   In the way of amusement an accordion and a few playthings are all that are necessary in the *Crèche*.   The accordion has the power of stopping their crying.   This is putting this musical instrument to a happy use, and it was a valuable discovery to ascertain that a kind of music so vile to adult ears can be made acceptable to those of babies.

It is not difficult, as they say, to accustom the children to go to sleep all at the same time, for they maintain that sleep is sympathetic; a fact which is well sustained by what we often have an opportunity of observing in crowded assemblages.   Although I doubt if a R. C. ever goes to sleep in Church.

In passing along the streets of Paris, I have been struck with the strange inscriptions over some of the shops.   These inscriptions are a kind of dedication.   Over a dry goods store, a grocery or shoe shop, you may read " au bon Pasteur," " à la bonne Providence," " à la Grace divine," " au diable à quatre," " au pauvre diable "; so that the eye as it glances along finds a curious mixture of sacred and profane things, and one cannot help thinking that the French have a strange way of associating holy subjects with ribbons, shawls, pork and vegetables, and a very droll idea of the " diable "—a person whom all good Catholics should regard with dread as man's great spiritual adversary, rather than sport with as they might be inclined to do with a Merry Andrew.

The names of many of the streets and places have been changed to adapt them to the republican fever: the old Palais Royal is now the Palais National.   What's in a name!   I had an opportunity in company with Mr. Degen, to make frequent inquiries amongst the shopkeepers, as to the present feeling of the Parisians in respect to the existing government.   With the exception of a barber, all were of one opinion: that things have not been bettered by the change; that the republic costs very dear, and that under its name little has been acquired in the way of political privileges; that there is nothing permanent in the present order of things; that although the socialists had been crushed, the three opposing parties—the Louis Philippe party, the legitimists and republicans—will keep France in a ferment, until there is another grand convulsion, and the political state of the country be reduced to its first elements. The traders, merchants and decent laboring people are for the government which will give them the best facilities and securities for gaining a livelihood. "To sit still is their strength." They dread any revolutionary movement that may disturb the tranquillity of the nation. I have seen in the passages pictures of Louis Philippe and of his sons, labelled with their royal and princely titles; also portraits of Henry V., King of France as he is styled. In the newspapers, although they are subjected to many restrictions, I have read very bold and able discussions of great political questions, where monarchism and republicanism are contrasted to the advantage of the former, and where it is maintained that there can be no stability in government, no tranquillity in the country, no guaranty for the prosperity and happiness of the people, without going backwards and reestablishing the French monarchy on the ancient foundation, by espousing and maintaining legitimacy in the person of the Duke of Bordeaux.

On the ninth, we engaged our courier, a young German by the name of Ferdinand Bauer, who as yet has proved himself to be all we could wish; and bought our carriages, one calèche which belonged to General La Moncière, and a britzska—the two together costing 1800 francs.

November 14th. Left Paris by railroad for Tonnerre, on our way to Nice, by Dijon, Lyons, Avignon, Aix, Frejus and Cannes. Mr. and Mrs. Degen and Mr. Eckford accompanied us to the station. After having received so much kindness from these friends on board ship and since our arrival in France, we parted from them with many regrets, and our sincerest acknowledgments of their many services and affectionate attentions. The station house is a capacious building, in an architectural point of view remarkable for its lightness and beauty, and admirable in all its arrangements for the accommodation of travellers. On showing your ticket, you are permitted to pass into one of the three compartments, under the same roof, as you may happen to be travelling in the 1st, 2nd or 3rd class, and from thence, at the ringing of a bell, you are conducted to the cars. The cars are like those formerly used on our railroads, with this difference, that those of the 1st class are much more luxuriously fitted out. Our carriages were placed on trucks, and we remained in them until we reached Tonnerre. There is one feature in the little French towns which flitted before us as we passed rapidly by on the railroad, which made a favorable, and I believe, a lasting impression. The houses all seemed to be clustering around the old Church, as if they had grown up around and were clinging to it, as if it was the nucleus, the sacred spot from which radiated peace and domestic happiness. There was no symbol of disunion; no evidence of dissent and religious bickerings and hostility, which stares us in the face as soon as we come in sight of some little pert American village with its four or five bright red or glistening white meeting houses. No one would think in France of asking where or which is the Church? In our religion, we appear to adopt the formula of traffic " Opposition is the life of trade."

Arrived at Montbard at ten o'clock. Rooms had been ordered for us at the Point du Jour. The fires in our rooms were all lighted, and we were soon refreshed with a capital dinner (trout, partridges, etc.). It is a dirty place, and only celebrated as the birthplace of Buffon.

November 15th. At nine o'clock started for Dijon. The roads are all macadamized. The villages we passed through today had a poor and desolate appearance, the houses of stone and sometimes stuccoed, with roofs hanging down almost to the ground. The only redeeming feature in the landscape is the old, quaint Church which is the prominent object as you approach each town. We arrived at Dijon at 7½ o'clock.

16th. Notre Dame is remarkable as a specimen of the purest Gothic. Its clock is mentioned by Froissart as the most curious one in Christendom or heathen lands. Several churches in this place have been desecrated, and are now occupied as warehouses, corn markets, etc.

" Les Puits de Moïse," in the old Chartreuse, is a curious specimen of ancient art. It consists of several beautifully finished statues, figures of Moses, Isaiah, Jeremiah, Zechariah, Daniel and David, ranged round a shaft, and was originally a centre ornament in a cemetery. The old woman who pointed out its beauties, in explanation of the two horns on the head of Moses, said that it represented " the glory," and that Moses was always thus distinguished among the Old Testament saints, because he alone was permitted to speak face to face with God.

The Chartreuse which is now rebuilt is occupied as an asylum for lunatics and idiots or " fous." On asking the old woman whether there were many fools in France, she replied " presque toutes."

We find every comfort in the Hotel de la Cloche, and I cannot help mentioning that half at least of our comfort and pleasure here is to be attributed to the amiable Mary Anne, the waiting maid, who by her engaging manners made a favorable impression upon us all. She is pretty, complaisant, bright and modest withal. Though cheerful she said she was " ennuyed " at times, when she thought of her father and mother who were living about twelve miles from Dijon. They were very poor, and she sent them more than half her earnings. Sometimes, she said, she was exposed to insult; not unfrequently scolded by the proprietor of the hotel, when the fault was in the peevishness of the travellers; and at all times regarded with jealousy by the other servants, who, as she said, if they only would take the same trouble to please that she did, would equally ingratiate themselves into the favorable opinion of the persons whom they served. She convinced us of her artless simplicity and honesty, by refusing to receive any present of money, assuring us that she was not permitted to receive for herself any gratuity, that she would be compelled to place in the servants' box anything we might choose to give her. Hers is a hard service. She has not enjoyed the privilege of going to Church since last Easter. Every night up to twelve o'clock; sometimes, as her turn comes round, watches all night; and her earnings, her portion of the gifts of travellers, amount to about 100 dollars a year. She is worthier of a happier lot. Would that all, especially those whose lot has, by Providence, fallen into a good ground, would be as contented as she is, and as cheerfully and faithfully fulfil the duties of the station in which God has placed them.

Left Dijon at two o'clock by railroad, passing through the Burgundy wine country, and arrived at Chalons 25 minutes past 4 o'clock.

18th.   Left Chalons in the steamer Crocodile at 10 o'clock, and arrived at Lyons 6½. The Crocodile is well named: it is a long, narrow, black painted boat. A passage in her was something like sailing down the river on a log. We remained in our carriages, it being a rainy day, and were right glad when we found ourselves rattling along the streets of Lyons.

19th.   At 10 o'clock left in the steamer for Valence. The river very narrow and shallow, shortly after leaving Lyons, and the passengers were obliged to run first to the bows, then to the stern, to get the boat off as she occasionally grounded. Near Tournon saw snow on the distant mountains. Arrived at Valence at 5 o'clock.

20th.   Next morning at 7 o'clock, by steamer, left for Avignon. Many soldiers on board; some look like mere boys. At one of the villages which we passed today, there was a " petite revolution " yesterday; a barricade was raised, one or two men killed, and several wounded.

Avignon was occupied by the Popes from 1305 to 1370, according to Petrarch, the Babylonish captivity of the Church. The Popes gained possession of Avignon by a grant made by Joanna of Naples while yet a minor for

80,000 gold crowns, which were never paid. The palace of
the Popes is now occupied as a barracks, the temporal in
fact supplanting the spiritual sword. We were disappointed in not seeing the halls of the Inquisition; some
alteration having been made in the building, as we were
informed, they can no longer be seen by the traveller.
Perhaps Murray's Handbook, Dickens' pictures and other
books of the same kind, have given so much publicity to
the cruelties and horrors perpetrated, under the name of
religion, within these walls, that they have been closed
with the hope of blotting out from memory, if possible,
this bloody chapter of ecclesiastical history.

November 21st. At 9½ o'clock left for Aix. A person is not long in France before observing that in this
land of gallantry, the fair sex are compelled to turn their
hand to many employments which in other less chivalric
countries are exclusively appropriated to the lords of creation. We met a woman driving today a public conveyance, filled with men, women and children. Another
woman passed us on the road, conducting a cart drawn
by 4 horses, with another horse tied behind. In Paris,
on entering the shops, it was often a matter of inquiry
to myself—where are the men? I once asked to satisfy
my curiosity, and was informed that the men superintend
the manufacture of the articles, generally in the rear of the
establishment, and the women attend to their sale in front.
Close to the road as we approached Aix, we saw olives,
almonds and mulberries. Stone crosses.

Arrived at Aix at 20 minutes past 5 o'clock. " Aix was
the ancient capital of Provence, the resort of the trouba-
dours, the home of poetry, gallantry and politeness, the
theatre of the courts of love and of gay fêtes."

22nd. Between 6 and 7 o'clock, went to the Cathedral;
a congregation of 30 or 40 were assembled for Mass. . . .
At 8 o'clock left for Frejus. For want of a postilion, I
was compelled to stay an hour at Le Muy, the other carriage, with the ladies, my father and courier continuing
their journey to Frejus. An *ouvrier* made himself very

agreeable to me during my compulsory stay in the village, and on giving him a franc to drink my health, he insisted upon doing the civilities of the place, and treated me first to a cigar and then took me to a café, where we regaled ourselves with a cup of café seasoned with cognac, and discussed American and French politics with the mayor and other official dignities of the village. Before reaching Frejus, Ferdinand met me with a one-horse wagon, and I reached the Hotel du Midi at half past 10 o'clock.

23rd. At 7 o'clock took a stroll and visited the Cathedral, adjoining which is a Baptistery of the 11th or 12th century, resting on eight columns of grey granite with marble capitals. I don't believe that any Baptisteries are to be found of later date than the 13th century, when the doctrine of the Roman Church was settled in respect to the seven sacraments, and the rite of Holy Baptism was levelled in significancy with Absolution, Extreme Unction and Matrimony.

Left Frejus at 8¼ o'clock. . . . The ride today exceedingly beautiful, along the shore of the Mediterranean at times, through olive groves, and by the side of orange trees ladened with fruit. We met with no inconvenience, thanks to a five-franc piece, at the *douane*, and arrived at Nice at 6½.

In a store where I was purchasing a few articles, I asked the shopkeeper whether there were many soldiers here. He replied " Yes, plenty of them. We have not yet emerged from a state of barbarism, where force rules instead of law." I see from the paper which is published twice a week, that the Sisters of Charity have been removed from the hospitals, in consequence of bad management, and their place supplied by others appointed by the city government. The differences between the Pope and King of Sardinia would appear, from what I read in the same journal, not yet to be amicably adjusted. Multitudes of priests, and monks bareheaded with bare or sandaled feet, loaf through the streets as if they had nothing to do, and found it difficult to pass their time. Perhaps they are forced to leave their hallowed retreats to sun themselves.

December 1st. *Advent Sunday.* In consequence of the carriage not coming in time, we arrived at the Church too late to find seats, and were obliged to return. We engaged in prayer in our room. Attended the Evening Service. Last Sunday evening attended a French Evangelical Service in an upper room; the congregation numbered about 12.

After leaving Nice the travellers ride along the delightful Cornice road—the old Aurelian way—which, " for a considerable distance, runs along the edge of a mountain overhanging the Mediterranean, offering views of the greatest beauty." San Remo as it appeared from the windows of the hotel, its houses pitched one upon another on the side of a mountain, is described as looking like a " gigantic hornet's nest." Departing from San Remo on the 3rd of December:

The weather is very much like one of our brightest September days. Along the coast, at intervals, perched on projecting rocks, are ruined towers, which were built to protect the villages from the piratical incursions of the Algerines. The streets of the towns are so narrow, that in some cases, they are obliged to close the doors of the houses to let a carriage pass through. The Churches we saw today are painted with the gayest colors, and a fresco painting of the Virgin is the chief ornament in the front. Several of the women which we met wore veils; some girls we saw engaged in unloading a vessel, walking two by two with a sack on their heads. The carriage never stops without drawing around it a swarm of beggars, but this is to be said in their favor—they generally are objects of charity from sickness or some bodily infirmity, and are thankful to receive the smallest coin,

so that a very moderate degree of charity, and a few
coppers, two or more of which would make a penny, go
a great way.

Arrived at Savona. Hotel de la Poste; magnificently
furnished, repairs not yet complete, cuisine tolerable only;
the proprietor seems determined to impress his guests
through the eye rather than the stomach.

Again travelling, our journalist notices the
frequent pictures or frescoes of the Virgin, on
Churches, houses, and garden walls. A stranger
might suppose that " the Ligurians were worshippers of a woman." Genoa is reached on the afternoon of the fourth. Here note is made of the receipt of letters from America. Naturally, much
attention is given, in Italy, to palaces, pictures,
statues, frescoes, as well as Cathedrals and other
Churches. At the same time the works of beneficence are never lost sight of.

Genoa is no less remarkable for the munificence displayed in its provision for the poor and afflicted, than for
the splendor of its palaces and Churches.

Albergo dei Pòveri. The building might be well
styled a palace. The object is to provide a home for the
poor and aged, for all in fact who are not able to take
care of themselves from age or other infirmity; accordingly it includes among its inmates men, women and
children, in number about 2000. There is a school for
the children, another for the " mutes." On a blackboard
which had just been used by one of these poor unfor-
tunates was written in Italian: " Faith is a principle in-
fused by the grace of God, by which one believes what
the Church teaches agreeably to the revealed will of
God." The men and women who are not incapacitated
by age or bodily infirmity, are engaged in manufacturing

towels, napkins, table linen, carpets and clothing of various kinds; the girls are employed in needle work, lace making, etc. Two thirds of the avails of the labor are received by the operatives themselves; the remainder goes towards the support of the institution. . . . The boys were at play when we passed through, and were amusing themselves with a game like marbles, only they played with oranges. The girls, as they were sewing, were all engaged in singing a hymn. . . . I have yet seen nothing in Genoa which has given me more pleasure, and impressed me with a more favorable opinion of its inhabitants, than this princely establishment, endowed and sustained with such munificent liberality.

In like manner, this benefactor of his race gives detailed attention in his Journal to the "Conservatorio of the Fieschine," an institution for orphan girls. On the 6th of December he writes:

San Siro. The oldest Church in Genoa, originally the Cathedral. Here was created the first Doge of Genoa with the acclamation of the people, when the oligarchy was destroyed.

December 7th. Woke up this morning about 5 o'clock by the ringing of bells, and was reminded of Nice where the bells were continually at work telling the hours and calling the faithful to their religious duties. If each stroke of the bell here and at Nice occasioned one humble earnest prayer, these two cities must receive each day from heaven a shower of blessings.

December 8th. At the Church of the Annunciation, at 9 o'clock, attended a military Mass. The Church was crowded, there being about 2000 soldiers in the nave. The glistening bayonets and the red caps of the soldiers, the rich uniforms of the officers, the beautiful costume of the Genoese women who wear a veil covering the head and falling on the shoulders, the gay appearance of the

Church itself, presented a most magnificent *coup d'œil*. In front of the altar were two military bands which seemed to take the part of responsive choirs, and to perform the entire music of the Mass. Not a voice was heard but that of the officiating priest. In spite of the roll of the drums, which might be condemned as un-ecclesiastical in its character, and rather secular if not irreligious in its associations, the effect of the brass instruments, bassoons, clarionets and hautboys, at first startling, became highly impressive. The sermon was in French. The reason assigned for this by a friend, was the circumstance of there being many Savoyards among the regiments quartered in this city.

Leaving Genoa, our musician noted:

On our way to the steamer in a small boat, we passed a Sardinian vessel of war, where the sailors were amusing themselves in the waltz, by the music of a hand organ, which a man was playing in a boat alongside. We found among our fellow passengers, Mr. and Mrs. Wolfe of New York, Mr. and Mrs. Spencer, etc.

[After a short stay at Leghorn.] As soon as we were in rough water, dinner was served and few were left to enjoy it. December 10th. Arrived at Civita Vecchia, 6 o'clock. French soldiers were doing duty at this port of the pope. At half past twelve on our way to Naples, where we arrived at half past two o'clock, A.M.

December 11th. As we passed along the streets even at this early hour, *Punchinello* was seen, surrounded by hundreds of admirers. Looking from the window of our apartment, facing the Villa Reale, much amused we all were at the gay scene below: men with huge baskets of bread on their heads; others walking along under a good sized cart load of vegetables; women with wet clothes,— a stone on the top to keep them down—conically piled up to form a curious headgear; everything is carried on the head except oranges, which are wheeled under our window in little wagons, prettily trimmed with green leaves; monks in every variety of costume; soldiers or officers in rich uniforms; beggars in picturesque attitude and dress· and elegant equipages of every description.

In my search for apartments . . . a funeral procession passed by. The attendants were all dressed in white garments entirely covering the person, with openings only for the eyes.

Many of the houses which we entered in search for rooms, are exceedingly offensive to the eye and nose; so that a short tramp through the city and but a look and glance at the interior of a few of its best habitations, immediately suggest a satisfactory reason why the Neapolitans prefer living in the open air. The Lazzaroni are philosophers, and men of taste after all!

In every street you find Lottery offices. In one, more showy than the others in its decorations, is the picture of the Virgin as Lady Patroness of the establishment. Certainly the Italians have strange ideas of the Blessed Virgin, and while they worship her with almost divine honors, nevertheless in spite of all their respect and reverence for her as the Mother of God, they extend the limits of her maternal influence and supreme dominion in heaven and earth, so far as sometimes to associate her with places and occupations, which some good Catholics would regard as disreputable and anything but moral in their object and tendency. This was, it is said, an old Greek settlement, and possibly the remains of Paganism have not yet been entirely eradicated. I should judge from the fact of seeing two priests in one of these offices, that there is nothing in Lotteries opposed to the religious principles of the Roman Catholics in this part of the world.

December 12th. I have not yet received from the Custom House, several books which were found in the " vache," and which must be examined by the censors before they can be delivered up. In an extract from a military journal of this city, which I found in the Galignani Messenger, among the proscribed books are: Cosmos of Humboldt, Schiller, Shakespeare, Molière, Lamartine, Ovid, Lucian and Sophocles.

15th.   Attended service twice at the English Chapel attached to the Consulate; the Rector or Chaplain, Mr. Pugh. The Church was crowded in the morning. Music good. Subscribers pay two dollars a month for a seat; non-subscribers are charged every time 50 cents. As far as I could observe, the stores today are all closed.

Museums and Churches are visited continuously. Referring to one of the latter, the journalist notes: "Too late to see the paintings in sacristy. The *custóde* said it was so many minutes of 24 o'clock, which is otherwise called 5 o'clock."

It takes some time for the eye to become accustomed to the style of architecture which prevails in this part of Italy, for sacred edifices. The classical façades and other Roman or Grecian features give them a secular appearance. So great is the contrast, within and without, of a Neapolitan Church and a Cathedral in the north of France, say at Rouen, that it can but with difficulty be imagined, that the two buildings were reared by persons holding the same faith, or could be occupied and used for the same sacred service. They would seem to represent two complete sets of religious ideas. At Rouen you see Roman Catholics in the shade, here in sunlight—too strong a light thrown upon it, its defects too apparent. There is so much flimsy ornament and tinsel in many of the most splendid Churches, that after visiting many of them, you leave with the impression that the Service of the Mass is growing to seed. There is a feeling of awe and reverence produced by the grandeur and massive ornaments of a Gothic Cathedral, whereas in an Italian Church you are at best surprised by the exhibition of wealth and at times lost in admiration when gazing on some masterpiece of the celebrated painters. Besides, in France you are not always repelled and excited to criticism by the miserable little dolls which are to be found in every Church and every street in Italy. I have not seen as much devotion in the Churches here as I observed at Rouen, Paris, Dijon and elsewhere in France.

Upon the 19th, visiting the Monastery of San Martino, after speaking of frescoes, precious marbles, and mosaics, he records:

In the choir, " The Nativity " by Guido, is particularly worthy of mention. Guido died before he finished this painting. His heirs wished to restore to the monks 2000 *scudi* which had been paid in advance, but they were so well satisfied with the picture, incomplete as it was, that they refused to receive back the money. In the treasury " The Descent from the Cross " by Spagnoletto, is one of the finest paintings in the world, in point of conception of subject and expression given to the different figures. In the hall leading to the Church is an inscription, historic, connected with the Carthusians who were obliged to fly from England, reflecting pretty severely on Henry VIII.

December 24th. Riding through the Toledo, found the street crowded with people. The fish sellers with their eels were decidedly the most conspicuous and noisy in the busy throng. Over each basket of fish or eels was a branch of bay-tree from which hung a picture of St. Pasquale. A marked contrast in the appearance of Naples and that of New York on the day before Christmas! Instead of sugar plums, fancy books and toys, nothing but the smell and sight of fish! This may be accounted for by the fact that the 24th December, as coming immediately before a great festival, is a vigil.

At 10 ½ at night, F—— and myself went to the Royal Chapel to attend the midnight service. After Vespers, the Mass commenced about 12 o'clock. The choir was

13

stationed above and in the rear of the altar. Besides an orchestra of about 25 performers, there were 7 singers, three tenors and four basses. The organ was almost too insignificant to deserve any mention. .I was surprised, however, by the musical performances of the organist, who in the solemn parts of the Mass, accompanied the priest in an *ad libitum* movement, which had a most ludicrous effect, and must have been very perplexing to the officiating priest, provided that his ears could discriminate between harmony and discord. As soon as their services were no longer required, the musicians and singers, retired, first blowing out the candles. The chapel was not crowded. I noticed great irreverence on the part of certain females who while on their knees were laughing‘ and joking. The sermon was on the Incarnation, or rather the Nativity, and I listened to it with pleasure al- though I could understand but a few words; the manner and voice of the preacher were so agreeable. We left the chapel at half past one o'clock. This service has helped me to realize the sacred season.

December 25th. This does not seem like Christmas. It is only with an effort that I can make myself feel that this is the same holy festival to which I have always looked forward with so much pleasure; and now I cannot bear to think of the Holy Cross, as the remembrance of our festival joys only excites feelings of regret. I hope that the girls of the school, and all my parishioners will pass a merrie and happy day. The English Chapel was opened for morning and evening service, and attended by good congregations. I must here express my dissatisfaction at the mode of conducting the Communion Service. There seems to be no rule or custom as to the postures, the majority of the congregation kneeling or sitting during the exhortations and the reading of the *Gloria in Excelsis*. I was moreover shocked by the irreverence of the officiating priests, who allowed the consecrated bread, which they had carelessly dropped, to lie on the floor of the chancel. The stores are all closed, as the festival is observed as Sunday. December 26th. The stores closed. 28th. Breakfast on board the Cumberland.

1851. January 1st. How little we know of the future! Little did I think as I was "watching" last January, that before the year passed around I should be here in Naples. How foolish and presumptuous to make any anticipations, when we cannot with all our shrewdness tell what a day may bring forth! I almost dread entering upon this year, but with sincerity I say "My times are in God's hand," and I am ready for all events and any contingency. Could we only live for eternity, how easily we could pass through life to the grave! Wherever we are we are in God's sight. How great the importance of each successive year when we consider eternity!

A high festival with the R. C.'s. Our Church is not open. The stores are all closed. There was some visiting among the Americans.

Record is made of a visit to the museum, especially to the rooms containing pictures and inscriptions from Pompeii and Herculaneum; also of notes in detail about the "Hôpital des Enfans trouvés," where the party is conducted "by a very interesting Sister of Charity."

Religion never appears under a more attractive aspect than when we see it presented to us in the humble offices and self-devotion of these holy women, who give themselves to the service of their divine Master and to attendance upon His poor.

January 7th. At the Church of St. Januarius of the Poor, my father and myself, with the courier and a guide, descended into the Catacombs. These Catacombs consist of three stories communicating with each other by steps cut in the rock. On either side of the corridors are shelves, as it were, on which bodies of the dead were laid, and furnished with slides into which passed stone or marble slab fronts. Near the entrance are three or more chapels, in which are frescoes roughly finished and now much obscured. On one of these chapels is pictured a saint with the title S. Desiderius. In another there is a ✠ with $A\,\Omega$; in another a picture of what the guide called a woman, but which we suppose to be our Saviour spreading out His hand to bless. One of these frescoes has been marred by an American of Boston, who has there cut in large letters his name. What stupidity, for a man presuming to travel for information, to go to the Catacombs, and then like a vandal deliberately set to work to destroy what has been preserved for centuries, and is among the most interesting monuments of early Christianity! There are pits, which have been opened, along the sides of the corridor through which we passed, that are full of bones and ashes. These Catacombs are supposed to be of great extent, some maintaining that they extend to Pozzuoli. L'Abbé Romanelli in 1792 and 1814 penetrated very far into them, and on the first story found a Church with altar, baptistery, etc. He asserts that his explorations extended beyond a mile. " Le clergé Napolitain y celebrait plusieurs fonctions, et celui qui y était agrégé devait promettre et jurer de visiter les catacombes au moins une fois l'an."

January 10th. In company with Mr., Mrs. and Miss Fanny Russel went by railroad to Pompeii—this railroad, by the way, being so far behind the age (we advance so rapidly in the path of improvement in this century that things very soon become old) that it was almost as curious to us as some of the antiquities at Pompeii itself. And it was a droll thing to find yourself in a railroad car *en route* to a city which was destroyed almost 1900 years ago. This is the second time that I have made this interesting excursion. I need not be particular in recording what I saw. One of the most extraordinary sights was a musical performer, real flesh and blood, who at the amphitheatre, while we were acting the audience standing on the stone benches, amused us highly with his ludicrous imitations, grotesque dancing, and his singing of national ballads. The whole affair seemed indeed to be a poor caricature of what had once formed the amusement of 40,000 persons. In their anxiety to pick up something antique, two of the party managed to get possession of the fragments of pipes. What was more strange still, one of the bowls of these pipes actually had tobacco in it! Mr. R. thought he would like to pull an orange from the tree at the restaurant, and to his surprise he found that most of the golden fruit was tied on to the branches. This restaurant is quite an accommodation. On their card we read: " For Dinner parties address Before to the Master of the Irons Crown Hotel at Toledo keept by the Same."

I could not observe that there were many changes since I was here in 1839. Certainly not many new objects of curiosity were presented to my view. I should judge from this that the explorations must proceed very slowly. During the revolution of 1848, the excavations were entirely suspended. About three fourths of the ancient city remain to be uncovered. Anything in the way of statuary or painting that is now found at Pompeii, is permitted by the King to remain where it is.

January 11th. Went to Baiæ; visiting Pozzuoli, Lakes Lucrine and Avernus, the Cave of the Sibyl, Nero's Bath and the Temple of Venus. Perhaps there is no part of Italy more rich in classical associations than the region through which we passed on our excursion today. I am not certain that our most pleasant reminiscences, gathered up in the past among the recollections of our schoolboy-days, are connected with Virgil and Horace and Cicero; still there is no little satisfaction to see the " facilis descensus Averni," the lake so celebrated by Horace for the oyster suppers of his friend Lucullus, and the remains of Cicero's villa where the orator and philosopher composed one of his best ethical works.

January 14th. In company with Mrs. S. and Mr. K. of New York went on an excursion to Capri. The weather not altogether agreeable; there was a little breeze and something of a swell, and Mrs. S. was laid out on the deck with a basin by her head. Although it was rather rough and there was some little danger of a ducking or something worse, I entered the grotto. The color of the water is a turquoise blue. During the five or ten minutes we were in the grotto, I was more concerned in thinking how we were to get out in case the wind suddenly rose, than in admiring the peculiar hue of the water. We were disappointed in not being permitted to land on the island, and notwithstanding we enjoyed some beautiful views along the bay, we were rather dissatisfied with our water party. We left the St. Lucia at ½ past 8 o'clock, and arrived at Naples on our return at 5 o'clock.

I have occasionally met in the streets an extraordinary looking equipage, a carriage or coupé painted gaily with blue or red colors and richly gilded. At first, seeing it in the distance, and only being able to observe its *outré* appearance and the curious fantastic dress of four little boys on the outside of the carriage, I supposed it was a part of some travelling show. I have at last found out that it is a funeral carriage for children. There is a rough box behind the carriage for the corpse. I presume the idea is that the death of children is not a subject of regret or sorrow. Our friend Spedicato (our Italian master) informed us the other morning of the sudden death of his little boy. He said that he had taken the body the evening before to the cemetery, and had left it to the monks to bury it, as *his feelings would not permit him to be present* at the interment.

Ladies, very richly dressed, are sometimes seen, seated in a sedan chair. This is the way in which mothers take their infants to Church to be baptized.

21st. Visited Royal Palace. The throne room and ball room very elegant. The apparatus to carry the queen up to her parlor is as comfortable a contrivance as could be designed. It is in fact a movable room. Her majesty has only to take five steps on the marble pavement, when she finds herself in this little room, and in a few moments she has reached her apartment. It is something on the principle of a dumb-waiter.

At Rome a large part of the Journal is devoted to the mention of pictures. Now and then a remark is added, as in the Sistine Chapel:

February 15th. I was not more impressed by Michael Angelo's " Last Judgment " than I was when I saw it for the first time on my previous visit to Rome. On looking at it you are more interested with the skill of the painter in foreshortening and anatomical drawing, than excited to fear and awe by the consideration of the subject which it depicts.

St. Peter's. I did not anticipate anything like the pleasure which I actually received on entering St. Peter's. My fondness for the Gothic style of architecture, prejudiced me against it. I had found previously all I had wished in the Cathedral at Rouen, and I did not expect to be impressed very seriously by the grandeur and magnificence of this stupendous edifice. But I was mistaken. In a few minutes I began to feel that St. Peter's was of all other sacred buildings most worthy of the service for which it was reared, most worthy of God's presence. Still I could not forget the means which were used to raise contributions for its erection, nor keep out of mind the great event which grew out of the sale of Indulgences. And I must confess that while I admit that this magnificent Church might be considered as the Tabernacle of God and the abode of angels, I must own it did not seem, in all respects, fitted for the worship of men. It seemed too much like heaven, to breathe more the spirit of the Church triumphant than the Church militant. You miss the props and aids of devotion. The soul is lost in the contemplation of the Supreme Glory of the King of Kings and Lord of Lords. . . . You are not drawn to Jesus Christ; you behold Him afar off surrounded by the dazzling rays

of His divinity. It is like standing on Mount Tabor.
We " wist not what to say," except " it is good for us to
be here."

Many interesting entries must be omitted for lack
of space. One of these, however, may not be
passed by; it shows whither the heart was turning:

From the Vatican we went to *La Trinita de' Monti*, to
hear the music at the Vesper service. I was disappointed.
The music was very simple and very indifferently executed
by a choir of nuns. It could in no way compare with the
afternoon service at Holy Cross.

In August, 1851, the traveller returned from his
second foreign tour, having devoted ten months
to the trip. At once he resumed his work at the
Holy Cross, which had been entrusted to other
hands during his absence.

Agitations and oppositions from without, were
not yet over: so it would appear from a story told
me by a Trojan parishioner.

In one of the fifties, about the time when Dr.
Coit was called to St. Paul's, Troy, it happened that
there was an informal assemblage of clergy and
others at the residence of Dr. Brinsmade. Among
the clerical visitors were to be found Dr. Coxe,
afterward Bishop of Western New York; Dr. Coit,
Mr. Tucker, and the Rev. Mr. Smith of St. John's.
Talk turned upon the services held at the Holy
Cross, which was then looked upon as advanced,
although nowadays it is considered mild; by certain objectors it was still termed " the Puseyite

Church." Mr. Smith entered a protest against the manner in which services were conducted at the Holy Cross; addressing himself to Mr. Tucker, he told him that he was driving people out of the Church. The Rector of the Holy Cross turned and said: "If it would help to save a man's soul, I would put on a red shirt and preach from a hydrant box." The "hydrant box" of that day referred to a flat-topped square wooden enclosure built around each fire-plug standing at a street corner; one such might be easily improvised as a temporary pulpit out of doors.

A correspondent writes to the *Church Journal* in March, 1853, affording a glimpse of a "bright Easter" at the Holy Cross. The order of service included: *Te Deum* and *Jubilate* by Mendelssohn; Anthem: "Behold now, praise the Lord," by Nares; Dr. Hodges' *Trisagion* and Novello's *Gloria in Excelsis.* At Evensong, the Anthem was the solo, "I know that my Redeemer liveth," with quartets and choruses from the "Messiah." The Versicles and Responses were sung as given in the *Directorium Chori Anglicanum,* "where the Plain-song is given—if we may trust the compiler—harmonized according to primitive purity and simplicity."

In June of the same year Dr. Muhlenberg pays a visit to the home and parish of his pupil. He accepts the position of preacher for the anniversary service of the Brotherhood of St. Barnabas, holden on St. Barnabas' day, June 11, 1853. Many of the clergy are present at the Holy Cross, and there is an unusual attendance of the laity.

The Morning Prayer was choral, the Service being " Nares in D " and the Anthem " Blessed be Thou," by Kent.

A few days later Mr. Tucker is in line with other clergy, upon the occasion of the laying of the corner-stone of St. John's Church in Troy. That there was need of a stimulating example like that afforded by the Holy Cross may be inferred from the words of one present at the ceremony: " I dislike to find fault when all were so well pleased, but I must say that the effect of black *coats*, mixed with black *gowns*, half and half in the procession, was neither good nor imposing. It had a shabby, unprepared, undecided, private-judgment look about it."

On the 20th of June, 1854, Mr. Tucker appears in the pulpit of St. Paul's Church, Albany, as chosen preacher for the first anniversary service of the " Church Brotherhood " of the capital city— an organization similar to that of St. Barnabas in Troy. Later, at a " Diocesan Convention of Church Brotherhoods," likewise assembled in Albany, the Rev. J. I. Tucker was elected President of the Convention.

At the consecration of the Rev. Horatio Potter, D.D., to the office of a Bishop, the services were held in Trinity Church, New York, on the 22nd of November in the same year. In the published report we read that " the procession entered from the South Sacristy, in the following order: Candidates for Holy Orders and students of the General Theological Seminary; unofficiating clergy in citizens' dress and in gowns and surplices, deacons and clergy officiating, and Bishops in their robes." What is more to the point, we note this: " In the middle of the choir the Provisional Bishop-elect was seated facing the altar, with the Rev. G. T. Bedell on his right and the Rev. J. I. Tucker on his left."

About this time, at a Thanksgiving office, celebrated in the Holy Cross, just before the announcement of his text, Mr. Tucker told his congregation that he availed himself of the first opportunity of informing them that he had declined the invitation to accept the rectorship of St. Peter's parish in Albany; that while he fully appreciated the honor conferred upon him by a call to one of the most important parishes in the State, there to succeed a friend who by reason of his eminent talents and Christian graces had been thought worthy of the high office of Bishop; yet he felt that there were holy ties and obligations which bound him to his present position—that there in the fear of God, and the hope of His blessing and the help of kind and sympathizing friends, he should continue his ministerial labors until forced to relinquish them.

Soon after the consecration of the new Diocesan, in the month of December, the Northern Convocation assembled in St. Peter's Church, Albany; the Provisional Bishop was present within the limits of his old parish, presiding at the services. At the opening Celebration on the morning of the 12th, the rendering of the music was of so pronounced a character as to call out admiration. Mr.

Tucker had much to do with it, as it will appear from the words of a correspondent printed in the *Church Journal:*

The music of this service was of a character, and performed in a manner, most worthy of remark. It is not often, or in many places within the bounds of our communion, in America or in England, that a more proper style of music, or much better executed, is heard, than that of the Choir of the Church of the Holy Cross of Troy. At the urgent solicitation of the Bishop, the Rev. Mr. Tucker and his competent Organist, Mr. Hopkins, gave the services of the Choir of the Holy Cross, to assist in St. Peter's on Tuesday morning: and their presence in full force, was one of the most interesting features of the occasion. The music was performed with great spirit and fine effect—indeed, some parts of the service were perfectly thrilling. Mr. Hopkins presided at the organ, the Rev. Messrs. Tucker and Shackelford in the Choir. The music sung was the *Venite,* and 9th Selection of Psalms— chanted responsively in *unison*—the first to a Gregorian tone, the Selection to Farrant's chant; *Te Deum* and *Jubilate,* Nares in D; Old Hundredth in G, sung in unison. Anthem, " Lord, what love have I unto Thy law," Kent. Anthem after sermon: " The Lord gave the Word: great was the company of the preachers," " How beautiful are the feet," " Their sound is gone out, etc.," Handel. The *Trisagion,* Dr. Hodges. And the old *Gloria in Excelsis.* It will be seen that it was a judicious blending of the congregational and the cathedral styles. Those who heard will never forget, in this world, the sweet songs they heard in the sanctuary, on Tuesday morning.

On Wednesday the Provisional Bishop held a special ordination in St. Peter's Church, when an ex-Baptist minister and an ex-Presbyterian were advanced to the Priesthood. At this service there was a choir made up of clergy, vested in surplices, who entered the Church and ascended to the organ loft. The Rev. Mr. Shackelford played the organ. His coworker of the day before was at the other end of the Church; the Rev. Mr. Tucker appearing in the pulpit, where he preached, as the paper phrases it, "an admirable as well as appropriate discourse."

The instances here cited will show the warm interest felt by the Rector of the Holy Cross in general Church work, outside of the limits of his own parish or city.

XI

THE BOYS' SCHOOL

Dr. Muhlenberg was never forgotten by any of his former pupils. On Christmas day in the year 1856, a number of his sons gathered at the Church of the Holy Communion in New York, to take part in a service which would remind them of the old days at the Institute and at St. Paul's College. They with other schoolmates had united in the purchase of a picture, " The Gospel at Home," painted by Hübner, which was then presented to the venerated school-father. The first name on the list of the committee having the matter in charge is Gregory Thurston Bedell, and the second John Ireland Tucker.

It has been remarked that the Rector of the Holy Cross was himself a witness of the fashioning handiwork of Dr. Muhlenberg. Certain it is that he followed his master in the æsthetics of divine service, in devotion to music and the use of the art, and in his passion for the duty of an educator.

The school of girls had been started before he came to Troy; it was the backbone of the undertaking. As soon as the new Rector arrived upon the scene, he entered into the plan with eagerness. He began his career of successful service as a teacher;

he himself instructed, five or more hours a day, and so he continued to do until the end of his life.

After matters had progressed for some years, he felt that there ought to be an enlargement of the beneficiary agency. He desired that boys as well as girls should be subject to the guiding influence.

As it turned out, he undertook too much. It seems to be a rule that when one man takes up the superintendency of two separate houses, one for boys, another for girls, that one of the two must go to the wall.

The ultimate discontinuance at Troy subtracted nothing from the fact that the Rector desired to render a full service, and that he rounded out the plan of Christian education.

A Boys' School was commenced. It lasted not many years, and yet its memory is cherished. Every now and then I hear a remark about it which shows the affectionate regard bestowed upon it.

For an account of the undertaking, I am indebted to one of the " old boys," now Rector of St. Luke's Church, Malden, Mass. Dr. Albert Danker sets down his memories; he kindly grants permission to quote from his manuscript:

I have attended the Holy Cross, more or less, since I was ten years old. It was a church which impressed the young, particularly by its ritual and architecture, so different from the other churches of the city at that day, for it was the advance guard of that mighty host which has spread throughout our whole land, worshipping the Lord in the " beauty of holiness."

The " Boys' School of the Holy Cross " was established by Dr. Tucker in 1855, as a first-class institution, to furnish boys with an English and classical education, fitting them for college or business life. It lasted four years only, but in that time sent forth many a youthful alumnus who afterward distinguished himself in trade or a profession. It held its sessions in the old Van der Heyden mansion— on Eighth street, nearly opposite the Holy Cross—destroyed in the great fire of 1862.

How well I remember the dear boys who recited together there during those pleasant years, under the instruction of Dr. Tucker, Dr. J. D. Lomax, now Medical Superintendent of the Marshall Infirmary in Troy, and others. The classmates and fellow pupils of my youth rise before me as I write, with their fresh young faces and bright, lively ways; they pass before my mental vision as though it were only yesterday;—Charles Sigourney Knox, and Hiram Nazro, who afterward bore off the highest honors in Columbia College; Jared L. Bacon, George M. King, Le Grand Cramer, Bernard Blair, Thomas Brinsmade Heimstreet, John H. Knox, James Knox, Matthew Vassar, Palmer Baermann, Samuel Tappan, Charles H. Dauchy, J. De L'Orme Reeve, James H. and Henry Ferriss, Albert Daggett, Samuel N. Rudkin, Charles R. Cross, Anson G. Gardner, Le Grand Benedict, and my own brother, Henry A. Danker. Some of these beloved comrades are waiting their joyful resurrection. Others have distinguished themselves in various walks of life in Troy and elsewhere.

One of the most pleasant features of our Saturday mornings at the school was our dramatic performance, which seemed to afford much pleasure to friends and relatives. Sheridan's " Rivals," Allingham's " Fortune's Frolic," " The Doom of the Tory's Guard," and many other plays were performed, either in whole or part, together with original dramas. We had a literary society with its paper, debates, etc., called the " Cadmean Society," which was of great benefit to us.

Dr. Tucker spent much time, hearing our recitations himself. The boys were all very fond of him, and owe much to the fine taste, critical scholarship, and genial manner with which he imparted instruction.

Professor William Hopkins taught us music weekly. I fear we were a difficult crowd to teach this divine art. One of our favorite mathematical instructors was Charles C. Martin, then a student at the " Rensselaer Institute," now chief engineer of the famous Brooklyn Bridge. C. Whitman Boynton was another instructor in the same department. He was one of the most rapid calculators in a problem on the blackboard I have ever seen, covering it with figures in a few moments.

I cannot close this article without at least a reference to Mrs. Mary Warren and her sons. They felt and expressed so much interest in the Church and the school and came so often to our exhibitions that we felt much attached to them. They always had a kindly smile and gentle word for all of us, and we never shall forget them, or the influence of the daily morning prayer at the Holy Cross, which we all attended, and which moulded the heart and after life of many a boy.

The noble Warren brothers and their beloved mother, Mary Warren, deserve their meed of honest praise as well, for efforts to introduce and popularize all the ancient and time-honored customs of the Anglican communion connected throughout the ages of the past with the grand old feast, the Birthday of the Blessed Christ. Dear Dr. Tucker and the brothers Dr. Nathan and Stephen Warren have done more than most of their contemporaries thus to revive, on this side of the Atlantic, those quaint and beautiful observances and customs which our own charming Washington Irving has immortalized in his " Sketch Book."

It was reserved for the Church of the Holy Cross to inaugurate a revival of the rites of olden time, which transported the young beholder back to those noble days of the Church of England, when, as Sir Walter Scott has written,

14

> Domestic and religious rite
> Gave honor to the Holy Night.

My Holland ancestry had trained me to appreciate peculiarly this revival in the Episcopal Church of ancient customs, ceremonies and traditions of " Merrie England " in days of yore; as the Yule log, the Mummers and Maskers, Lord of Misrule, the " Boar's Head Carol," and " The Good St. Nicholas," also the Christmas table smoking with good old plum pudding, mince pie, furmity and many another dish which the ancient Puritans proscribed and ordered to be abolished in the endeavor to rule Christmas with its sports and pastimes out of the calendar.

Our Boys' School always had a special celebration of their own in the school-house on Eighth street. Here during Christmas week Dr. Tucker had an appropriate stage erected with curtain and scenery, and the boys performed " St. George and the Dragon," " Bombastes Furioso," and other plays and burlesques suitable to the season, to the great delight apparently of our admiring friends.

Later on, in the years after this building was burned and the school was closed, the good doctor and myself, then in deacon's orders, and assisting him in the Church, arranged a series of Christmas plays and pastimes in the " Mary Warren Institute " in imitation of the olden sports, masking and mumming in the ancient baronial halls of old England.

Most laughable and amusing was this entertainment to the crowd of children and friends who filled the building. What screams of laughter greeted the breaking asunder by accident of the " Guyascutus," the strange animal with a head at both ends of his body, and the discovery thus of the two young fellows within who guided the creature's movements! And what a wonderful giant Mr. Wagstaff, the sexton, made with a false face elevated far up in the air upon a pole, draped with a concealing cloak, and whose advent in the hall caused some of us actually to grow pale

with affright at our own creation, like the monster in
Shelley's " Frankenstein " !

Then followed the festal banquet, where the tables
groaned with the viands, plum pudding, roast goose and
all the mediæval delicacies which Dr. and Stephen Warren
had hospitably served with the generosity of the ancient
lord of the manor.

As may well be imagined, the establishment of
the Boys' School brought an additional tax upon the
time and strength of the Rector, as well as a heavy
drain upon his financial resources.   Dr. Lomax
writes:

Although the school was called a pay-school, a very
large number of pupils received their tuition free.   In fact,
in every instance where it was known to the Rector that
the circumstances of the parents were such that they could
not pay, the bills were sent to them receipted, and those
who paid no attention to the bills were never reminded of
their indebtedness.   The income from tuition was therefore very small.   Indeed I do not believe it was at any
time sufficient to meet half of the expenses of the school.
To carry on an educational institution of the character of
the Boys' School of the Holy Cross, involved no small
outlay of money.   Many of the pupils not only received
their tuition without charge, but they were even furnished
with text books, copy books, slates—in fact with whatever
they required in pursuing their studies.   The cost of these
things during the term formed a considerable sum.   The
deficit at the end of the year was paid by the Rector, and
no matter how large it was, it was always paid cheerfully.

Further, Dr. Lomax refers to the Rector as a
" very careful teacher.   He was progressive, and
never hesitated to change his methods when he

became convinced that others were better. He used the most approved text-books, some of which he had imported expressly for his school."

He was very popular with his pupils. I do not believe that there was ever a boy in the school who did not respect him, and whose good feeling he did not have.

As an associate, Dr. Tucker was just and considerate. He was always cheerful, apparently looking on the bright side. He was even-tempered to a very remarkable degree. During the five years I was with him in the school, I never saw him lose his mental equipoise even for one moment. Our relations were always of the most cordial character.

The assistant teacher retires from the school; his principal writes him:

LENOX, August 29, 1859.

MY DEAR MR. LOMAX:

In a batch of letters waiting me here, I found one from you informing me of your determination to retire from your position in the school of the Holy Cross.

You do not tell me what are the circumstances which lead you to the determination. Whatever they may be, I regret most heartily that anything should disturb our pleasant relations and deprive me of your valuable co-operation, and would be most glad could I induce you to reconsider the matter and direct you to different decision. But I am not so selfish as to wish you to do anything which might interfere with your interests. I am anxious on the other hand to promote your welfare. Still it is a grievous thing to me to think of your leaving the school, for I know not how I can supply your place. Possibly your determination may tempt me to abandon the Boys' School. However, I do not mention this to influence your conduct. You are bound to consider yourself and future career, and not my wishes and wants.

I expect to return to Troy on Saturday, and should be happy to find there a letter containing more full information as to your plans. In the meanwhile believe me as ever,

Most affectionately yours
J. IRELAND TUCKER.

Mr. J. D. Lomax.

There was a difficulty about the finding of a suitable person to take Dr. Lomax's place, and without increase of expenditure. At any rate, the school never reopened. The enlarged attention bestowed upon the other school by the Rector gave indication of the fact that he had not changed his opinion about the importance of Church education.

XII

THE LATER FIFTIES

A series of old scrap-books has come to hand, filled with cuttings collected years ago at Troy by the Rector; many of these refer to the Holy Cross and the Mary Warren Institute.

There is one—undated, but presumably belonging to the year 1856—which furnishes a record of happenings at the time. The Editor of the *Church Journal* prefaces the printed correspondence with his own remark, " At a distance from the city, perhaps Troy will furnish as choice a specimen of Christmas celebration as can be found " :

On Christmas eve, at about dusk, the Christmas Tree, sparkling with a hundred wax lights among the boughs, was unveiled at the residence of Mrs. Warren, and shone in the eyes of seventy or eighty children, mostly the orphan inmates of the school founded by their munificent entertainer. Carols were sung, and congratulations were exchanged, and happy with gifts and enjoyment, the little ones went home delighted.

At midnight precisely the chimes began their merry noise from the tower of the Church of the Holy Cross, and kept it up with varying changes for half an hour: and then, in the clear moonlight and the mild atmosphere of this December, a lusty choir of singers filled the streets with their resounding *Carols*, beginning under the windows of the Rector of St. Paul's, and thence extending their visits to others also. This charming feature of Christmas celebration, will, we trust, spread as fast and as far as the Christmas Tree.

At the Church of the Holy Cross, on Christmas Day, there was full choral service, the *Venite* and Psalter being sung to the grand old Gregorians, *pure*. The sermon was preached by a clergyman visiting the city from New York. The Anthem was "For unto us" from the "Messiah," and was well done; as were also the *Te Deum*, *Jubilate* and *Gloria in Excelsis* of Ouseley. The whole day's service was delightful in the highest degree.

Here is a counterpart of the foregoing—a cutting taken from the Troy *Daily Times*—which gives account of an Easter celebration, probably in the year 1857. From the record it will appear that Plain-song was still in the ascendant, that its value had been appreciated after full trial. It will be seen also that music of the highest grade was adopted as an integral part of divine service. The reporter says:

At this Church the ancient custom of decorating the altar at Easter with the early flowers of spring, is continued. The collection yesterday, considering the earliness of the season, was remarkably beautiful. It is a long time since we have feasted our eyes on so many beautiful flowers in one collection.

All the services were choral throughout; and were performed with the skill for which the choir of this Church is celebrated. At the 11 o'clock service a Choral Litany was performed, and an appropriate sermon preached by the Rev. Mr. Tucker; after which the Holy Communion was administered.

The large double choir of this Church performed the

morning and evening choral service throughout with admirable effect. The Responses, both morning and evening, together with the Easter Anthem " Christ our Passover," were taken from the " Plain-song of the Church "; the Proper Psalms, both morning and evening, from " Helmore's Plain-song "; the *Te Deum* and *Jubilate* at morning service, and the *Cantate* and *Deus* at evening service, from the music of Joseph Corfe. But the crowning glory of these rich musical services, was the grand " Hallelujah Chorus " from Handel's Oratorio of the Messiah —a work trying to the best of Church choirs, and even to more extensive musical bodies; and the admirable production of which reflects the greatest credit upon the able organist of the Holy Cross, and the efficient choir under his management. We must say that we think the Plain-song particularly adapted to congregational chanting. We hope to see it more generally introduced.

The last remark will show an intelligent interest in the matter, which in these days is not customary on the part of a secular reporter. Nevertheless, the narrator is inclined to look on the whole business as a " performance," and he so phrases it. But there is no doubt that the function was planned and carried out as an act of praise to Almighty God.

The Rector of the Holy Cross had a care for matters of general concern outside of parish limitations. We have found him already officiating at services of the Church Choral Society held in New York City. It was a custom with him to visit his neighbors and be present—anywhere within reach—upon special occasions, such as the laying of a corner-stone, at a confirmation or ordination service, or the meeting of a convocation.

Mr. Tucker showed strong interest in the "Brotherhood of St. Barnabas," a general Church organization devoted to works of benevolence, to the giving of help in sickness and for burial, and to the support of a " Church Asylum " in the city of Troy. Many special services, participated in by the assembled brotherhood, were held in the Church of the Holy Cross. We read of a sixth anniversary, holden on the Feast-day of St. Barnabas, in one of the later fifties, when Dr. Cooke of St. Bartholomew's, New York, was the preacher, and when the annual report was read by the Rev. John Scarborough, then deacon of St. Paul's, Troy.

In the summer of 1858 the Rector of the Holy Cross received from his *alma mater* the degree *Sacræ Theologiæ Doctor*.

Bearing the new honor, he comes into prominence in August of the same year as preacher at St. Paul's Church, Troy, upon the occasion when the Rev. John Scarborough—now Bishop of New Jersey—is advanced to the Order of Priests. The Rt. Rev. Horatio Potter is in charge. Many visiting clergy are present. There is a quartet choir in the gallery, which sings " How beautiful upon the mountains " as an " opening piece."

The preacher had chosen for his subject " The Polity and Ministry of the Church." He referred to the polity as outward and visible, arguing that its facts must be determined " by the Bible record, with the assistance of such light as is thrown upon the subject by profane history." After reviewing the statements made about the ministry of the

Apostolic Church, he gave attention to the period of the Reformation. In the address to the candidate, the preacher said:

It is but natural, I would repeat, but proper that you should associate high thoughts, and glorious anticipations with the holy office to which you seek to be admitted. You " have used the office of a Deacon well," and " purchased to yourself a good degree." But with that degree —that promotion in the Church of Christ to which you aspire—remember, is bound up by apostolic injunction " great boldness in the faith which is in Christ Jesus." As you prize, then, the good degree to which you have attained by your faithfulness in a lower grade of your ministry, be bold " in the faith which is in Christ Jesus." Be bold in preaching the truths of His holy Gospel, bold in maintaining the use and the dignity of His sacred institutions. Let me affectionately urge you never—through a cowardly concession to expediency, or at the dictate of a selfish policy—to shrink from an open and uncompromising profession of your religious principles; of your real, earnest convictions of truth, of right and of duty. " Let no man despise thee " or thy office for a base compliance ·with error, and the violation of the most solemn vows.

Two days after the ordination the Rector had a slight experience of them that break through and steal. Upon a Friday night, the Church of the Holy Cross was entered by burglars, who broke open the alms chest, carrying off—as the reporter expressed it—no one can say how much gold, silver, and copper, also surplices, stoles, and other matters. The same reporter entered into argument:

It is but fair to presume that the robbers were not
Ecclesiologists, and were, therefore, possibly deceived by
the iron bands and the multiplicity of locks, into the idea
that the well secured chest contained great treasures. A
taste for Mediævalism may thus expose a parish to other
attacks than those of "the brethren" who are opposed to
the revival or imitation of middle-aged Christianity, even
in the shape and decorations of an alms chest. Perhaps
to put temptation out of the way of thieves, it would be
well to have it understood that these boxes for alms are
opened every month. The burglars complimented the
attendants at Holy Cross, by supposing that they were
liberal in their alms; and in return they ought to be held
up as an example to all other Church robbers for the
decency in which they carried on their depredations.
Nothing, I am happy to say, was injured by the thieves
through mere maliciousness.

On the 1st of March, 1859, the Missionary Convocation of Northern New York assembled in the
Church of the Holy Cross, thirty-six of the clergy
being in attendance. As upon other occasions, the
records of the time speak of the music as noteworthy, in particular the Plain-song as "hearty
and spirited."
The session is memorable as taking action about
a sad loss which had come to the Rector and people
of the Holy Cross, and which was felt by multitudes
in Troy and elsewhere. A resolution was adopted,
unanimously, giving expression to the feeling called
out by the recent death of Mrs. Mary Warren.
One Sunday in the following month, Bishop
Horatio Potter paid a visit to the Holy Cross,
confirming fourteen candidates; it was the second
Confirmation within the year, which showed thirty-

three in all as a portion of the fruits of faithful labor. At the end of his sermon the Bishop spoke touchingly of the peculiar loss that had come to the parish. He dwelt upon the virtues of Mrs. Warren, Founder of the Holy Cross. He was surrounded by the sad memorials of her departure from among the living; but there were grander memorials still to recall her charity and devotion— the very walls of that Church were her monument. The Bishop spoke of the kindness of Mrs. Warren, in particular, to the clergy; of her zeal and benevolence, and said that the effects of her holy example were to be seen in places far distant from the scenes which witnessed her pious works of faith and love. There were many weeping ones in the crowded congregation when the Bishop delivered his eulogy.

Soon there was another sad burial, at Burlington, New Jersey, fittingly associated in time with the loss of Mrs. Warren. The body of the noble-hearted Bishop Doane of New Jersey was laid to rest in the green God's acre which surrounds the impressive St. Mary's Church.

We read about the solemn beauty of that Wednesday in Easter week, when the extended line of vested clergy wound along the margin of " Riverside "—" on the left, the broad, flashing surface of the Delaware, with its moving sails, seen through the trunks of the new-leafed trees, among the branches of which the birds were making music as merrily as if there were no grief below." The body of the much loved Bishop, covered by a purple pall, was borne by the faithful all the way from

Riverside into the choir of St. Mary's Church. Afterward in the churchyard, when the great company gathered around the open grave, Doctor Tucker had a place in the memorable scene. The sentence, " I heard a voice from heaven," was sung by three priests—the Rev. Messrs. Pecke and Shackelford and the Rev. Dr. Tucker. The music sung was a Trio adapted from Mozart's Requiem. The three voices blended in a fine balance of harmony; the sounds, swelling and dying away in the open air, gave exquisite expression to the feelings of the grief-stricken multitude.

During the year, an important enlargement had been effected in the fabric of the Church at Troy. Then was built the picturesque tower which now stands as a landmark, also the spacious ante-chapel which added much to the seating capacity as well as the architectural effect of the building.

The extension had been contemplated by the founder. After she had gone, the plan was carried out by her children. The purpose is inscribed upon a stone tablet let into the west wall: " This Church, free to all people, was founded by Mary, widow of Nathan Warren, A.D., MDCCCXLIV. The Ante-Chapel, contemplated by the founder, was built by her children as a memorial of their venerated mother, who on the VIII day of February, A.D., MDCCCLIX, in the LXX year of her age, entered into that rest which remaineth to the people of God."

Together with the rectory, built two years earlier, the structure now presented an imposing frontage of eighty-three feet. The material was solid, the construction permanent: blue stone in the walls, a checkered stone pavement within, Aubigne stone in piers, arches, and window tracery. A screen of wood carved in open-work was put in place between ante-chapel and nave—the earliest example of the sort within the limits of the American Church. A great rose window was inserted as a memorial of the foundress. The figures in this and the other window lights formed the subjects of informal instructions, delivered by Doctor Tucker to the girls of his school.

Like the original structure, the improvements were designed by Dr. N. B. Warren, who had received a suggestion from the ante-chapel of New College in Oxford.

The first service held in the re-opened Church was one of mourning for a close friend and a faithful co-worker. It was a year of sorrows; three times the dark messenger had come to the intimate circle of those dear to the Rector and his people.

Harriette Louise, wife of Edmund Schriver, was the only daughter of Mrs. Mary Warren; the child had walked in the footsteps of her sainted mother. Like her, she went about doing good, and maintained a lively interest in school and Church.

On Thursday morning, the 15th of December, Mrs. Schriver drove to the Holy Cross, where she entered the tower and watched the hoisting up into its place of the last bell of the chime. Much work remained to be done about the building; as Mrs. Schriver left she made the remark, " I do not think it will be possible to have the Church opened for service on Sunday."

The visitor returned to her sleigh. In the descent of the hill the horse became restive; as he turned a corner he appeared to start upon a run; Mrs. Schriver jumped from the sleigh and was dashed against the icy ground. She was carried into the house of a physician, but before husband or brother could reach her, her earthly life was done.

On the following Sunday the Burial Office was said at the Church of the Holy Cross. Doctor Tucker wrote about the occasion:

The Rev. Dr. Coit, and the Rev. Messrs. Twing, Mulchahey, Potter and Scarborough were with me on that solemn occasion, to express, along with many others, their sympathy.

After the Lesson, I informed the congregation, that we had selected that very day for the re-opening service of the Church—had requested Bishop Potter to be with us on an occasion of so much interest to all who were familiar with the history of the parish—and that a compliance with our request had only been prevented by previous appointments. "*This*," I said in some such words as these, " is our opening service. And could there be one more solemn and impressive; one better fitted to promote the glory of God by making all of us who are here today, deeply sensible of the shortness and uncertainty of human life, and of the necessity of watchfulness and diligence in the performance of our religious obligations?"

I then read, as most expressive of my own feelings, from a letter of condolence addressed to me by Bishop Potter.

The sad service was held on the Fourth Sunday in Advent. Upon the Christmas day following immediately after, Doctor Tucker preached a sermon, which has been published in pamphlet form; it is headed " Christmas Consolations for the Sorrowful."

After dwelling upon the fact that " the good tidings of great joy " and the full chorus of the celestial choirs were associated with the gloom of night, he went on to say:

May there not be something congenial with Christmas tidings and Christmas joys, in that stillness and gloominess of the soul, when gladsome hymns and friendly greetings sound "like songs in the night when a holy solemnity is kept," and as the clouds of affliction hang heavy, shutting out all signs of worldly festivity, heaven seems to be nearer and God's words reach us in tones more clear? . . .

If ever, one might think, a messenger from heaven would be greeted as the bringer of good tidings, it would be when all the beauty and glory of life is covered over with a drapery of sorrow. . . .

One present at the service tells me what an effort it was for Doctor Tucker, overcome by his own sorrow, to deliver this sermon. At times he would break down, almost sobbing. So it was, toward the end of his sermon, when he struggled to say:

I love to think here amid these signs of Christ's presence and glory, of one who was very dear to me and others, and dear to most of those who now are before me —of one who was here in the morning, and in a few minutes after leaving this house of Prayer was sud-

denly by angels conducted into Paradise. . . . With
mind and heart now full of Jesus, the Incarnate Saviour,
I love to speak of her, who so unexpectedly was parted
from friends on earth, to join her friends in eternity,—
who, in an instant, passed from the threshold of the
temple into the special abode of the Divine Presence.

Among the names of clergy, present at the sad
funeral, appears that of the Rev. Mr. Potter, introduced by one of the newspapers of the day as " the
son of the Bishop of Pennsylvania." The Rev.
Henry C. Potter, now Bishop of New York, had
entered upon the rectorship of St. John's Church in
Troy. Soon the young Rector found himself subject to the attraction, the winning way of Doctor
Tucker. The two became friends and then companions; they travelled together upon certain summer journeys. Bishop Potter's own remembrance
of the period will be given.

One thing remains to be mentioned in connection with an eventful year. It was a quite usual
occurrence for the Rector of the Holy Cross to be
" called " to some other field of labor. Upon different occasions he was asked and urged to accept
the rectorship of influential parishes.

Beside these, there came at least the suggestion
of another line of duty. At the Second Annual
Convention of the Diocese of Minnesota, assembled
on the Feast of St. Peter, the chief business was
the election of a Bishop. Upon the first ballot, the
Rev. John Ireland Tucker, D.D., was nominated by
the clergy, by a large majority of votes. The timid
laymen failed to confirm, by a vote of 10 to 11.

15

Again the clergy nominated upon a second ballot; again the laymen rejected by the majority of a single vote.   Afterward, by a correspondent of the *Church Journal*, it was asserted that two of the lay voters did not possess the right of suffrage.   By that time, however, the Rev. Henry B. Whipple had received the election.   The result was no doubt a relief to the parson dwelling upon Mount Ida, for he had declined offered positions showing stronger attractions than the Diocese in a new land.

XIII

BISHOP POTTER'S REMINISCENCE— ELECTION OF THE FIRST BISHOP OF ALBANY

The beginning of the sixties has been described by a participant. Not long ago the Bishop of New York kindly gave his impressions reminiscent of a time when the future Bishop began to be a neighbor of the Pastor of the Holy Cross. The Bishop said:

My acquaintance began when I became Rector of St. John's Church, Troy, in 1859. Doctor Tucker had then been in Troy some fifteen years; he had already made large place in the affections of the people, overcoming the original prejudices which many had entertained.

My first impressions of him were those of a very young man, barely of age, who was daily surprised by the courtesy and kindly interest of a man greatly older than himself. I was frequently indebted to him for assistance in the services of the Church, and always for the most generous encouragement in all intellectual work and in the problems which saluted the inexperienced stripling in charge for the first time of a parish of considerable importance. Our relations became more intimate, and once or twice during my seven years' residence in Troy, we spent part of our summer vacations together in travel. We were members of a literary and social club, to which

belonged many of the leading professional men in Troy
and others, including the Hon. David A. Wells. In that
fellowship, I gained a very strong impression of Doctor Tucker's wide reading and large intellectual sympathies. He was not only an educated man in the best
sense of the term, with a trained mind and good classical
foundations, but he was a constant and various reader of
the best books.

In such intercourse, not only the knowledge but the
prejudices of men come to the surface; and it was a revelation to one accustomed to the ordinary experiences of
life, to find how free from prejudice, intolerance and ac-
rimony, one could be, and nevertheless hold his own
convictions in a very strong grasp, and feel most deeply
concerning all that he believed. The secret of it all was
to be found in the singular nobility of his nature—absolutely free, I think, from all pettiness, jealousy, censori-
ousness and acerbity, more so than almost any man
whom I have ever known.

With these characteristics, he came to exercise an influence in Troy which was absolutely unique, and no
man or woman who was striving for the right, in how-
soever blundering or eccentric a way, had any doubt about
his substantial sympathy. He had rare wisdom, practical good sense, a fine and true quality of discrimination,
but he could be both just and generous to people who
were without these characteristics; and most of all, whoever was striving in whatever agency for the triumph of
the eternal righteousness, knew that Doctor Tucker was on
his side. From this fact, there came to pass a very singular result. He was never a public man in the merely
popular sense of that term—now and then in great emer-
gencies he came to the fore, and allowed the eminent
weight of his name and co-operation to be counted upon
the side of some grave moral or civic issue—but ordinarily, his life was lived in the modest circle of his own
parochial relations and obligations; and yet notwithstanding this he came to be felt in Troy as a power for

good everywhere, among all classes, with a force and weight that increased steadily to the end. I do not recall more than one other instance in this generation of such largely silent influence of character.

To those who knew and loved him best, it seems to be something almost a profanation, the attempt to speak of Doctor Tucker in his more intimate personal relations. The charm of his presence, singularly high-bred but most gracious in dignity, and his bearing absolutely without ceremoniousness or stiffness, but with a courtesy so unfailing and a charm so irresistible—who that knew them will ever forget them? A man without family, his home had always the warm charm of a delightful hospitality, and his conversation the rare quality of invariable sympathy, vivacity and responsiveness. Never surely was there a more beautiful illustration of the fact that graces of mind and character make age a forgotten factor in our estimate of friends. Doctor Tucker was as young, the last day that I saw him, as the first; and yet nearly forty years had stretched between them. He had indeed great charm of presence, the face of a saint and a scholar, but his merely physical characteristics seemed always to me simply like the porcelain shade which reveals the steady and gracious light that burns within. There may be other men in the ministry, of his generation, who resembled him in his rare qualities; but I think that to those who knew him he will always stand apart, in the life of the community in which he lived and in the ministry of our American Church, as a figure of absolutely singular and unmatched graciousness, of benignity and habitual and unaffected self-sacrifice.

-When the Civil War came on in the year 1861 Doctor Tucker was roused up to an ardor of patriotism. At one time he had almost made up his mind to enlist in the army; from this he was dissuaded by arguments adduced by an old friend and parishioner, who quoted the words of God addressed to David: "Thou shalt not build an house for my name, because thou hast been a man of war and hast shed blood." But the Rector's abiding interest in the topic—especially in its bearings on Church unity—is witnessed in the subject-matter of many cuttings from newspapers preserved in one or more of his scrap-books.

Doctor Tucker was never a political preacher. He never forgot that he was a priest. Nevertheless, he looked upon loyalty to his government as one of the ordinary Christian virtues, and as having no intrinsic connection with politics; accordingly, during the war, when Thanksgiving days came round, he was accustomed to "speak his mind," and to "speak it warmly"—so I am informed by a devoted parishioner of long standing.

On the tenth of May, 1862, a great fire occurred in the city of Troy, now famous in its annals. A terrible gale was blowing; the high wind distributed the sparks and burning fagots. In this way the Van der Heyden mansion, standing in Walnut Grove and used as the parish school-house, took fire and was consumed. The Church escaped. I have been told of a fact, apparently incredible, testifying to the power of the wind on that fateful day. Sheets of music belonging to the Holy Cross, showing signs of fire, were found in Lenox, Mass., whither they had been carried by the gale.

Although the Church fabric was not destroyed, some of its furnishings gave token of the ordeal. The altar-piece was so blackened by smoke that the scene portrayed upon it became almost invisible.

Originally the picture had represented the Cross at the time of the removal of the Saviour's body.

It had been painted by Weir of West Point for the chapel pertaining to that military institution. As the offence of the Cross had not yet ceased, the authorities objected to the setting up of the picture in the place intended; they would not permit its introduction into the chapel.

Captain Schriver, himself a graduate of West Point, heard of the dilemma. He suggested to the artist that there was a Church of the Holy Cross up the Hudson, where the subject would be most appropriate. Mr. Weir gladly offered the picture to the Church, over whose altar it acted as reredos for years.

After it was begrimed by smoke and changed into " a dark and gloomy object," it maintained its position until the chancel was lengthened at the time of the last enlargement. Then the altar-piece made way for stained glass windows. The former was hung upon the wall of the ante-chapel until, at a later day, it was again displaced to make room for a memorial tablet. At the present time the canvas is preserved in the attic of a private house.

The great fire had another effect upon the fortunes of the Holy Cross: it perpetuated the pastorship which otherwise might have ended prematurely. Doctor Tucker received three separate calls to accept the rectorship of St. Mark's Church, Philadelphia.

Strong persuasion was brought to bear. Just when the St. Mark's people were trying their hardest to induce Doctor Tucker to come, and while he was balancing the question, the day of fire overtook his parish. He said at once, " There is no use in talking. My poor people are in trouble: I cannot go."

A heavy loss was borne by Rector and people when William Hopkins was called away from earth, on the 18th of February, 1866.

Mr. Hopkins had been the first, so far the only, teacher of music in the school and organist in the Church. In the connection he had served faithfully for twenty-five years. He began his labors when the girls were first assembled as an Industrial School associated with St. Paul's parish. Even then, when the effort was new, his success was rapid. His little pupils appeared in a public performance.

I have before me a copy of a boldly printed programme which reads:

CONCERT

The pupils of the School of Industry will give a

CONCERT OF VOCAL MUSIC

On Monday Evening, July 31,

At their School-room in State Street.

They will be assisted on this occasion by their teacher, WILLIAM HOPKINS. The receipts will be appropriated to the support of the Boys' School of St. Paul's Parish.

This Concert will be given under the superintendence of the Ladies' Industrious Society of St. Paul's Church.

PROGRAMME

PART I

1. INTRODUCTION—Piano Forte .   .   .   *Rossini.*
2. CHANT—Psalms for the Day .   .   .   *Lord Mornington.*
3. TRIO—Oh, say not, dream not, heavenly
    notes .   .   .   .   *Keble.*
4. DESCRIPTIVE PIECE—Hark, the Vesper
    Hymn is stealing .   .   .   .   .   ——
5. TRIO—The Sabbath Bell so full and
    swelling .   .   .   .   *Neukomm.*
6. ANTHEM—Great is the Lord .   .   .   ——

The second part included a Chorus from Weber's " Freyschütz " and other selections.

William Hopkins was a conscientious Church musician. He had to do with that first partly Choral Service, ever celebrated in America, at a children's office on Easter day in 1842. He had intimate connection also with the starting and continuance of the Choral Service at the Holy Cross, where the sung office has been heard within its walls ever since the opening. He trained the girls and other singers for the rendering of the important anthems, at once adopted as a part of the offering up of praise.

Moreover, he was a communicant member, a loyal son of mother Church; so, when it came to be the time that the words of burial should be said in his behalf, it was fitting that there should be an outburst of real prayer and praise.

At one o'clock on a Tuesday afternoon, the body of William Hopkins rested upon a bier in the ante-chapel of the Holy Cross. It was partly covered by a pall of cloth, purple and white. At three, the children of the school entered in procession, wearing their uniform of scarlet cloaks and drab bonnets. The banner of the Mary Warren Free Institute was carried in line by a former member of the " Parochial Choral Society "—another organization in which the one remembered had been active. After the Trustees of the Institute, marched the officiating clergy—Doctor Tucker, Messrs. Cooke, Danker, and Cady.

As the procession advanced, the choir sang the opening sentences. The first roll or tide of harmony, sweeping through the Church, was remarked upon in reports written at the time. That pervasiveness of rich, soulful vocal harmony has always been characteristic of services sung at the Holy Cross.

Merbecke's music was given as the setting for the sentences. The Burial Chant was Gregorian—taken antiphonally. After the lesson, the clergy gathered about the coffin, when again the Merbecke music was sung, this time set to " Man that is born of a woman." Doctor Tucker intoned the Committal. " I heard a voice " was arranged to phrases taken from Mozart's Requiem. Mr. Cooke intoned the concluding collects.

As the procession passed out it sang " Lord, now lettest Thou Thy servant depart " to a setting by John Smith, Vicar Choral of St. Patrick's, Dublin.

Thereafter it was said: " The music was the best eulogy of the dead man, over whom it was sung, that could have been made." It was a witness to his own labor, and to his appreciation of beauty in the worship of Almighty God.

The interests of the Church at large, in Europe as well as America, were much in the thought of Doctor Tucker. Naturally, his view went out toward his own national communion, and in particular toward his own Diocese.

When the jurisdiction of Albany was set off from the parent stem, there was not an entire unanimity of feeling about the naming of a Priest who should be elevated to the Episcopate and entrusted with the charge of the new spiritual commonwealth. Many of the Church people in and around Troy had made up their minds in favor of a candidate who—as it turned out—was not elected. The man of their choice was passed by, and as a consequence some of them felt sore; in certain neighborhoods opposition became threatening.

Doctor Tucker saw the need that some one should stand up and preach for Church order and for the support of the constituted authorities. He preached upon the subject on the Sunday occur- - ring next after the election of the first Bishop of Albany.

Some of the remarks made by the Rector are outspoken and resolute, but the public agitation which called them into being was of a character which demanded plainness of speech.

The text was chosen from the Epistle to the

Romans, 15th chapter and 5th verse.   The speaker began:

The Diocese of Albany being now fully organized, I feel that it is due to the people committed to my spiritual charge to present to their consideration some facts respecting the Diocese of which this parish forms part, and in whose concerns it should entertain therefore a wise and hearty interest.

After referring to the apportionment of territory and the strength of the district, the preacher continued:

The Convention assembled at St. Peter's Church, Albany, on Wednesday last. Bishop Potter preached the sermon. . . . On Thursday at 12 o'clock, after a most solemn and impressive religious service and silent prayer, the Convention proceeded to elect a Bishop, and on the ninth balloting the Rev. Dr. Doane, Rector of St. Peter's Church, Albany, was elected first Bishop of the new See, he having received a majority of both the clerical and lay votes. The *Te Deum* was then sung. Soon afterwards, Dr. Doane at the request of the Convention appeared before it, acknowledged the kindness and confidence of his brethren, clerical and lay, evidenced by their choice; assured them that " if he thought the office had come to him through man's device, and not from God, he would die sooner than take up the load that is laid upon his soul," and closed his address with these words: " I give myself, my life, my all, through you, to God. I ask from you your confidence, your sympathy—I had almost said your pity, and your prayers that when the Chief Shepherd shall appear I may have some part, with you, in the crown of glory that fadeth not away."

The election was as unexpected to Dr. Doane as to his

friends. And inasmuch as it has been intimated that there was some secret combination of the clergy to further and secure the election of the Rector of St. Peter's, Albany, or prevent the election of some other prominent candidate favored by a majority of the laity, I here publicly affirm that if such a combination existed, it was unknown to myself, and I also state the fact, that before the first balloting, I only knew how two men would vote, myself and one other. I did not rely on the coöperation in Dr. Doane's favor of one lay vote. I had made up my mind after due consideration how I should cast my own vote, when I was assured by a clerical brother that he concurred with me in judgment and purpose. Under the circumstances I could not be very sanguine of success. I determined to do my duty honestly in the sight of God, and submit graciously to the allotment of His Providence. More than a year ago, in conversation with a friend, a layman, I frankly avowed my own preferences, acknowledged that I could not anticipate the election of the clerical brother whom I might choose, and assured him that I was ready in good faith, to sustain any man as my Bishop, who with good heart, in all sincerity and faithfulness, believed in the Bible and the Book of Common Prayer. I thus showed myself not very difficult to please or satisfy, while at the same time I honestly avowed my own preferences, and recognized the rights of the majority of my lay and clerical brethren. I think more of the office than I do of the man who fills it, and I was ready to honor and obey any Diocesan whom the majority of my brethren might distinguish by the prerogatives and dignity of the Episcopate. I should distrust my own faith in the use, the expediency, or the necessity of the sacred office of the Bishop in the Church of Christ, if I could allow my individual likes or dislikes, my notions or conceits, my opinions or convictions, to make me falter in my allegiance to my Bishop.

Obedience and submission to an ecclesiastical superior, are not however, as I feel, inconsistent with the self-respect of a man, and the inalienable rights of a Christian priest. . . . I say this to guard against the imputation of holding and teaching blind submission on the part of the clergy and laity, to the will and judgment of a Bishop. I do not believe in the infallibility, even in the most modified sense, of the Bishop of Rome, nor do I believe any more in the infallibility or indefectibility of the Bishop of New York, Albany, or any other See, whoever may be the temporary incumbent. . . . But this I do believe with all my heart, that if our reverence for the holy office of Bishop is so flimsy, so identified with persons and things of a mere temporal interest or concern, so associated with the accessories, which belong to individuals, circumstances and places, then, if our reverence be dependent upon such contingencies, as fleeting, as shadowy, as deceptive, as the overhanging branches or the passing clouds which picture the mirrory surface of the lake, we can put little confidence in our assumptions and protestations about Episcopacy, our loud and factious pretensions concerning its Scriptural and Apostolic claims. . . . What would become of an army where the officers and men faltered in their obedience, and withheld the conventional signs of respect, because they questioned the general's political wisdom, or doubted the expediency of a stratagem, or the plan of a campaign? . . . Or to come nearer home. How far could we look forward into the future for the preservation of our republican rights and institutions, if the respect and obedience, which we manifested toward "the President of the United States and all others in authority" were dependent on our personal regard, our esteem, our liking for the successful competitor for national gifts and honors? . . .

The point that I am aiming at is this, that even though the individual who is elected to the Episcopate differ from us in opinions and notions of Church policy, still our reverence for the holy office of Bishop should carry us beyond the control of personal sympathies and preferences. I am as yet maintaining only an abstract principle, which is this: that it is a duty imposed upon all who consider themselves Churchmen living in this section of the State comprised within the limits of the new Diocese, to give their allegiance to the Bishop who shall be entrusted with its spiritual jurisdiction, and this in spite, though it may be, of individual wishes, of partisan or local interests; and to assist by a liberal contribution of their worldly means, by active sympathy and hearty coöperation, by their counsels, by their words and deeds, in giving efficiency to his administration of the affairs of the Diocese. If every man, who happens to be disappointed in the selection of the incumbent of a vacant see, can withhold his charity, his zeal and energy, from the authorized instrumentalities established to promote God's glory by the extension of the Church, then I say there is an end of ecclesiastical authority and allegiance, and we are but a step removed from the barest and wildest scheme of Congregationalism. . . . If we as Churchmen presume to stand before the world as Episcopalians or Bishopmen, or men who profess to believe that the government by Bishops is a divine appointment; that a Church Episcopally ordered is the Church established by the Lord Jesus Christ as His kingdom upon earth, the establishment divinely founded, divinely authorized, blessed with the promise of perpetuity by the Lord Himself, thus established and blessed to evangelize the world—if this be the conviction of Churchmen who choose to designate themselves " Episcopalians "—how without the sacrifice of our religious principles can we forbear, whatever be the motive, from giving according to our Christian faith and ability, aid spiritual and material to the only institution agreeably to our professions, which, on Scriptural grounds, and in accordance with Apostolic and primitive practice, can claim divine authority or sanction for preaching Christ and administering His sacraments? If a man who professes to be a Churchman or an Episcopalian boldly avows his determination to withhold all sympathy and support from his Bishop, because he would prefer some other individual as his Diocesan, I would say: " Well, be it so: only be consistent and manly; throw aside principles, or the profession of principles, which at heart you have abandoned. Let there be no cant, or shallow, empty professions. Remove, so far as you can, by your words and example, the obstacles which hinder the efforts and labors of other zealous religionists. If you are unwilling to help the Church over which a Bishop presides to do its work of evangelization; if your convictions in favor of the authority of a divinely established Church cannot control your preferences for men, or your predilection for peculiar theories and schemes—O then, if not for consistency's sake, for the sake of principles and of duty, for Christ's sake, for Religion's sake, for the sake of the dying souls of your weak and sinning brethren—if you are unwilling, whatever be the motive, to help your Bishop and, *in and through him*, the Church over whose spiritual interests he presides, then be honest and manly. Don't prate about the divine rights of the Episcopate; drop your exclusiveness, and give a fair chance to Presbyterians, Baptists, Methodists, Congregationalists and R. Catholics to work the field which is white for the harvest."

I know this is plain talk. When the election of a Bishop in the Prot. Epis. Church is regarded by men, who call themselves Churchmen, as the ordinary election of a civil magistrate, or the appointment of an individual to the Presidency of a Collegiate institution, and what are considered his peculiar fitnesses for the office, or his claims to the high dignity, are regarded by individuals as the marks on the scale to indicate the amount of pecuniary support, moral aid, and efficient coöperation they are expected to give to the successor of an Apostle, then I hold that those who associate other ideas more sacred with the ministry established by the Lord Jesus Christ and His Apostles, must not hold their peace, but boldly expose what they believe to be the inconsistencies, the errors and dangers of a most treacherous policy.

I do not consider myself an illiberal man either in my sentiments or acts. If I know my own heart, almost to an infirmity, I am disposed to please all men. One thing as a believer, I often wish, that there were no such men upon earth as Presbyterians, Baptists, Universalists, Congregationalists, Methodists, R. Catholics, and High and Low and Broad Churchmen. I mean to say that I often devoutly wish that there were no denominational titles to distinguish the disciples of Jesus Christ, but the one which at first was given to them, " Christians." But we are not living in Apostolic times. We cannot appeal immediately to an Apostle for an opinion or judgment. We live in the midst of circumstances very unlike those among which S. Paul, S. Peter and S. John moved and acted. A man is obliged to adapt himself to the persons and things which surround him. He has his convictions, say, about the peculiar form of the Church which the Lord Jesus Christ established. He identifies Episcopacy with that form or ecclesiastical organization. *I* thus associate the order of Bishops with the name and authority of the Lord Jesus Christ, and with all the purposes of His incarnation, death and resurrection. According to my conception of spiritual things, then, it appears sacrilegious to say the least, if not positively blasphemous, to molest or thwart a Bishop in his holy endeavors, and this to gratify a mere suspicion, whim or prejudice.

Now let me say a few words about the Bishop elect. He is a son of Bishop Doane; and can therefore boast the name and lineage of one who, in talents, zeal, labors and self-sacrifice, I may add in cares, troubles and trials, has not, in my opinion, his superior on the roll of our American bishops. As evidence of sincerity in my words: I travelled hundreds of miles to pay my respect to his memory, chanting with two other priests, at the open grave, the words " Blessed are the dead who die in the Lord."

16

The preacher then recalled another occasion, three months earlier, where he had joined in the singing of the same anthem, and when Bishop Doane himself committed to the earth " the body of his and my own dear and much revered friend." He told the story of the firm friendship subsisting between the two, the Bishop of New Jersey and Mrs. Mary Warren. When the telegram arrived announcing her death, the Bishop said: " Alas, how few are left to us! Who next?" " And the next was himself. So soon God heard the prayer of his parting words over her sacred and beloved dust, 'Sweet spirit! be it ours to follow thee as thou hast followed Christ, to bear with thee His Cross, to wear with thee His crown.'" The speaker continued:

But we must pass on. It is the son and not the father that now claims our attention. The Rev. William Croswell Doane does not owe his election to his name; on the contrary, a name identified with extraordinary zeal and exertions for the Church of Christ, is not always the surest pledge, in these days, of favor and patronage from Churchmen.

It was thought that Dr. Doane possessed physical, moral and mental qualities, which in a peculiar way, adapted him to the labors of organizing a new Diocese, and taking charge of its missionary work. He is strong and able to work, and is just as willing as he is strong and able to work. In a section of country like that which forms the larger part of this Diocese, where the Church has to be planted, religious services maintained by means of missionary agencies, places for public worship built, precisely as if organizing a Church in heathen lands—where we expect little sympathy, and look for much opposition; a large field, that rather rough and stony; few laborers and with little money to pay those few laborers and to hire more; no end of work, and but small resources to do it with—in such a section of the country by no means congenial to our ecclesiastical polity, we want a Chief Pastor who loves work, who never shirks toils and labors, who is able and willing to carry his full share of the burden, and help others who are not quite so vigorous and enduring as himself. We want a man in this new Diocese who not only loves to work, but *knows how to work*, how to lay plans and organize, how to devise and use expedients; who knows how to work himself, and how to make others work with him. This is a great want. It magnifies the power of one man a thousand fold. . . .

And as our Bishop is to open for the Church, as it were, new territory, in portions of which our creed is unknown and our customs strange, we need in this Diocese a man who knows *what* he believes and *why* he believes; who can give a reason for the faith that is in him, and that without compromising his honesty as a man, his charity as a disciple of the loving Jesus, and his dignity as a Christian Bishop. . . .

Now have we chosen such a Bishop? If we have not secured such a man for our Diocesan, then I am deceived in my hopes and expectations.

And if the testimonials are signed by a majority of the Standing Committees of the Dioceses, and the Bishop elect is consecrated, and thereby commissioned. as it were, by Apostolic authority to minister the affairs of this Diocese, then who, I ask, that recognizes the authority of a Bishop in our ecclesiastical organization, can withhold his cordial sympathy and active coöperation?

I speak not as a partisan, with a mind and heart pinched up by the bands and rivets of intolerance, bigotry and faction. I hold firmly my religious opinions and convictions; but I dare not measure other men's sincerity and wisdom by my own opinions and convictions, tenaciously as I grasp them. Neither do I speak now as the personal friend of the dear brother who has been elected to the Episcopate. I am not the advocate of a party or the apologist for a friend. I speak as the minister of Christ. I am trying to effect something for His honor and glory, and for the spiritual good of my fellowmen.

The preacher urged his brethren in faith and worship not to withhold sympathy, prayers, and pious endeavors; not "to punish a Christian brother and a Priest for being elevated to a holy office, which he neither sought nor wished," closing by the plea:

If he fail to accomplish what his Divine Master has commanded and commissioned him to do, through our jealousies, strifes, contentions, or through our neglect, our apathy, our lack of interest, love and zeal, *whose* glory is impaired, who is contemned, who is slighted and dishonored? And whose souls must bear the shame and remorse of that contempt and dishonor?

XIV

SHALL IT BE LOWELL MASON OR DR. DYKES?

Let it be remembered that uniformly and from the very beginning anthem music has been prominent and influential at the Holy Cross. Nevertheless, constant attention has been bestowed upon the simpler sections of service. The Church on the hill has been noted for its singing of hymns. There never existed any tendency to belittle the lyrical or metrical numbers, in which the congregation had a part. The large and famous choir did not take up with the feeling of the old-style quartet, and account the hymn as a flippant trifle—to be rattled off without serious thought and with the smallest expenditure of time and breath. On the contrary, they—choir and people—made each recurrence of congregational song distinctly worshipful.

The Rector himself was always a happy participant in the music, both of anthems and hymns. He had so sturdy a throat capacity that he was competent to read or sing all through a service and at the same time conduct and take part in other portions, the leadership of which is ordinarily delegated to the choir.

Therefore, all the more did he bestow care upon the selection of that which was to be sung. He was anxious to find tunes which would best answer their purpose, and he began to make a collection of those which might be serviceable within the limits of his own cure. Naturally, his first thought was for the little ones, and we hear about a " Child's Book of Praise," a design which soon expanded into " The Parish Hymnal."

As this was the beginning of Doctor Tucker's public duty in a new department, which carried his name throughout America and on the far side of the Atlantic; as many know him now—however imperfectly—only as the Editor of a Musical Hymnal, it will be right for us to pause and try to ascertain the state of affairs which existed in our churches during generations gone. If we glance backward, recalling successive steps in the progress of psalmody, we may the better understand that which was accomplished by our independent thinker.

What were the tunes sung by our fathers? What were the characteristics of their music?

It is not needful that we shall devote much space to the recounting of the story about the beginnings of music in America. There was a day when each Puritan congregation was acquainted with not more than four or five tunes, of which " York tune," still extant, is an example. The members of this limited repertory were repeated *ad nauseam ;* they were sung as simple melodies " on the air " without harmony, vocal or instrumental. As time went on, individual worshippers varied the tune each to suit himself, or the several participants would select different melodies out of the small stock of four or five, and sing them all at once. The result is described as chaotic.

The state of the case was parallel to that recorded by George Eliot in " Felix Holt ": " The preacher gives out the tenth Psalm, and then everybody sings a different tune, as it happens to turn up in their throats. It is a domineering thing to set a tune and expect everybody else to follow it. It is a denial of private judgment."

In the matter of *tempo* and unity of attack, there was the like independency. One would reach the middle of the second or third note before another had left the first. " Go as you please " was the motto. A reverend writer working for reform in 1721, complains about the amazing slowness of delivery; he urges " not to fatigue the Singer with a tedious Protraction of the Notes beyond the Compass of a Man's Breath, and the Power of his Spirit: a Fault very frequent in the Country, where I myself have twice in one Note paused to take Breath."

Thereafter came on a struggle to introduce " regular singing," or singing by note, which was bitterly opposed as " Quakerish and Popish, and introductive of *instrumental* musick." Against the new way it was argued " that the *names* given to the notes are *bawdy*, yea *blasphemous ;*" again, " that it is a *needless way*, since their good Fathers that were strangers to it, are got to heaven without it."

Neither may we linger upon the narratives having to do with William Billings and his compeers, the famous line of Singing-school masters in New England, throughout whose reign there flourished the "fugueing" tune, and other lively productions.

Some of us can recall the "Oldde Folkes' Concerts," at which the choir sang "Russia" set to words apportioned in this wise:

> False are the men of high degree,
> The baser sort are vanity;
>   (*Bass*) Laid in a bal-
>   (*Treble*) Laid in a bal-
>   (*Alto*) Laid in a bal-
>   (*Tenor*) Laid in a bal-
>   (*Full*) ance, both appear
> Light as a puff of empty air.

Each verse ended with a slice from a madrigal. The method, applied to the make-up of hundreds of tunes, was once immensely popular in religious service. A pleasant reminder of it still subsists in "Antioch."

Others of us will remember "China" and "Windham," examples of another huge shoal—this time of unmelodious and mechanical tunes. We may thank our stars that we have got beyond them. They come down from the latter half of the eighteenth century, but in them we find no flavor of antiquity, no "voice of the ages." There is a radical diversity between the enduring strength of a genuine antique—such as a Gregorian melody—

and a faded weakling which is known merely as an
" old-timer."

After the day of " China," we reach a period
identified with two much-used collections: the
" Modern Psalmist," appearing in 1839, and employed so long that its title became a misnomer;
and the " Carmina Sacra," first copyrighted in
1841. These and other tune-books of the age
were shaped oblong—very long sideways. When
one held in his hands the open volume, he felt as
if he had to manipulate the top part of a mercan-
tile ledger cut short. The " Carmina Sacra " was
issued under the sanction of the Boston Academy
of Music. A later edition was edited by Lowell
Mason. In due time the book came to be almost
omnipresent; its gray boards were a familiar sight
in every choir loft.

People adopted with energy the original tunes
composed by Lowell Mason. Of him it has been
remarked that he did more to awaken interest in
psalmody, and to depreciate its standards, than
any other man of his time. Says a writer back in
the fifties: " No one has done as much as he, in his
day and generation, to extend the practice and
lower the taste in sacred music. In the mechanism of getting up books of psalm and hymn tunes,
and in making money out of them, he has been
facile princeps—out of sight ahead of all com-
petitors." Concerning " The Sabbath Hymn and
Tune Book," then just published, the same reviewer continues: " The music is entirely Mason-
ical. Of the vast quantity of tunes embodied in

this large octavo a few are good, many are bad, and all the rest are indifferent: but for *quantity* we assure every purchaser that he will get his money's worth."

Surely it may now be asserted with slight fear of contradiction, that when Church congregations came to like " Hebron " and its class, they deceived themselves and made choice of a tasteless inanity; before long they succeeded in the importation into service of a weariness from which the soul must turn away. Fancy nowadays that our people should set themselves to work with grim determination and a compulsory diligence at the singing of " Hebron " or " Balerma " or " Martyn."

Our younger readers may not comprehend the use of these appellatives; but let them be reminded that we speak about an age in which each tune received a distinctive name, just like a new-born child.

Many of the tunes set down in the " Carmina Sacra " have now gone out of use; others survive in occasional employment. Among the latter we find Zeuner's " Missionary Chant "; also " Park Street," " Italian Hymn," and " St. Martin's "—the last-named being still sung with gusto at St. Thomas' Church, New York, to the wording, " Not to the terrors of the Lord."

Among the side-long tune-books there was one of especial interest to us because it had a connection with the Apostolic Succession; it was edited by Church organists, and its selections were to be sung to the Prayer Book Psalms and Hymns.   The title of the work was the " Cantus Ecclesiæ," published under the certified sanction of the Musical Fund Society of Philadelphia, and edited by Messrs. Darley and Standbridge. The copyright is dated 1844.

Its assortment of tunes belongs to the same category as those of the " Carmina Sacra "—" Mendon," " Blendon," " Park Street," and the like. The solid English composers are represented— Handel, Dr. Arne, Dr. Arnold, and others. There is a local flavor in the names given to original tunes, then first published. " Morton," by A. G. Emerick, recalls Dr. Henry J. Morton of St. James', Philadelphia. Other popular clergy then living and laboring in the same city receive tribute; we find " Tyng " and " Suddards." Beethoven is impressed into the service to form the melody " Doane." The tune was the forerunner of many fashioned in the same way; for " arrangements " were coming into vogue. In the book, bits were taken and altered from Donnizetti, from Michael and Joseph Haydn.

The Greatorex Collection came out in 1851, offering " Manoah " and many other settings, which became prime favorites.

About this time it happened that tune-books were multiplied at such a rapid rate that the stock of tunes would no longer hold out; accordingly the number of " arrangements " increased yet more alarmingly. Operatic composers were much called upon. Secular melodies were fitted to sacred words. I remember when " O ye tears " was sung to a hymn, and " When the swallows homeward fly " to another. National airs were incorporated. In like manner folk-songs were appropriated; the latter stood the transition better than most, as they are cast in the mould of melody likely to stand the rack of time. Even Bacchanalian ditties were transformed; it would not do " to let the devil have all the good tunes."

At last the shape of tune-books took a change. It began to " square up "—in form, a prefigurement of the alteration of taste which should happen after a while. A book was issued, entitled " A Tune Book proposed for the use of the Congregations of the Protestant Episcopal Church "—ordinarily spoken of as " The Tune Book." It was a semi-official production. The House of Bishops appointed a committee to prepare or adopt a collection of tunes to be used in connection with the " Psalms and Hymns." The membership of the committee included the Rev. Doctors Muhlenberg, Bedell, and Geer.

The contents of the work show an adherence to a dignified standard. There is no trace of the ditty. A decided tendency toward the chorale may be discerned—which is not surprising when we remember the early Lutheran associations of the Rev. Dr. Muhlenberg. The stately notation by minims was chosen as in consonance with the character of the compilation.

In its day the " Tune Book " had a great run. It was not superseded until after the " Additional Hymns " had made their appearance.

Nevertheless, Church people in America had gone on singing the " Psalms and Hymns," those formerly bound with the Prayer Book, largely to tunes made up in the style of the glee, varied now and then by a folk-song, in rare cases by a ditty. " Retreat " and " Rock of Ages," by Thomas Hastings, also " Heber," by Kingsley, are excellent examples of worthy favorites fashioned purely after the method of the glee or part-song.

The chorale had little hold upon us. Unless the congregation sings sturdily as in Germany, or at least universally as in England, a chorale setting must be a failure. Church folk think about " Old Hundred " with enthusiasm; but sometimes it happens, however hard they try, that their singing of it is apt to make one weary. Just before it begins, they say within themselves—" now something grand is coming " ; they call up zeal and energy; but after the event they feel depressed, dissatisfied with their endeavor. Once, at an annual service held before the Commencement of a Girls' School, I heard as a Recessional, " Now thank we all our God," sung to Crüger's Chorale, by light treble voices only, and accompanied by a timid organ of six or seven registers; and the effect was disastrous.

In England the history of psalmody shows variations like our own. The glee style had its exponents, but many of the older composers adopted the form of the chorale, as Mr. Croft in " St. Ann's." By the beginning of the nineteenth century the standard had fallen far below that of Tallis

or Ravenscroft. Two tendencies may be traced:
the one running parallel with the chorale, the
other patterning after the secular song of the time,
a debased sort of lyric. As a witness of the degra-
dation of taste, it may be mentioned that about the
year 1800 and for a considerable period thereafter,
the most popular hymn-tune in England, sung to
the Advent wording " Lo, He comes," was, note
for note, a secular air probably composed for the
amatory verses beginning

> Guardian angels, now protect me,
>   Send me back the youth I love.

The air was sung by Mistress Anne Catley at
" The Golden Pippin "; moreover, it served for
the accompaniment of a hornpipe danced at Sad-
lers' Wells. Serious objection may be urged
against it, not only on account of its low origin,
but because it is intrinsically unfit for association
with sacred subjects.

Gradually there was a struggling effort to attain
to better things. Dr. Gauntlett came forward,
drawing attention to Gregorian music and yet in
touch with modern feeling, for he was chosen by
Mendelssohn to play the organ part at the first
performance of " Elijah," at Birmingham in 1846.
Helmore was working at Plain-song. Richard
Redhead was in the field.

There was a stir of life in religion, in Church,
which demanded a new expression. It craved
sacred songs for all the people, but it needed a

variation from strict Plain-song or the chorale. The later English school met the requirement. It grafted " time-motive " and melody upon the stock of the chorale. When " Hymns Ancient and Modern " appeared in 1861, the light shined out complete and clear; the old tree put forth abundance of blossoms having fragrance and grace. Some of us remember the times when the book " Hymns Ancient and Modern " was working its way in America. Many sympathetic singers felt at once the innate beauty disclosed by Dykes, Elvey, Gauntlett, and the rest. Parsons tried hard to find Sunday-school services and other unrubrical offices in which these settings might be introduced. After our " Additional Hymns " came out in 1865, they gladly availed themselves of the opportunity to announce, in regular service, " Abide with me " and " Sun of my soul!"

No doubt the English book was received with reservation of opinion. Among its selections, certain of the more mechanical sort did not take hold. I remember the reluctance about the acceptance of Ewing's setting for " Jerusalem the golden "; it gained ground slowly, and only by association with the uplifting and inspiring poem. Other tunes were unpalatable. I recall the satirical receipt given by a cleric for the making of a hymn-tune like some of these. Said he: " Put your eight notes in a bag; shake them well and draw them out as they happen to come—that gives you your air.' "

There was a world of good, however, in the new compilation, and it made its way. One clergyman met another in his study. Said he, " I have found a good tune for ' Oft in danger ' " ; forthwith he proceeded to sing, solo unaccompanied, Gauntlett's setting in " Hymns Ancient and Modern," now a household word. After the English manual was licensed for use in the American Church, Dykes' splendid strain, " Holy, holy, holy," and " Our blest Redeemer " soon found ready adoption.

In spite of the direction taken by foreign psalmody, the tune-books published among us continued to follow the old fashion. Thrall's " Episcopal Common Praise," of date 1867, shows scarcely a trace of the awakening. In the preface to that book, the editor speaks still of Lowell Mason as " Patriarch in the cause of sacred music."

On the other hand, Dr. Batterson put forth his " Missionary Tune Book," which gave recognition to the new style, although it did not forsake the old. Dr. J. S. B. Hodges was writing and publishing tunes framed after the later English fashion.

Early in 1870—the preface is dated Advent, 1869 —Doctor Tucker brought forth his " Parish Hymnal." In so far as American tunes-books went, it was like a lightning flash in a clear sky. It was a radical departure; it cut loose from all of our past. There was not merely a diminution of the accepted bill of fare; the supplies were stopped. Think of it! —a tune-book without " Martyn " or " Brattle Street," or even " Hebron! " Here were brought forward, herein did the people gain happy acquaintance with strains written by Redhead, Dykes, Ouseley, Barnby, Monk, Elvey, and Gauntlett. German

masters—Mendelssohn, Schumann, Haydn—were
called upon. What bravery there was in the print-
ing of " From Greenland's icy mountains " without
Lowell Mason's tune! The audacity is empha-
sized by the fact that no fitting tune had yet been
found to take its place. Dr. Muhlenberg had offered two, but both had failed of adoption.

American composers were not wanting. John
Henry Hopkins was in evidence. Dr. Hodges
contributed " O day of rest and gladness " and
" Bread of the world "—now sung practically in
every parish of the land. Doctor Tucker's " We
sing the praise of Him who died " began a long
career of beneficence; the same may be remarked of
Mr. Rousseau's " Ride on, ride on in majesty " and
his ever popular " Soldiers of Christ, arise." Since
the day of its appearing, Dr. Warren's Easter Hymn
has been incorporated into the order of thousands
of services.

Even the lighter style was not despised, so long
as it had something to offer. The Tune Book of
St. Alban's, Holborn, and Boosey's " Household
Music " furnished that which was tripping on the
tongue.

The book was not ? Church Hymnal. It was
planned primarily for use in schools, in Bible or
Confirmation classes, or upon special occasions.
Nevertheless, it could help directly the music of
service. As a portion of the wording was already
included in the authorized hymnal, these hymns
could now be sung to their proper tunes.

Of the enlightened psalmody, the " Parish Hym-

17

nal" was the introducer; toward this it was the educator. It stands single and alone. It accomplished a new thing of inestimable benefit. Through its instrumentality our Church singers made acquaintance—and that a pleasant one—with the better way, and they came to crave it. Before the "Hymnal with Tunes" was issued, the work of adoption was well advanced.

It was in the year 1872 that our people first looked upon the Church Musical Hymnal, now known as the "First Tucker." Herein and hereby the work was completed which had been begun in the preliminary compilation. Tunes first published in that book were transferred to these later pages. Here was a happy selection, showing thought and skill, with a prevailing adherence to the higher standard. Compromise there was, but only as the music followed the words. The larger part of the tunes is the workmanship of modern English writers. That school is supreme.

Nevertheless, soon after the publication of this work, Doctor Tucker made the remark, in conversation, that he did not pin down his musical faith to the limits of "Hymns Ancient and Modern." He had a liking for a freer and more flowing style, which yet conformed to the new type. For example, he introduced in his new book Dr. Cutler's "The Son of God goes forth to war," which has become almost exclusively "proper" for the words. And as in the former publication, St. Alban's Tune Book—representing the glee side—is made use of.

John Henry Hopkins contributed his Plain-song

setting of " The Royal Banners forward go," and other standard compositions. Dr. Muhlenberg sent the music for " Jesu, the very thought of Thee."

It is pleasant to recall the enthusiasm with which this book was received, and to follow the change of taste brought about by its extensive adoption. The book was scattered all abroad; it appealed to multitudes; it was found in the hands of almost every chorister; and the appetite changed. Our people—in general—began to want a purer providing. They stepped to the nobler level, of which they had learned by means of the Tucker message and ministration. It is not too much to say that the " First Tucker Hymnal " wrought a revolution; it achieved the victory; it made the new style not only tolerable but popular. It won the masses to the liking of its own lofty method.

Whereas, Christian people used to stand round an open grave and sing " Hark! from the tombs a doleful sound," set to a tune which answered the description, viz., to Timothy Swan's " China," now under similar circumstances we hear " For all the saints, who from their labors rest " set to Barnby's noble lyric. And what a transformation it is! We do not appreciate it, do not realize the importance of the step upward, to the highest grade of psalmody. And the remarkable feature of it all is, that this stricter and grander style has been popularized. Many is the time that I have noted the fact that even small boys belonging to amateur choirs show unfeigned delight in these strains written by a master of music.

After this the way was made easy for all future compilers of our tune-books. The standard had been set up and multitudes had rallied to its support. In large degree an axiom had been established that the music of the Church must be Church music even in regard to the hymn-melodies. It was only natural thereafter that musical editors should make use of the new style. It was a fresh application of the working of a principle of imitation referred to by Tennyson:

> All can raise the flower now,
> For all have got the seed.

The tendency was so wide-spreading that it influenced the compilers of tune-books who worked for Christians of other name, representing a less ecclesiastical sort of piety. Witness the considerable representation accorded to the modern English school in Dr. Robinson's " New Laudes Domini." Or note the " Evangelical Hymnal " compiled by Dr. Hall and Lasar; the book might almost be considered as prepared for adoption by the revived Church of England.

Think, then, of the world-wide influence exercised by the modest man, priest-musician, sitting in his study on Mount Ida!

Doctor Tucker used to say that there were two kinds of music—good music and bad—and that he believed in the use of the good, at any rate for the service of God. So he set up his banners for tokens, in the " Parish Hymnal " and in " Tunes Old and New Adapted to the Hymnal." And he converted the whole land to his way of thinking; he raised the standard of psalmody from Atlantic to Pacific.

The choice of hymns—of the words—pertaining to the American book had been determined by the General Convention of 1871. Thereafter ensued a controversy in the Church papers about the desirability of certain selections. Mr. James S. Biddle published critical essays in the *Episcopal Register*. In one of these he refers to Doctor Tucker as the "accomplished hymnologist," and, further, "fears that we are drifting into a sweet, dreamy sort of Tennysonian Kebleism—a love-lorn pietism." The Rector of the Holy Cross writes to his old-time schoolmate:

Troy,
Jan'y. 16th, 1872.

My Dear Biddle:

I have read with much interest the articles in the *Episcopal Register*. But I must say at the outset, that I do not agree with you in your judgment of Keble and his brood. Yet I am heartily in sympathy with you when you condemn the silly, sickish and sensuous idea which some good people seem to entertain of heaven. Their ideal of heaven is hardly as real and reasonable as that of the pious old soul, who was anticipating the pleasure of wearing her Sunday gown, an everlasting clean white apron, and eating perennial strawberries and cream.

Why should we not be real and reasonable in religion as well as in other matters, and forego all "cant" with respect to eternal and temporal things?

No one will probably recognize the Parson of Holy Cross in the expression "accomplished hymnologist," and yet, I must own that it is pleasant to be remembered by a friend in such a flattering way.

You refer to hymns which are to be used in connection with *adoration*, such as "The God of Abraham praise," and I agree with you in thinking that this is the sort of hymns which should be used all but exclusively in a Church Hymnal. But I imagine that the Committee acted under the conviction that they were appointed to provide religious poetry or poetry of a devotional kind, which could be used elsewhere than in Church. But I incline to the opinion that many of the hymns will never be used, in private or in public.

Again, the Hymnal is lumbered up with many hymns which from the *crankiness* of the metre are not singable, and never can become popular. Two hundred hymns might very well be thrown out at random, and no harm done to the interests of the Church and evangelical piety.

The Committee did not in my humble opinion give enough care to their work. They did not rely enough upon their own taste and judgment, but condescended too much to old grannies to whose ignorance and prejudices they seem too much disposed to pander. Think only of their inserting a hymn for "The Churching of Women," and not providing a hymn for the Annunciation of the Blessed Virgin Mary!

I am very glad that you have called attention to the distinction of O and Oh!—an exclamation, by the way, that has become somewhat more common since the production of the Committee's labors has come before the eyes of the Church.

Your articles, I am sure, must do good eventually.

Ever most truly as of
old, your friend
J. IRELAND TUCKER.

James S. Biddle, Esq.
 Phil'a.

Not long before the assembling of the next

General Convention, Doctor Tucker writes again; he still objects to the selection of the hymns.

TROY,

April 8th, 1874.

MY DEAR MR. BIDDLE:

Please excuse my tardiness in replying to your note of the 12th ult.

I have the best authority for attributing No. 433 to Prof. John De Wolfe. One of his relations now living, I believe, in Providence, R. I., claims it as a family heirloom. . . .

With respect to alterations in the Hymnal, I am in favor of omissions. When I return from a visit to New York, I will write you again, and tell you what I would throw out. I need now only say that in some instances the hymns are unsingable and can never be used as "Spiritual songs."

I am very glad to know that you are giving your attention to this matter of revision. I would advise in the interest of the publishers not to make too many alterations.

Ever yours most truly

J. IRELAND TUCKER.

Mr. James S. Biddle, Pa.

When Mr. Biddle kindly forwarded the letters here quoted, he wrote: "We were not correspondents, and I believe he was wont to neglect answering letters. You know Palmerston used to say that it was all fudge—this punctuality about replying immediately: that if you let things be, most letters answered themselves in three or four days. This was Dr. T.'s practice, I suppose."

Every now and then I have heard remarks, made by those who knew him best, to the effect that

Doctor Tucker did not like to write letters. A complaint has come to hand, from one who by letter had begged permission to reprint a tune from the Hymnal, that no answer was vouchsafed. Farther back in time, when I was the ecclesiastical neighbor of Doctor Tucker, I once wrote him, asking for suggestions about a question of service: up to the present no answer has been received.

The appetite grows by what it feeds on, for it became evident later that he went so far as not to open many letters addressed to him. He deferred the ceremony associated with an unpleasant result. After he had been called hence, a considerable number of unopened letters was found among his effects.

The Doctor used to plead for himself in justification of his neglect about correspondence, that as his mail increased it brought so many begging letters—by the wholesale—also missives asking what organ builder should be employed, or what bell founder; or what priest should be called to a vacant parish, or where a family servant might be procured, that it became impossible to keep up with the rapid ratio of the multiplication of these epistles. He was forced to take refuge in a masterly inactivity.

His matured feeling was evidenced by a remark made when his organist and coworker was abroad. Mr. Rousseau had found illustrated postal cards, containing pictures of European resorts. Some of these he had used in the writings sent to his home. They contained a few condensed phrases in the style of a telegram.   One of these was picked up by Doctor Tucker, who looked at it and said: " How much better that is than a great long letter! "

The failing—if such it be—has been referred to as the only flaw in the character of Doctor Tucker. No one knew of any other.   And whenever this little foible is remembered, his dear friends smile affectionately, as when they used to be gladdened by his genial, joyful presence.   They are happy to think that their saint, true exponent of the title, was yet a human being.

Despite the peculiarity, correspondence went on briskly about the time of the appearance of the first musical Church hymnal.   To its editor many letters were sent, some of which are at hand.   It will be interesting to quote portions of these answers to inquiry; so we may have a glimpse at the inside working, the making of a renowned manual.   Further, it may be a satisfaction to unprofessional folk to note how musical composers talk when they make use of the ordinary language of speech. Some of their names are recorded high up upon the tablets of the temple.

Glebe Field,
Stoke Newington,
Jan. 5, 1872.

My Dear Sir:

Your first letter did reach me, and I congratulated myself on the good fortune which had brought me so kind a greeting from the " other side of the Atlantic."   But I had the ill-luck or ill-management to lose the letter: how, I cannot tell, in coming home from King's College: and I could not recall your address: so I had it not in my power to thank you.

I now lose no time in acknowledging your second favor, received this morning, and hope to post the tunes for which you ask me, by the mail following.

You seem to " reckon up " the doings in the old country at short intervals, or you would not have been aware of my concern with the Scottish Hymnal.

I had a copy sent me, some time since, of the volume brought out in 1859 by the " Committee appointed for the purpose by the House of Bishops " at New York: but it has not struck me as exhibiting a high taste in Church music. In the intervening 20 years you have been, I dare hope, able to make some advances, tho' one picks up from American friends, now and then, little bits of information which do not, so far as they go, indicate anything like strictness, in the popular feeling.

We must, of course, labor on to keep up and improve that feeling, while we try, too, to give the people something they can sing with pleasure.

With all good wishes for the New Year,

Very truly yours

W. H. Monk.

The Rev. J. Ireland Tucker, &c. &c.

The same correspondent writes on the 7th of April:

You will be interested to know, perhaps, that I am just asked to correct for the press a collection of Chants for the Scotch Presbyterian Church—the authorities of which are about *for the first time* to try to introduce the practice—not, as some of them think, to succeed *in our time*.

Tenbury,

Jan. 1st, 1872.

Rev'd. and Dear Sir:

I am a bad hymn writer; it is by no means my *forte*. But if you will send me some words to which you wish music set, I will do what I can with pleasure.

You speak of *terms*. Under ordinary circumstances I would of course make you a present of any work of mine. But I am collecting money for rebuilding my organ, and therefore, without naming any sum, I will merely say that I will thankfully receive any contribution you may like to make towards the above object, by way of acknowledgment of the hymn tunes I hope to send you.

I have by no means forgotten our intercourse at Rome in 1851, especially our very pleasant musical evenings at Miss Seeley's. If ever you come to this part of the world, I hope you will come to see me, and I will let you hear some really first-rate Church music, and I can introduce you to some of the finest organs, organists and choirs in the world.

Believe me

Yours very truly

FREDERICK A. GORE OUSELEY.

Dr. Dykes is modest when he comes to speak of remuneration, although his contributions are second to none in value.

ST. OSWALD'S VICARAGE,
DURHAM, ENGLAND,
Jan. 13, 1872.

MY DEAR SIR:

I must offer my sincere apologies for my long delay in answering your obliging letters.

Two difficulties have presented themselves to me in reference to your letter: 1st, the question of terms; 2nd, the character and authority of the proposed book itself.

To begin with this second point. I was puzzled, not long after receiving your first obliging letter, by receiving a communication from Mr. ——, informing me that *he* was appointed musical Editor of the American Hymnal to which you referred, and requesting me to help him in his work.

So the question arises: are yourself and he engaged in the same work? Is *yours* a mere private speculation, or *his*, or *both?* Or are they both undertaken with the sanction of the Convention? Are they, in fact, opposition works, or are they not? For it seems a pity that there should be a division of energy and forces, a frittering away of resources. Much better that there should be a combination, so as to have one strong book instead of two weak ones.

Then as to terms. I have never been accustomed to write for money, although I have frequently had an " Honorarium " sent me for work done. I therefore seem hardly to know what is a fair remuneration to ask for tunes sent.

As far as feeling is concerned I would much rather not take anything. But when a man has a large parish, and a family growing up, and is not overburdened with this world's goods, and finds considerable difficulty in making both ends meet, I suppose there is nothing objectionable in his resorting to any legitimate means which GOD'S good Providence may throw in his way for enabling him to pay his just and lawful debts, and obtain a little help for those who are dependent on him.

Often as I have contributed to Hymnals, the first and only time that I ever received so much per tune, was in the case of the very last work that I wrote for. In this case the Editor insisted on sending me 3 guineas for every tune. I told him that it seemed to me a good deal: but he never would send less.

There is one benefit in keeping the remuneration rather high, as it prevents the needless multiplication of tunes. And really, we are being so deluged with tunes nowadays (I myself am sometimes quite bewildered with applications from all kinds of quarters) that I am disposed to consider any reasonable check upon their too exuberant production a real benefit.

However, I would almost rather that you yourself should suggest what you consider a proper remuneration for tunes, as I have no desire to do anything unreasonable.

Enclosed I send you tunes for the 3 hymns you were good enough to forward to me. " Rock of Ages," of course, is a beautiful, almost unequalled hymn. But why not have all 4 verses?

The other two hymns I do not think much of. I hope they are not a specimen of the average hymns in the Authorized Hymnal. I have done my best, and set them to tunes of a rather melodious character, as I suppose in your country there is a feeling for and appreciation of melody; and if the people cannot get good religious melodies, they will get hold of secular melodies for their hymns.

Any more hymns that you may think good to send me, I shall be happy to endeavor to set, to the best of my power.

With kind regards and renewed apologies for my delay,

I beg to remain

My Dear Sir

Very faithfully yours

JOHN B. DYKES.

P. S.—I am not now Precentor of Durham. I resigned that office when I took my present living.

Dr. Dykes writes again, on the 29th of April, from Firgrove Lodge, Weybridge, Surrey:

Having been away from home for some little time, and on the move, it is only a few days ago that I received your kind and friendly note with the enclosed cheque, for which I beg to offer you my best thanks.

I am glad to hear of you, explanation of Mr. ——'s relations with the General Convention, that they are not of any direct and formal nature; for I had rather gathered from his communication that he and he alone was authorized to edit the musical edition of the Hymnal.

Would it be possible to obtain a copy of this Hymnal

in England? For, if so, it would probably be more convenient (in case, at any future time, you should require
help from me) that you should simply refer to the number of the hymn or hymns for which you are in want of
a musical setting, than that you should send me loose
slips which are always in danger of being lost.

Moreover I should feel more interest in the work, were
I to see it in its entireness, and learn something of its
general tone and character. I am sorry to hear your
account of it: but with the divided state of parties in
the Church, what is one to expect from an *authorized*
manual representing all parties, but a somewhat colorless
and timid production? Our " Hymns Ancient and Modern " being a private work, has been an immense boon
to our Church at home, and has stopped, at least for a
time, any attempt at an authoritative hymnal. It has
been wonderfully blessed by GOD in greatly raising the
tone of the Churchmanship throughout the English Communion.

Let the many American composers be represented by a single example, as follows:

BURLINGTON, VT.,
Feb. 5, 1872.

REV. AND DEAR BROTHER:

Yours is just received. I leave tomorrow for Malone,
to attend the Convocation of Ogdensburgh, and shall not
be back for several days. So I send you the music for
the *Dies Iræ* at once, without the words—not knowing
how *they* may have been cooked by the Committee. If
the last *three couplets* have been arranged as *two trip-
lets*, you will set them to the *first* of the three strains.
. . . It is a botch if they have done it, though! Those
couplets are an exquisite relief after the long continuance of the other.

I can't bear the idea of setting the *Vexilla Regis* to

anything but its own tune, but the compressed form of the melody is more manageable to modern ears than the more expanded which is given in H. A. & M. I send a barred and countable modernization, which perhaps may answer.

I send you also an arrangement of the glorious old *Pange Lingua*, which is less cranky than some. It may not be unwelcome.

As to brother X—may brother X be——criticized!

Yr. ob't. serv. in the Church
J. H. H.
[John Henry Hopkins.]

The Rev. Dr. Tucker.

The first " Children's Hymnal " came out in the year 1874. Among the letters at hand, there are some dated that year, signed by names to be remembered, such as Arthur S. Sullivan and John Hullah. The book of 1874 was notable not only on account of its contents—which according to its own announcement were planned for little ones who " may be disposed to sing Sacred music more frequently than on *one* day of the week "—but also for the quite charming illustrative pictures scattered through its pleasant pages.

XV

THE MIDDLE AGE

It was not until the year 1873 that the present writer paid his first visit to the Church of the Holy Cross and to the Rectory which stands by its side. There he was impressed first of all by an unfailing hospitality. There too he breathed a pleasant atmosphere, that of a home where the priest dwelt in the midst of music and pictures.

Acquaintance was made with the Church building, both as to exterior and interior. The first suggestion conveyed by the structure was the flavor of an old-world existence, also of a style of Churchmanship representing culture and religion.

Conducted into the school by its pastor and chief instructor, the visitor was introduced to a class of bright girls gathered about a grand piano. One of the teachers took a seat at the instrument, to play an accompaniment. Doctor Tucker, by means of a baton, conducted the singing of one of the exercises by Concone. These well-known compositions have been made use of, in many localities, for the cultivation of the solo voice. Here they were applied to the vocal training of a large class, and with eminent success. The unison was delivered smoothly as by a single well-trained soprano, the intonation was true and the phrasing just. The singing of that exercise is remembered vividly even to this day.

After a return to the Rectory, there was afforded an illustration of the playfulness which welled up in the every-day life of the Rector.

It has been said that he, early in life, made choice of an ascetic career. Distinctly and resolutely, he did renounce the pomps and vanities of the world. But he was never an ascetic in disposition. He was a happy man himself, and he cared more than all else to make other people happy.

The example referred to occurred in the way of table talk. For some cause the conversation had turned upon the administration of Baptism in Church. Speaking of the deportment of babies under the circumstances, Doctor Tucker remarked in passing that he had noticed this: that if infants cried at all, they were accustomed to begin just when he would reach that part of the service which told them that they were to " hear sermons."

Another visit and a Sunday spent in Troy brought further disclosure of the interest attaching to the work. Along in the seventies, some of the best men singers were engaged to help only at the Choral Evensong on Sunday afternoons. These would drop in after morning service, to take part in a full rehearsal. At such a practising-time it was that I received first suggestion of the " swelling anthems " as sung by the famous choir.

At Evensong I made further discovery about the basis of that fair fame.

18

The Choral Service was impressive, pure, and round-toned. Manifestly it meant praise. There was a trace of independency about the method of the Choral use, owing no doubt to the fact that the Church was a pioneer, starting out with no traditions. For example, not only in Gregorian tones, but at the beginning of the Lord's Prayer and the Creed, there was no " Priest's intonation "; cleric and choir began together, " full " at once. At the time, the choir was using the Helmore Psalter. The delivery of the psalms was unhurried, thoughtful, and reverential.

But especially notable was the music of anthems, now soft and persuasive, now rising into a rolling tide of vocal harmony, a solid and satisfying reverberation of chords. There never was anything else just like it.

The quality of tone, loud or gentle, was always musical. The altos were phenomenally rich and effective. Both sopranos and altos, and they were many, sang with voices fresh and yet mature. One must think perforce about the cultivation of tone and of its unusual effectiveness. The results of skilful training were evident in every note. Yet the art was concealed; no chorus singing was ever more spontaneous and unshackled.

The voice culture of the choristers and the musicianship of their reverend instructor found their peculiar province in that part of the service devoted to the anthem. It will be remembered that this Church started in the one way—assigning a prominent position to the standard compo-

sition of florid music.   So it has continued without
variation, and so it gave example to the Church in
all America, as influential as the other initial suggestions about Choral use, or the surplice in the
pulpit, or flowers over the altar, or the Offertory as
an act of worship.

At a later day, when Bishop Doane wrote a brief
introduction to a pamphlet containing the words
of anthems, he gave testimony about the singing
of standard compositions at the Holy Cross.

Dr. Warren at my request has made the following
selections of anthems from those in use of late years
at the Church of the Holy Cross in Troy. I have
greatly desired that our Cathedral use should take its
flavor from this most dear and sacred place, which has
been the *fons et origo* of Choral worship in the American Church; of whose beloved foundress Dr. Warren
carries on the name and the benefactions; and where
my dear friend and brother Dr. Tucker has ministered
for so many years, pattern of Priests and pioneer of
Precentors.

As I left the place, I recalled a phrase of the same
Bishop, occurring in an address, in which he speaks
of the " lovely Evensong of the Holy Cross."

Is it any wonder that Doctor Tucker was accustomed to boast of his girls?   Indeed it seemed to
be only by virtue of Christian fortitude that he
could tolerate any other sort of choir.   I remember
one morning in Albany, at the temporary Chapel
of All Saints, when the first Cathedral choir was yet
new and little trained.

As was their custom, the boys were in the chapel,

practising for the daily Choral Evensong. They had just rehearsed the Psalter, to be sung that afternoon. Immediately after, I went out into the chapter room, where Doctor Tucker happened to be waiting. He spoke of the progress made by the new choir, and in particular of their success in chanting, mentioning their unanimity and distinctness in the enunciation of the words. " But," said he, " they sound like cats. All boys' voices sound like cats." He was thinking of his girls at Holy Cross.

The healthful popularity of the incumbent was not subject to change or diminution. Somewhere about 1874 he received a call to accept the charge of St. Paul's parish in Troy. The invitation conveyed an especial compliment, as it was addressed to one, resident in the midst of this people during thirty years; it issued, too, from the mother Church of the region. It was thought for a time that Doctor Tucker would accept. He had the matter under serious consideration. Some of his own parishioners were so sure of his going that they made application at St. Paul's to secure pews, so that they might be ready to follow their shepherd.

This was one of the many calls to other posts of usefulness. Besides those already mentioned, invitations were extended by the parishes of the Advent in Boston; St. John's, Washington, also by the authorities at Nashotah, seeking a successor for the lamented Dr. De Koven. Moreover, far back at the beginning of the Troy rectorship, it was given out by Major Tucker that his son was soon to go to Dr. Muhlenberg, to labor with him in New York City.

Between the mother parish in Troy and the daughter upon the hill there has always existed a kindly feeling. The circumstances connected with the origin of the latter, of its going out from the parent hive, were indicative not of strife or contrariety, but of a religion pure and undefiled.

The St. Paul's people always cherished for Doctor Tucker himself an admiration second only to that prevalent among his own parishioners. The sentiment came to the surface when there was an informal celebration of the fortieth anniversary of his Rectorship.

At Christmas time in the year 1884 there happened a " Surprise Party." The Doctor had no premonition of the celebration in so far as it related to himself. He was completely surprised.

The report of " A Notable Christmas " may be quoted from a newspaper of the day, dated December, 1884:

One of the most noteworthy of the Christmas gatherings that have taken place this season was the Christmas-tree celebration at the Mary Warren Free Institute, Christmas eve, commemorating, as it did, the fortieth anniversary of the Rev. Dr. Tucker's pastorate over the Church of the Holy Cross. Although appreciating Dr. Tucker's well known aversion to anything like ostentatious parade, yet the trustees of the school individually determined that an occasion that rounded so unusually long and successful a ministry should not pass unnoticed. At their request the Bishop of the Diocese kindly accepted their invitation to be their representative, and accordingly on Wednesday evening at the school-room of the Mary Warren Free Institute, where the pupils of the school and a large number of the congregation and the friends of the Messrs. Warren had assembled, Bishop Doane presented to Dr. Tucker, in behalf of the trustees, elegant and unique testimonials, in solid silverware, of their love and affection for their revered Rector. The Bishop prefaced his remarks by alluding to his being the representative of Albany, which was originally settled by the Dutch, whose patron saint was St. Nicholas, and that he therefore was the direct representative of that good saint, a most happy fact in view of the pleasant task before him. He also paid a high tribute to Dr. Tucker for the good he had done during his long connection with the Holy Cross Church. He said that as a Bishop one of the most discouraging as well as unpleasant features of his work was the oft-recurring changes between pastor and people, and that, therefore, he felt most strongly the force of the occasion they were then commemorating. After the presentation and Dr. Tucker's reply, in which he alluded also to the Bishop and claimed the honor of having first associated his name in connection with the bishopric, another surprise was in waiting for Dr. Tucker, for the Rev. Dr. Harison came forward and in a very happy preface presented the Doctor a massive silver "loving cup"—a *poculum caritatis*—a gift from the Vestry and Wardens of old St. Paul's Church. Dr. Tucker in his reply referred to the early history of the Church of the Holy Cross as an off-shoot from St. Paul's, and feelingly alluded to Mrs. Mary Warren, the founder of the former Church, paying a most affectionate tribute to her memory. Nathan B. Warren acknowledged the tribute paid to his mother. After the singing of carols, bountiful gifts were distributed to the scholars from a beautiful Christmas tree, when the assemblage departed, all wishing the Doctor a very merry Christmas and very many of them, in which wish the community heartily joins. Dr. Tucker also received a number of costly gifts from members of the congregation.

Mrs. H. C. Lockwood, parishioner and friend, was absent, detained on account of sickness; she sent her own greeting in the form of a poem, which made so strong an impression that I have heard it spoken of to this day.

Five years later brought on another celebration retrospective in its character. Then it was that the Trojans kept the one hundredth anniversary of the naming of their city.

On " Church Night," at a great public meeting held in Music Hall, Doctor Tucker was one of the speakers. That which he had to say is of enduring interest—as follows:

Mr. Chairman, My Reverend Brethren of the Clergy and Fellow-Citizens of Troy : Some men have honors thrust upon them. The honors which I bear this evening have grown upon me, like the ivy upon the Church wall. No one, I fancy, would covet or claim the honors which are conferred only by the lapse of years. As a minister of the Gospel, I have gone preaching the kingdom of God among you for nearly fifty years—not a century plant, but something more than a semi-century plant. I am not to the manor—Van der Heyden manor—born, but am an adopted citizen of Troy, "a citizen" in the language of St. Paul, as I feel, " of no mean city."

Why have I stayed here so long? Why have I resisted the alluring solicitations of occupying "a larger field of usefulness? " Because I love my work, and my faithful, generous fellow-workers at Holy Cross, and because my feelings have helped my conscience, and every year I have grown less willing to sever ties of friendship which bind my heart with the hearts of my fellow-citizens who have so generously extended to me since the first welcome their affection, sympathy and regard, and I am glad that I have been allowed to stay long enough to be with you on this joyous occasion, when we are celebrating the naming of our city. This is a matter of interest to us all. But what, I ask, is the naming of a city in comparison with the incident of giving a name to the richest, most generally enlightened and principal nationality in the world? The familiar synonym, wherever the English language is spoken, of the United States, " Uncle Sam," originated in this city on Mount Ida or along our wharfs in the year 1812, where the provisions for the army, which were marked " U. S.," were facetiously said to stand for " Uncle Sam "—Uncle Sam Wilson, one of the inspectors of military stores that passed through this city.

But this is wandering beyond my province. When I came to this city there were three Episcopal Churches. We have now seven, with a large and growing interest in the Cathedral of All Saints, Albany. Among my clerical associates and pastoral friends four have been elevated to the Episcopate, Scarborough, Starkey, Worthington and Potter, the Bishop of New York, once so closely and dearly associated with St. John's parish; and who, from his elevated position, might seem now to rank as metropolitan of our Church in this country. Dr. Van Kleeck, for many years Rector of St. Paul's parish, through faithful and efficient service as a parish priest, was promoted to the more arduous and prominent position of secretary of our Board of Domestic Missions. Rev. Dr. Fairbairn, for years Rector of Christ Church, is now President of St. Stephen's College, Annandale; and there, by his talents, tact and energy, has acquired for himself and college, distinction and public esteem. Dr. Eliphalet Potter, President of Hobart College, who, with personal traits and gifts that win affection and respect, bears, along with his brother, the Bishop of New York, a "*clarum et venerabile nomen*," may be regarded as the founder of the free Church of St. Barnabas. Dr. J. Pelham Williams, late Rector of St. Barnabas', who recently left us with regrets and good wishes, is a brother honored for his scholarly attainments, genial converse, and the faithful maintenance of his opinions and convictions. And here I have to recall the names of Drs. Walter and Cox, once Rectors of St. John's, the deep theologian and sharp controversialist Dr. Coit, the faithful, hard-working Harison, a man who, by his knowledge of canon law and zealous energy, belonged to the Church at large rather than to St. Paul's parish.

St. Paul's Church, which we fondly call our mother Church, like the eastern banyan tree, has dropped her branches, and those branches are growing up into good and stately trees; while the old mother Church herself seems to renew her youth and blossoms forth in "the beauty of holiness," and her boughs are richly graced with "the fruits of the Spirit."

St. John's Church is closely identified with the first enterprise of the Episcopal Church in the foreign field. . . .

In this city was introduced the Choral service through the energy and liberality of my worthy friend and parishioner, Dr. Nathan B. Warren, a name identified with the progress and improvement of ecclesiastical music in this country.

Here was established the first or second missionary Church in our communion. Here was the first observance of Saints' days and the Festival of the Ascension. Here the first Episcopal minister preached in a surplice. Here were first heard in one of our Churches the old Gregorian tones. I might refer to other novelties, as they were once called, introduced in this city, and which are now well-established usages throughout our communion. The name of Troy has been wafted by a tide of sacred melody over oceans to the Azores, Japan, Greece and Rome, and brought back a cheering response even from the Lord High Chancellor of England, the author of the "Book of Praise."

By reason of circumstances I feel as if I stood here this night as a kind of representative man among the ministers of Troy. We, as I proudly and boldly claim, are the guardians of the palladium of Troy. When the wily Greeks captured and destroyed that sacred image of Pallas, the patroness of Ilium, Troy fell. The palladium of our city and country is the religion of the Lord Jesus Christ. For that religion is the safeguard of our civil rights and social blessings. The clergy are the sworn defenders and champions of our holy faith. May I not, then, my fellow-citizens, claim for us, to whom are entrusted the care and custody of your choicest privileges and dearest hopes, your hearty sympathy and generous coöperation, while I express what I believe is the sentiment of every priest and minister on this broad platform, that we are endeavoring, each according to his convictions, his conscience and ability, " to keep the unity of the Spirit in the bond of peace? "

The same year, 1889, was marked further by an important enlargement of the Church fabric—a considerable addition to the length of the chancel. When this new chancel was consecrated by the Bishop, the men of the choir were habited for the first time in cassock and cotta. Fortunately, the girls retained their uniform, that of red cloak in winter and white in summer; the girls have never been vested in men's ecclesiastical garments. Their head-covering took the form of a " Tam-o-Shanter " cap, still in use.   In the connection it has been remarked that the motto of the founder of the Church was " She is not afraid of the snow for her household: for all her household are clothed with scarlet." The words are chiselled into the stone, around the fireplace at the school.

Processionals were started, a crucifer taking his place at the head of the line.

By the latest alteration the effect of the imposing architecture is much increased. There is now an unusual length of nave and chancel. When the choir is in place, and the lights burning, at a Sunday Evensong—always held at five o'clock—the impression which the soul receives through the eye is fit counterpart of that conveyed by the organ of hearing.

The Rector referred to the last improvement of the structure in a sermon preached in April, 1894, on the semi-centennial anniversary of the laying of the corner-stone of the Church.

When I look back nearly fifty years it is with difficulty that I can identify myself with the first pastor of the Church of the Holy Cross. He has seen so many changes in the edifice itself and in the look of things! The Church has grown in dimensions and has gathered fresh grace and beauty with its years. It does not look like the little Church in which I once ministered. Friends have come and gone, how many dear, loving and much loved friends! I have many more parishioners, as I feel, awaiting me with prayers and hopes in Paradise than I now can reach with look and voice.

XVI

THE LAST HYMNAL

The editor of the " First Tucker," which in its day wrought a musical revolution, was not likely to intermit his labors in the one department. From time to time he put forth manuals having connection with the service of song either in school or Church. Among these there is a compilation entitled " Selections and Proper Psalms Set to Gregorian Tones," which has been approved by use in many congregations where the Psalter is sung in such wise that it is possible for the people to take part.

After great labor, incommensurate with the result, the General Convention of 1892 put forth a new book of words authorized for use; it was followed by the musical " Hymnal Revised and Enlarged." This was published in January, 1894, near the close of the beneficent career. Naturally, the chief editor did not bestow personal work upon the compilation to the same extent as in the case of the " Parish Hymnal " or its brilliant successor. Much was left to the coworker, who had known for years the wishes and opinions of his *primus*.

That Doctor Tucker was personally concerned, however, in the preparation of the last Musical

Hymnal will appear from an examination of his correspondence. For example:

5 Park Side, Cambridge.
Feb'y. 23d, 1893.

My Dear Sir:

I am greatly obliged for your letter of Feb'y. 7th. It is always a great pleasure to find that anything one has written has been acceptable in choirs. I now send you *two* settings of the hymn you enclosed. If you prefer a plain, diatonic version, you will probably prefer No. 1. In No. 2 I have allowed myself considerably more freedom in harmonies and sentiment. . . . I receive 3 guineas for a tune. My contributions to the completed " Hymns Ancient and Modern," the " Quiver " and other collections have been paid for at this rate.

Believe me
Yours very truly
George Garrett.

The Rev. J. Ireland Tucker.

The result of the above correspondence will be noted in No. 256 of the Musical Hymnal.

Dr. John Stainer returns the words of a hymn, because he deems it " unfitted for music owing to the irregular grouping of the lines." Later he writes again:

Oxford, England.
May 22, 1893.

Dear Sir: I am much obliged to you for sending me some more words of hymns. As soon as I get a little leisure I will try my hand at them, but I cannot, I fear, hope to do better than those tunes of mine already much used; e. g.:

The Saints of God.
I need Thee, precious Jesu.

The roseate hues.
Author of Life Divine.
There is a heavenly home.
There's a friend for little children.
Christ who once.

As these were published before the present law of copyright, they are, of course, at your disposal.

In the *latest* revision of " Hymns Ancient and Modern " two of my tunes seem to be much liked and used.

" The God of Abraham praise (2nd tune) "; this makes a useful Processional; only if you adopt it, please make the last line as I wrote it.   .   .   .

" The Voice that once in Eden " is also in this Appendix. As the copyrights belong to me, I will gladly give you leave to use them.

Of course, I am not so vain as to assume that you wish to include *any* of them, but I shall esteem it a great favor if you will let me know which, if *any*, of my tunes you are intending to insert. I am

Yours faithfully
JOHN STAINER.

Sir Robert Stewart addresses the coeditor, referring to the demand for melodious writing:

Friday, 14th April 1893.
40 UPPER FITZWILLIAM STREET, DUBLIN.

MY DEAR MR. ROUSSEAU:

I have to acknowledge with thanks your draft on Dublin, and your very courteous letter accompanying it. I shall hope my American cousins will like the tune. I am one of those who believe music, devoid of melody, is but " a body without a soul," and I also believe that this object—melody—can be. attained without falling into a vulgar or a meretricious style.

I don't suppose my wife and I shall have the pleasure

to see your Chicago marvels; I dread the sea voyage
too much. And I only hope *your* shrewd, sharp-witted
countrymen and women, will not too hastily judge of
the Irish art of music, by specimens of it from those who
are ill-fitted to represent it. I hear of some who will
visit your shores very soon, in similar capacity, but who
go solely " on their own hook " (forgive the vulgarism)
and are not sent out by any respectable or respected organization, to represent this singular, curious, but generally gifted nation.

Always yours
ROBERT STEWART.

Many tunes written by Arthur Henry Brown
have become established favorites. His setting of
" The day is past and over " is often on the lips of
them that sing. A message from him will be of
interest:

BRENTWOOD,
April 8, 1893.

MY DEAR SIR:

I hereby desire to thank you for your draft, duly received, and am pleased to find that both tunes are quite
to your satisfaction. By this post I am sending a copy
of my new book of the Festal Harmonies, for your acceptance, together with an Easter Carol that has recently
appeared in one of our English Church periodicals. I
will not forget to send you a copy of the Festival Book
[probably of the extensive Gregorian Festival in London]
which will doubtless be issued in a week or so. The first
two Processionals will, I think, be quite to your liking.
The Anthem is not my choice, and I wanted to have
something by one of the old Cathedralists, or in the old
Church style, at least. For all the other part of the book
I am entirely responsible.

I am not at all likely to cross the Atlantic, and much

prefer *terra firma*. The English Channel or the German Ocean have sufficient terrors for me, and these I have frequently braved.

Yours very truly
ARTHUR H. BROWN.

The new book is now making its way. It was adopted at once in places distinguished by the setting up of a standard of pure music. Others are finding out what a storehouse of good is here.

Some have been dismayed, their attention distracted, by the apparent overplus—and consequent over-weighting—of new compositions, and in particular of the elaborated sort called " choir tunes." There may be a larger supply of the latter variety than that required by the average congregation; but there was an evident desire on the part of the editors to meet the peculiar demand which exists in places where they give especial attention to musical culture—as at the Holy Cross, or at St. Paul's School, Concord.

Nevertheless, simple tunes are not wanting. If sought, they will be found. Neither do the standard favorites fail us. An examination will show that each distinctive attribute of the first Musical Hymnal is retained in the second. Those who have learned to like tunes in the former, will find them in the latter.

As to the introduction of new melodies. People fancy that they have an exclusive partiality for the " old tunes "; but at the same time they do not care to sing " York tune " all the while. Their repertory must be enlarged at times; fresh blood is needed now and then. Besides, all the favorites were new once, some of them at a recent date. It has been less than half a century since Lowell Mason's tunes were first learned as novelties. Many of us can remember when "Sun of my soul" and "Our blest Redeemer" were unknown in America. Dr. Hodges' "Bread of the world" was not in existence then. Ward's tune to "O Mother, dear Jerusalem," started *de novo*, printed on a choir festival programme, only a few years since. It gained ground so rapidly that it was heard in many diverse localities before it was printed in a book.

New tunes are in demand; people ask for variety. The novelties, however, have to be tried before they are approved. The time of trial for the latest lot has not yet passed away.

It is not at all unknown that one familiar with the second Musical Hymnal will every now and then make a fresh discovery of beauties before unnoticed. Recently a clergyman, who uses the book in his parish, spoke with enthusiasm of H. W. Parker's simple but charming setting of "All my heart this night rejoices." He had just heard it sung, had found it a gem of pure water; hitherto he had passed it by, as the words happen to be classed under the heading of "Hymns for Children." The like experience may be met with having reference to Doctor Tucker's noble tune composed for "Thou art the way, to Thee alone," and to many other compositions.

The last Hymnal is more cosmopolitan than the

first. The ideal standard set up in the " Parish Hymnal " could not be maintained in its entirety; for example, the General Convention had seen fit to incorporate into their book some of the Moody and Sankey words, and perforce the ditties must follow them.

Nevertheless, this latest " Tucker Hymnal " is a credit to the land of its birth and to the national communion. It is the last effort in the domain of that art much loved by him with which Doctor Tucker had connection; and it is still, in the main, an embodiment of the principle with which he started out—that the music sung in Church must be Church music, and that it must be good.

THE CHOIR OF THE HOLY CROSS

XVII

THE JUBILEE

The night before Christmas — year 1894 — brought with it joy, brightness, and brotherly kindness even more than that which pertains, in the ordinary course, to the festival of good will. It was a time to be remembered.

Then, at the Holy Cross, began the celebration of a triple Jubilee—fiftieth anniversary of the dawn of this pastorship, of the opening service of the Church, and of the establishment of the Choral office in America.

Already at half-past six the light shines cheerily through the Gothic windows, streaming out into the darkness. Bells are chiming in the tower. The organ tone is swelling, jubilant, reaching far abroad, where multitudes are crowding to enter in; soon they fill the place.

Happiness was in the air. Faces glowed with enthusiasm. The sacred precincts were made sweet with roses, fair with lilies, and fragrant by the branches of evergreen. There were to be seen loving cups and other lasting testimonials—silver and golden—likewise resolutions, graven upon parchment, of imposing proportions.

The clock strikes seven. After a sudden hush; the distant sound of voices signalizes the prompt beginning of the office. A long line of choristers marches in, singing Henry Smart's melody, ever young, set to the wording " Angels from the realms of glory." There is a crucifer at the head, a youth of fixed devotion, who is habited in red cassock and white cotta. In the like manner are robed the men singers all. Their vestments are in harmony with the red cloaks and white dresses of the girls. An onlooker remarks the appearance of these many maidens, as they journey on, turning to enter the chancel, and likens them—in after writing—to a joyful singing band of Little Red Riding Hoods gathered together especially for Christmas eve. At the end of the great line walks a band of clergy, among whom two personalities had been assigned to the post of honor; the one was the Bishop of the Diocese, the other—at the Bishop's side—" a man of fourscore years less five, whose name will be remembered and whose life-work will be honored when most of those who pray and preach today have been forgotten."

As it is a night unforgettable, it will be well to recall the names of some of the eminences appearing in procession. Here were the Rev. Doctors Enos, Rector of St. Paul's, and Maxcy of Christ Church; the Rev. Messrs. H. W. Freeman of St. John's, James Caird of the Ascension, G. A. Holbrook of St. Barnabas', and E. De G. Tompkins, formerly of St. John's; the Rev. Mr. Silliman, Grace Church, Albany, and Dr. Nickerson of Lansingburgh. From the Cathedral of All Saints' at Albany came Dean Robbins and Canon Fulcher, while the Bishop and Rector—the one for whom thanksgivings were to be offered—were preceded by Gen. Selden E. Marvin, chairman of the General Committee.

Doctor Tucker intoned the office. Dean Robbins read the lessons. The *Magnificat* and *Nunc Dimittis* had been composed especially for this Jubilee by Dr. E. J. Hopkins of London.

At the close of Evensong the choir sang—in worshipful manner—an Anthem, including the Recitative " Comfort ye," also the chorus, " And the glory of the Lord," from Handel's " Messiah." Then followed prayers and Mendelssohn's setting of the Christmas hymn, " Hark, the herald angels! "

During the Offertory Dr. Enos presented a set of resolutions in behalf of the clergy. In obedience to an order given by the Diocesan Convention, which had assembled in November, he read:

Those who were your companions in the old Diocese of New York, and stood with you when the Diocese of Albany was born and cradled, have already put on record their appreciation of your high character and distinguished services. The Bishop in his annual address, and eminent priests and laymen in congratulatory resolutions on the floor of Convention, have eloquently voiced what I am charged to assure you is the universal thought and sentiment of the Diocese, viz., that the primacy of honor which you earned and enjoyed so long ago is still yours in more abundant measure, if possible, than ever before.

This festival to-night in the crescent glow of Christ's nativity, is a triple Jubilee. It marks, first, the formal opening, fifty years ago, of Holy Cross Church; secondly, the beginning of your pastoral relations here, and in this connection your mastership in the Mary Warren Institute; and, thirdly, the introduction into this country of the ancient Choral Service, in its correct form and as a settled parish use. . . .

For half a century, by the simple law of fitness, you have been a leading figure in the religious, educational, musical and social life not only of Troy and Albany, but of those territorial divisions of the State of which these cities are the centre. When the time came, you assisted efficiently in the erection of the new Diocese of Albany; you were a member of its primary Convention; and have been a full sharer in the burdens and joys of its eventful history.

But the influence of a life like yours cannot be confined within the boundaries of a single city, or diocese; it reaches forth and stirs the world outside. Especially in the field of ecclesiastical music, the whole Church is your debtor. Not only has "the word of Christ dwelt in you richly in all wisdom," but you have "taught and admonished in psalms and hymns and spiritual songs," until your name is a household word throughout the land.

Testifying to the graciousness and worth of your personal character, fifty changeful years agree. They tell of your modesty, consideration for others, unswerving loyalty, high sense of honor, chivalric courage.

After the reading, he continued:

With these greetings I present to you, in the name of the Convention, this silver testimonial, a gift from the Bishop and clergy of the Diocese. It bears an inscription dictated by your Bishop, in a tongue you know and love so well.

"JOHANNI IRELAND TUCKER, S.T.D.
SACERDOTI FIDELI. PASTORI PRAECLARO,
DOCTORI DOCTISSIMO. SACRAE SYMPHO-
NIAE MAGISTRO. VIRO VERE VENERATO.
FRATRI IN CHRISTO DILECTISSIMO. IN
GRATAM MEMORIAM CULTUS DIUTURNI AC
DEDITI PER L. ANNOS.
D. D. D.
EPISCOPUS ET FRATRES SUI IN DIOCESI
ALBANIENSI. VIGILIA NATIVITATIS DOMI-
NI JESU CHRISTI.
MDCCCXLIV.   MDCCCXCIV."

I also hand to you the official copy of the resolutions
of the Convention in the matter of your Jubilee.

These and this to you, dear Dr. Tucker, with the Convention's affectionate congratulations.

The Bishop then presented to the admired Doctor a purse of gold, offered as a tribute of affection
by the Woman's Guild of the Parish. Afterward
the Diocesan ascended the pulpit and delivered
one of his always graceful and fitting addresses.
In part, the speaker said:

The mystery of the manufacture of headlines in a newspaper office is one that must always puzzle the brains of
a layman, not admitted into the secrets of that most
astonishing profession. But sometimes their reason is
clear and good. And when a newspaper writer of this
city, last April, described this Church, in which we are
gathered to-night, as "a Church of the First Things,"
I am inclined to think he builded better than he knew.

Dr. Tucker said to me just after the last Diocesan
Convention, "Please remember that Christmas eve is
the Jubilee of the Church of the Holy Cross and not of

the pastor," and I must remember it. I would not dare
to say, in his presence, what I feel about him as a man,
what I owe to him as my brother in the ministry, what
he has been as a priest in this Diocese of Albany, or what
I know the congregation, the city and the Diocese would
have said, if my tongue were free. His presence, his
wish, this place, and the proprieties of the service make
it impossible. Only this much is true, that not even the
holy purpose of the saintly foundress of this work, not
even the loving service of her life, not even the devotion of her children, not even the true hearts and help-
ing hands of other helpers, not all these together could
have accomplished the great and gracious results of
these fifty years, without the leader whom God sent
here; fearless and faithful, with his untiring devotion,
his invincible courage, his inexhaustible patience, his unusual gifts, his incomparable character. Let us note with
reverent thankfulness, in the glance backward which we
take to-night, how this is "a Church of the First Things."

It has been always a Church, whose sittings have been
free to all, with no demand of money equivalent, for the
right to, or the choice of, seats. . . .

Secondly, the Choral Service was first really introduced in America, actually reintroduced into this century,
in this House of God. . . .

I believe I am not an extremist in this matter either.
I recognize the intense solemnity of the simplest and
plainest " use " in this great act of worship. I deny that
it can be made either " high " or " low," by lights or
music or the number of officiants. I deprecate pro-
foundly the tuneless and discordant distractions of attempts and imitations, when the music is beyond the
reach of the choir. I greatly dislike the twisting and
turning of English words, to fit Roman Catholic mass-
music, no matter how beautifully written for a foreign
tongue, and a purpose of devotion as foreign as the language. And I deplore the mutilation of the Liturgy by
organ interludes, by the " vain repetition " of words, by

the prolonged elaborations of ornate services. But I believe that the consecration to the worship of Almighty God of the art of music, and the dignifying of our great act of worship, with a wealth of sacred harmony, is an act of devotion acceptable to God, and conducing to the adoration of man. And I thank God for its cradling here, under the guidance of this true Precentor, whom we have well called to-day " magister sacrae symphoniae," master of holy harmony.

More even than this, there began here the due observation of the Holy Days of our Lord and of His Saints. The pastor of this Church was one of the leaders, if not the leader, in this State at least, in the recognition of the Church's purpose, to make the Celebration of the Holy Communion a frequent, and not an unusual act. The observance, with a Celebration, of Ascension Day is now, thank God, so practically universal, that it seems difficult to believe that fifty years ago it was almost unknown in America. The careful and niggardly economy of the Holy Communion, which omitted the Celebration on the first Sunday of the month if Easter or Whitsunday came just before or after it; the neglect of the plain requirement for a Celebration whenever a Collect, Epistle and Gospel were provided, have passed out of the memories of most of you, and were never known to our younger clergy. And the leaven which was hid, which has wrought out the blessed change, was in large part first used here. Through what suspicions, criticisms, distrusts, estrangements, oppositions, these unusual, because disused, customs of Catholic worship were introduced and maintained here—when every minor act of ritual that accompanied them, like preaching in the surplice, or turning to the east in the *Gloria*, was popularly considered popish—only one can realize, who remembers, as I do, the attacks and the assaults, the abuse and accusations heaped upon my father, who was doing just this sort of work in St. Mary's Church in Burlington, half a century ago. And it is proof enough, that these were only the loyal carrying out to their fulfilment of the spirit and the letter of the Book of Common Prayer, to note, that everywhere now, in the deepened and enlarged life of the Church, they are the prevailing custom and rule. But the first promoters of it, the men who were ahead of their time, the men that caught and comprehended the revival of Catholic truth and worship before their fellows, are the men to be held in honor for their insight and their farsight, their convictions and the courage in which they held them.

But this is " a Church of First Things " in other ways than these. This Church is really the chapel of the Mary Warren Free Institute. There is intense pathos in the story. . . .

Behind and underneath the outward and visible signs of the character and conduct of service, lies another element, another " first thing," the holding and maintaining of the Catholic faith. Here the old truths and doctrines, which indifference and ignorance had overlaid, whose utterance was well nigh drowned in the babel of the discordant and dissenting voices of those who held half truths, and in distorted proportion to each other; here, the " first things " of the faith were proclaimed—when to preach them was counted disloyalty to the Reformation— the mystery of the Incarnation, the grace of Sacraments, the visible reality of the Church, the Communion of the saints on earth and in Paradise, the apostolic authority and the apostolic power of the ministry; " the first principles of the doctrine of Christ." And the power of all that has been wrought out here, the salt that saved it, the leaven that quickened it, the light that made it incomprehensible (unable that is to be swallowed up by darkness), was in the fast and firm holding, the clear and constant proclaiming, of the Catholic faith.

There are some " first things " that come home, to me, personally here to-night, with an overwhelming flood of recollection: associations from young childhood with Mount Ida; my father's warm affection and admiration for dear Mrs. Warren; his sense of sorrow, which spread itself through our home, in the sharp and sudden passing into Paradise of the only daughter of this house; his English visit, made, as his diary reads, "With N. B. and S. E. W., two sons of my dearest friends"; the life-long romance, with infinite pathos in it at times, through which this house was builded as it was begun; failing eye sight, lasting just long enough to draw the plans of the Church, at whose consecration they so fitly chose and sung for the anthem that true Eucharistic Introit, "O send out Thy light and Thy truth that they may lead me and bring me unto Thy holy hill and to Thy dwelling"; an Advent Sunday in my diaconate and very early married life, when I preached here; and then an interval of fifteen years, when, before the Northern Convocation, I preached a sermon in this Church, about which my brother said to me, "That ends my hope of your election as our Bishop"; and since then five and twenty years of close companionship, of constant sympathy with my plans of work, of generous hospitality and helpfulness; with the looking forward on my part to my official or casual visits to this Church, as a chief pleasure, in the enjoyment of the unique beauty of the service, which has come to have the same finish and completeness that the English gardener described in his grass as due to constant care and a thousand years.

And so I come, not Bishop only, but loving brother and old friend, to speak to you, and to speak for you, on this festal evening, when the old Glastonbury legend repeats itself in spiritual reality; and the staff, that was set here fifty years ago, blooms with the fresh and fragrant flowers of hope and happiness on this Holy Night.

The Jubilee idea, as we get at it in the old Hebrew customs and laws, had varied meanings. It had its root in the old purpose of God to make a social system, in which inevitable injustices should heal themselves; by the equalizing of possessions every fifty years; by the opportunity given to reclaim whatever had been lost by misfortune, and to redeem what had been mortgaged in an hour of trouble, and by the freeing of all slaves who asked for freedom. These were its chief characteristics. But you began, and have held on to equal rights and privileges in this House of God, which have never been lost. There has been never any servile bondage here, but the free rendering of mutual service, from which no one asks relief. And inasmuch as the old Jubilee law expressly exempted, from the duty of restoration to its original owner, land that lay within walled towns, this property is safe from any danger of reversion to its gracious givers. What is there left to us then of the thought and spirit of the Jubilee, whose wonderful seven times had in it the thought of completeness, and the essential idea of rest, crowning the Sabbatical month and the Sabbatical year? Just this: Wherever the word comes from (and that is not clear) it has sometimes, as its alternative expression in the Septuagint, " Voices and trumpets." And the trumpets which usher in our Feast of Restoration and Renewal shall set their silver voices to the words of the Psalm for the sons of Korah, singing of this House of God, " The singers also and trumpeters shall He rehearse: All my fresh springs shall be in thee." And then we will add our voices to the trumpet notes and say to this true and Holy House, " Peace be within thy walls, and plenteousness within thy palaces "; and to its beloved Priest, for all who are gathered here to-night, in person or in heart, I say, " for my brethren and companions' sakes, I will wish thee prosperity."

After the Bishop's address, Dr. Warren's Festival *Te Deum* was sung, a true voicing of the feeling of each thankful heart.

At the close of all, the procession retraced its steps, singing H. W. Parker's lovely carol, " All my heart this night rejoices."

That was the way the people felt, all of them, as
they retired from the holy place. The service in
which they had been absorbed was referred to by
a local secular paper as " making perhaps the most
remarkable epoch in the Church history of this
city."

Let it be noted that up to the time of service the
ground had been green, not covered by snow; but
when the congregation came out at the close of the
first Jubilee office, they found the air white with
falling flakes; and so the Christmas picture had
been completed while they worshipped.

At once all repaired, through the snow, to the
rooms of the Young Women's Association, where
a reception was tendered to Doctor Tucker by Mrs.
George Henry Warren. Christians of many diverse titles were in attendance, pressing forward
to shake hands with the one remembered. There
was an abundance of flowers and music. The
Committee of St. Stephen's Guild proved themselves competent managers of a social function.

Among the many gifts offered to the Rector
there was a massive gold loving cup from the children of the late George Henry Warren and a surplice of fine linen from the Mary Warren Guild.
A large floral offering had been sent to the Church,
which carried the inscription:

Symbols, dove with branch, peace; circle of white
flowers, purity; " '44 " in white flowers, youth; " '94 " in
yellow flowers, ripened age; " '50 " in white and yellow
flowers, saintly life. To Rev. Dr. J. Ireland Tucker from
the corporation and members of St. Barnabas' Church.

On the Saturday preceding the Jubilee the trustees of the Rensselaer Polytechnic Institute had waited upon the Rev. Dr. Tucker and presented a handsome engrossed copy of congratulatory resolutions adopted by that body.

On Christmas morning the splendid exercises of the triple Jubilee were resumed. Bishop Potter of New York had left his home, travelling throughout the night, that he might be present and preach at this especial Celebration.

After the office, Doctor Tucker gave a luncheon to the Bishop, to Mrs. George Henry Warren, and a few invited guests. Among the gifts late in arriving was a silver loving cup from old friends in St. John's parish, including Bishop Potter and others.

The Christmas tree festival, given by Mrs. George Henry Warren and Dr. Warren, fell in with the mood of the time.

Thursday evening—in accordance with his custom—the Doctor entertained his young friends at a Christmas feast held in Harmony Hall, for which cards of invitation were issued. An orchestra was secured, and the young, men and maidens were partners in the dance.

In connection with the fiftieth anniversary, the vestry of St. Paul's—mother Church of the entire region, which had once invited Doctor Tucker to become its Rector—took action, paying their tribute to the priest—then living in their midst—revered both in his own city and throughout the land. There was always a singular unanimity in the exercise of good will, having reference to him. St.

Paul's vestry passed a minute which included the following:

We speak only simple truth when we designate him as the brave, courtly, Christian gentleman. In earlier years he brought into his worship what must then have seemed startling innovations, yet steadily retained the respect of Churchmen, even though they followed him but slowly. He was a pioneer in the restoration of forms and accessories of worship of the earlier Church; yet none less than he ever sacrificed the substance of true worship to the mere form. The personification of priestly dignity, no trace of affectation is found in him. In social position the peer of the highest, the humble citizen has no warmer friend than he. And this is by no means confined to his parish or his communion. . . . He was a priest, a sage, and a man. Through his good deeds and gentle manners, he had filled the town with a sort of tender and filial veneration.

On the Sunday following the Jubilee the Rector himself had something to say. Taking for his topic the song of the Christmas angels, at first he recited reasons why glory should be given to God. Then he continued:

Glory to God in the highest that He put it into the heart of that saintly woman, Mary Warren, to build this house of prayer for poor and all people; and glory to God in the highest that the same divine impulse, touching filial love and reverence, inspired the hearts of her children to hallow her memory and their own affection by enlarging and beautifying the Church which the mother built, and maintaining it now for fifty years by their devotion and munificence. Glory to God in the highest that those children had the means and the willingness to fulfil a mother's wishes, and even to transcend in their affection and endeavors that good, loving and wise mother's most ardent wishes and fondest anticipations.

"Peace to men of good will." I have read and heard with mixed feelings of pleasure and humility the encomiums that have been written, printed and spoken about the clergyman who has completed the fiftieth year of his pastorate in this Church of the Holy Cross. With pleasurable emotions I have read and listened to the kindly expressions of men of good will, men, friends and acquaintances, prompted by a generous impulse to say, write or print what the heart felt and wished publicly to express to a friend upon a memorable epoch of himself and of the Church in which, by God's providence, he ministers. It would be churlish to reject or depreciate such heart-offerings of love and respect. My own heart most keenly sympathizes with tender hearts that "rejoice with those that do rejoice and weep with them that weep." I warmly and thankfully appreciate all the kind words of commendation and respect which I have read or heard. I cherish with pride and pleasure the eulogiums of my reverend father in God the Bishop of Albany, and the loving tribute of affection of my friend the Bishop of New York. What man would not be moved by such expressions of love and honor? I cherish with gratitude and respect the proofs of confidence and regard offered so generously by my brethren, clerical and lay, of the Diocese of Albany. I cherish most heartily with the sacred associations of this Jubilee the friendly and cordial greetings of other ministers of "the everlasting Gospel," that love our Lord Jesus in sincerity, and with us can rejoice in the birth of "a Saviour which is Christ the Lord."

I cherish, too, with proud and grateful feelings the congratulations of the citizens of Troy, irrespective of religious designations, who by their good willingness or good pleasure inspire my heart with fresh energy, zeal, love and courage, and I take the utterance of their good willingness as a kind of "God speed."

My heart responds, like the strings of the harp to the
gentlest touch of the musician, to every expression or
look of love or respect awakened by this strange and
happy Jubilee. But I must confess that after letting my
heart beat and vibrate with every word and look of good
will, while thoroughly, most sincerely, most heartily appreciating the motives or the feelings that prompted kind
words and the gentle and generous offices of love—when
I come, as it were, to myself and look sternly at facts, I
feel as if the picture has been, to say the least, as I am
prompted now to say, somewhat too highly colored. The
artist with his cultured eye and cunning hand can idealize
nature, so that while every feature of the landscape is
traced truthfully upon the canvas, yet the picture merely
shows that the painter chanced or chose those particular
features. Thus it happens not infrequently that the picture is even more striking and beautiful than the scene or
place depicted. This seems to be the modern style of
writing history and biography.

But to drop imagery, I feel as if my good-willing
friends, the men of pleasure, have unwittingly, no doubt,
bestowed more praise and commendation than I indeed
deserve. I am not disposed at the present moment
through any mock or false delicacy to disclaim any fair
share of praise and congratulations which I feel belongs
to me; nor am I tempted by the occasion to grasp at
honors which I know, and here I am glad to confess,
may be rightly claimed by others. This let me frankly
state: I had nothing to do with the inception and building of this Church of the Holy Cross. The idea originated with Mrs. Mary Warren. This Church, which we
trace back to its origin, the heart, or the faith, the charity
and devotion of a loving and saintly woman, was built
by that good and charitable woman. It was afterward
enlarged and embellished by her children. I had little
to do with the introduction of the Choral Service in this
Church, and its consequences throughout this country in
connection with the musical and ritualistic proprieties in

20

the order of the divine service in the offices of public worship throughout the whole extent of the spiritual domain of the Protestant Episcopal Church of the United States. The credit and honor of the introduction of the Choral Service into this country belong, without dispute, and must be frankly and gratefully conceded, to my much revered and devoted friend and parishioner, Dr. Nathan B. Warren.

I have had the opportunity, offered rarely to my clerical brethren, of conducting a service conformable to my own conviction, the usages of the Holy Catholic Church and the Liturgy of the Protestant Episcopal Church in this country. I accept, then, the commendation which I have received, so far as I have shown the desire and endeavor to use the opportunity for the glory of God and the diffusion of peace and good will among men. I have had my ideal, and I now find out by the experience of fifty years how imperfectly I have tried to work up to that ideal—like the artist who, when he is putting the last touches on the canvas, with feelings of disappointment, with sadness and regret, feels as no one can feel, how poorly, how imperfectly he has embodied in figure and color the conception of his genius, his great thought, his mighty purpose.

" Peace on earth to men of good will." ·I have received congratulations and testimonials of respect from the Diocese of Albany, from the Vestries of St. Paul's Church, Christ Church and St. Barnabas', from Bishop Potter and his former parishioners of St. John's parish accompanied with a beautiful and costly piece of plate, from the President and trustees of the Rensselaer Polytechnic Institute and from the trustees of the Church Home.

Extract from a letter addressed to me by Colonel Le-Grand B. Cannon: " Your jubilee reminds me of the origin and early days of your parish and my great-aunt's 'Saturday Sewing-school' for the children of the poor —culminating in your parish with its parish school and thus perfecting a great mission work, which through its hundreds of educated girls, not a few now mothers and grandmothers, has through their agency influenced in no small degree the growth of the Church throughout the nation. It is rarely that one is permitted for half a century to continue his labors in one locality and direction, and I beg the privilege to add my congratulations and that you will accept the chalice and paten as an evidence of my great personal regard for your admirable life."

Extracts from a letter of Bishop Knickerbacker (who died Monday, December 31): "Indianapolis, Ind., Dec. 21, 1894.—My first impressions of the Church as a boy I received in the beautiful services of Holy Cross. I rejoice that you have been spared to see the wonderful advance in the Church's growth and that you have been permitted to see great results from your own faithful ministrations. I pray that you may be spared many more years of usefulness. I can envy your blessed Christmas, believing that you are remembered in more households in Troy than any living man; that you have the good wishes and benedictions of many Bishops and clergy of the Church. May God bless you and your work is the prayer of your old friend, D. B. Knickerbacker, Bishop of Indiana."

I have received letters of congratulation from former pupils residing in Michigan, Massachusetts, Rhode Island, New Jersey, Pennsylvania, Maryland and our own State, and a kind letter and a gift from the husband of a former Sunday-school scholar and parishioner of many years, now residing in Colorado.

Extract from a letter received from C. Rowland Mason, Baltimore: "As one of your old scholars, who nearly forty years ago had the privilege of singing in the Church at Troy, I could not refrain from adding my word of congratulation and good wishes on this anniversary. In many wanderings in the past forty years I have often looked back to the pleasant days spent in Troy, and have always felt the benefit which I derived from your instruction and example."

It seems strange to me that in the many notices of the Jubilee of the Holy Cross and the fifty years' pastorate of its Rector there have appeared but two or three allusions to the time and labor which I have devoted for nearly forty years to the instruction of the young. As I view things, looking back through many years and out toward the never ending future, my best and most lasting work as the pastor of this Church was done, as I believe, in the Girls' and in the Boys' School. I am now weighing things by their results. It is a great privilege and honor, fraught with the most solemn and anxious responsibility, as I feel, to mould boys into high-minded and generous-hearted men and fashion girls into gentle, companionable, modest and Christian women. To train and teach boys and girls and fit them to meet life's work, temptations and trials I count as higher art and skill than to sculpture marble with the genius and the deft hand of a Phidias or Praxiteles. Besides, what I have done as a teacher, burdensome as it might seem, has been lightened by the impulse of love and hallowed by the restraints and incentives of duty. I have been willing now for many years to take as my daily motto " Feed my lambs." My reward is the affection of my pupils, their obedience to my precepts, their virtues or moral conduct in the world and their hopes and confidences for the future, as " members of Christ and inheritors of the kingdom of heaven."

Extract from a letter from F. E. Hale, M.D., Providence, R. I. After offering congratulations he asks for my photograph as a special favor which he would cherish beyond expression, and he adds: " It is hardly necessary to have the picture to remember the face, as it is imprinted indelibly upon my brain. I should like it as a memento, to make me a better man. I have not forgotten you and the interest you took in me by teaching me to write between your knees. May God keep you .for many years to come is the earnest prayer of your former pupil, ' Neddie.' "

In conclusion I wish peace on earth to all men, but my subject and the text prompt me to salute with the benediction of Christian peace the men of good will.

> The great God of truth
> Fill all thine hours with peace.

Now the God of hope fill you with all joy and peace in believing, that ye may abound in hope, through the power of the Holy Ghost.

XVIII

A GLANCE BACKWARD

The celebration of a fiftieth anniversary is always suggestive of a retrospect. Naturally one looks back and recalls separated factors which help to make up the life in its entirety.

Doctor Tucker's sphere of activity went out beyond parish limits. Forgetting that he was a busy man, occupied week-days and Sundays in school and Church, he started a mission in South Troy, now St. Luke's Church. In those days there were no street cars, and he used to accomplish the long distance on foot, going every Sunday evening after he had finished his services at the Holy Cross.

In the Diocese he was always an interested and industrious worker. The estimate of his associates in the Standing Committee will be found elsewhere.

His Bishop once made the remark, "Doctor Tucker is faithful and helpful in every way." In truth, such a priest is a fortunate right arm for his Diocesan. From the beginning of the Cathedral he was connected with its General Chapter, an active participant in all that pertained to its prosperity.

His relations with St. Stephen's College, and his personal service, will not be forgotten. About this,

Dr. Fairbairn writes: " He was one of the original trustees who were named in the charter which the Legislature granted in 1860. His interest in the institution never flagged. He has proved it by the valuable gift which he has made to the College. The second item of his will is the bequeathing of his valuable library to the institution. It was not the last item, as if now he was at a loss to know what to do with his books, but the second one, as if the College were uppermost in his mind."

Time and again he was elected a deputy to the General Convention. Of the Church at large he was a servant through the instrumentality of his hymnals; so he was kept in touch with the wants of a continent.

In his adopted city he maintained a lively interest in public matters. Since 1869 he had been a trustee of the Rensselaer Polytechnic Institute. So late as June, 1894, he preached the Baccalaureate Sermon to the Graduating Class of that institution, when, speaking to scientists, he chose as his theme " The Imperfection of Human Knowledge."

When a city armory was erected in 1884, at the laying of the corner-stone Doctor Tucker appeared upon the stage, pronouncing a Benediction. At the " Troy Centennial," in 1889, he was chosen a member of the committee of one hundred representative citizens in charge of affairs.

He was a philanthropist in private as well as public. His acts of beneficence, of practical assistance offered to those in need, were judicious but almost

measureless—of them no one knows the extent—
and the sphere of their application was never limited by creed. In the Troy *Daily Times*, issued
on the day of his death, a leading editorial gave
utterance:

Dr. Tucker was a man of boundless charity in thought
and act. No one ever heard him speak ill of others,
though he may have had his differences of opinion, as
was inevitable with his strong personality. But he was
tolerant, patient, forbearing. Deeds without number in-
dicating his generous, unselfish regard for his fellow-men
might be recounted by those who were his beneficiaries.
They were never revealed through his telling of them.
How many a saddened soul has been ministered to by
him, what gifts most helpful and timely he has given,
what aid to the young and struggling he has extended,
only the Keeper of all secrets knows. Dr. Tucker, with
his modesty and quiet bearing, was one of those who
" do good by stealth, and blush to find it fame."

In like manner, his priestly service rendered
to the sick was unrestricted. A physician, who
had known him long, testifies as follows:

November 26, 1896.

I was brought in contact with the good Rev. Ireland
Tucker many times in visits to the sick, and admired his
tender devotion to them, notably during the cholera epi-
demics of the '40s & '50s. I found him at early morning
hours and at midnight giving consolation and administering the Sacrament to the dying, whose screams and
suffering were painful to witness; and this he did in a
deliberate, sympathetic and faithful manner that betrayed
no fear or timidity. At his Jubilee 50 years later, as I
was with the multitude congratulating him, he detained

me, holding my hand, and said: "Do you remember those cases of cholera at night down in those wretched tenements?" "Yes," I replied, "and you were brave!" "Well, Bontecou," he said, "I went with fear and trembling, for I had a mortal dread of the disease."

[Signed]
R. B. Bontecou.

So there was an abundant performance of pastoral duty having no connection with school or Church, especially in summer time, when the one parson who stayed at home was pastor for Christians of every name.

Indeed, at any time of year he would be called upon. In his early ministry he happened to be summoned to bury a Roman Catholic, very indigent. When he entered the room he found evidences of the wake just ended. The Rector read the service, and then helped the undertaker to carry the dead.

One New Year's day he was interrupted in the midst of his reception and asked to visit a man at the Pest-house, then filled with patients suffering from black small-pox. He hesitated not, and found that the victim was one who had been a boy in his own Sunday-school.

Soon after the celebration of the Jubilee the Rector said, "All these good people are making a mistake. If I have done any good work in the world it has been, as a teacher of the young, not as a Priest."

He had a real passion for teaching; otherwise he never would have kept up his five or six hours a day in the school to the very end. Herein, as in other matters, he showed himself the successor of Dr. Muhlenberg. Said Bishop Coxe, in his printed tribute: " To say that the beloved old instructor of his school-days left a deep impression on his mind and his life is not the whole story: to him Dr. Muhlenberg seems to have left his mantle. Dr. Tucker accepted it and bound it about his spirit, and so continued the labors of that saintly presbyter."

It was his pleasure to make real the connection between school and Church. Pupils of the Mary Warren Institute form the choir of the Church of the Holy Cross. So it was planned from the beginning that they should be taught in religion and in music.

In the early days the department of music was included merely as a part of the general scheme, which came under the supervision of the directing head and active principal. Mr. Hopkins, when organist, drilled the girls only in the music which was to be sung on Sundays; in his time there were no exercises in *Solfege*. But after the death of the first organist, Doctor Tucker took upon himself the entire duty of instruction in the department, enlarging its scope and sphere. Here he found use for the technical training which he had received from Italian and French masters. We are not surprised to find that he introduces the " Exercises by Concone."

Wednesday afternoon was the Doctor's especial period devoted to the training of his pet music class. On other days he would interest the less advanced children in singing, principally by the practice of hymn-tunes.

There lies before me a series of books once blank, now containing manuscript closely written, the pages of which display an assortment of different chirographies. The little volumes are of especial interest because they contain a story original with Doctor Tucker.

The Rector was accustomed, in the performance of his school duties, to devote an hour now and then to "dictation." Somewhere about the year 1869 he varied his programme, as he gave a "story" to be written down by the pupils. It seems likely that the narrative was improvised at the time; for the copy here preserved is in the varied and pencilled handwriting of different scholars.

Surely it will be worth our while to examine the only story from the hand of the priest-musician. We are not surprised to find it simple and childlike. It contains many touches characteristic of the author. One of these is a quality of happy playfulness, very familiar to those who knew him well. A niece of his once made remark: "He was full of life, full of fun. We children were in great glee whenever we heard that Uncle John was coming."

The same characteristic of gentle sportiveness, of the sort of merriment that gives pleasure, wells up and overflows in certain sections of the story.

It is a tale about "the day and not the night before Christmas." At breakfast Mrs. Cobham tells her daughter Bessie that the sleigh will be at the door soon after luncheon, when they will go out with their Christmas baskets. They make a tour, in which the Lady Bountiful distributes benefactions in the pleasant guise of holiday remembrances. One of the places of stopping was " The Snells."

Mr. Snell, a tall reverend-looking man with his white cravat and long black coat, was seated by the stove, apparently much interested in looking over the pages of the *Church Almanac.* As he afterwards informed Mrs. Cobham, it seems that he could not leave off his old professional habits, and was looking out the " lessons " for the Nativity.

For many years he had fulfilled the duties of sexton, in the Church which Mrs. Cobham had attended as a child. That was in the days of big square pews, high " reading-desks" and higher pulpits. Mrs. C. well remembers the care with which the sexton, " Poppy Snell " as the boys somewhat irreverently called him, provided during the cold, wintry weather, the warm coals for her mother's Dutch foot-stove. And this perhaps may be one reason why her heart now warms up to the strange and rather crabbed old man. I am not at all sure in my own mind that the duties of the sexton's vocation in any remarkable way conduce to sweetness of disposition and gentleness of manners. . . .

He was not partial to Deacons or Assistant Ministers, and once was heard to say that " one parson could give enough trouble, and two were much more than any ordinary sexton could comfortably get along with." As he saw himself getting crowded by the special observance of Saints' Days and the introduction of the Daily Service, he became more and more conscious of his need of additional help, and accordingly sent the following petition to the Rector and Vestry:

Saint Philip and St. James's Day.

To the Very Reverend the Rector of St. Stephen's Church, the much respected Wardens and the worthy gentlemen of the Vestry.

Although "I would rather be a doorkeeper in the house of my God, than dwell in the tents of ungodliness," and although I devoutly trust that my heart may never fail to respond to the sentiment of the Royal Psalmist "I was glad when they said unto me, Let us go into the house of the Lord," yet notwithstanding what the wise man declares and therefore must be true, that "there is a time for all things," I must own that *I* can neither find time nor strength to get the Church ready for Daily Service, for early Celebrations, look after the gas and furnaces, to seat strangers, and discharge with apostolic order and decency my chancel functions on the Holy Day. I therefore respectfully, and with due regard to those in authority over me, as the inspired Paul enjoins in his Epistle, ask the favor of your considering whether among the things that are not only "lawful" but also "expedient" may be reckoned the furnishing your humble servant with a coworker, assistant or "helpmeet," if I may be allowed to use a word familiar to all readers of Sacred Writ.

Wishing you much of the grace you need, and many of the virtues which belong to the names of the chosen saints which our holy mother the Church "throughout all the world" this day commemorates in her Table of Lessons for Holy Days,

Your much favored and obligated
Servant of the Sanctuary
ABRAHAM SNELL.

It is scarcely necessary to add that the petition was granted. Under the new arrangement, things worked pleasantly enough for years, until Mr. Snell, like many other persons at least as knowing and intelligent as himself, got obfuscated in the mysteries of Ritualism. He could not for the life of him keep clearly in his mind the distinction of colors—ecclesiastically speaking he was color blind—and as if he was uncertain which rule to follow, that of Sarum or of Rome, he would sometimes put on the wrong altar cloth, the purple frontal or super-frontal when green or red would be more fitting to the season, and would offer the Rector and the Curate a plain black when they expected a white and embroidered stole. He could not tell an alb from a chasuble, nor a chasuble from a vestibule, and never had been taught the difference between " ablutions " and " absolutions," " confessionals " and " processionals."

From sheer mortification, as I believe, he resigned his situation as sexton of St. Stephen's, another unfortunate victim of Ritualism, and as a " retired officer," was living at the time of our story a pensioner of the parish.

When the manuscript volumes containing the story were forwarded, there came with them an explanatory letter as follows:

All through the story the Doctor seems to have woven his own character, full of love and charity and joyfulness. His picture of the old-time sexton is so good, and the description of the family, joining on Christmas eve in the hymn " While shepherds watched their flocks by night " sung to old " Antioch," in which the voices take up the last line " And glory shone around, round, round " is excellent. My wife and I can never forget his reading it to us—this part especially—and as he repeated " And glory shone around, round, round," he would burst out with the merriest Christmas laugh, his very face illumined with that glory which he now shares.

Again to the story-book. Later, on Christmas eve, there was a household assemblage in front of a cavern carved in wood; at the back of the cavern appeared a stable, and in front a Cradle and the Holy Family. It was a piece of Swiss mechanism, and the figures acted their part. The Magi knelt, then camels and asses, then the shepherds and the sheep. While the action was in progress distant music was heard—*Adeste Fideles*, a chime as from fairy bells, then John Henry Hopkins' Carol.

" Bethlehem does not now seem so far away as it used to," ᵣaid Miss Bessie.

" Come, Mrs. Ayscough, what do you say for ' While shepherds watched their flocks by night ' to the old tune ' Antioch '? "

" Who can pitch it? " asked, in a loud and animated voice, Mr. Cobham. " Why I, to be sure," replied Uncle John. " Didn't I go to singing school in my younger days along with Sally Dorson, and sing out of the same Psalm-book? What is the use of learning without also ' practising as they know,' as Tate and Brady have it:

> ' Who know what's right; nor only so,
> But always practise what they know '?

Now mind, Bessie, you and Carrie and grandma must pitch in with me on the air; your father of course will take care of the Bass; your mother may choose between Tenor and Alto—one part is about as easy to her as another; our friend Thomas, the butler, may double on the Bass. And no ' shining,' sir. It is s-h-o-n-e—not ' shyned ' around."

By the time they reached the fourth line, " And glory shone around," the choristers were in full swing. The Bass were tremendous on the " round, round, round, round, round " in the repeat. When Thomas got the hang of the tune, he kept shouting " round, round. round, round " until he almost got dizzy.

"Once more the same verse," shouted Mr. Cobham, who had not much faith in his own memory. "And you, Mr. Thomas Plumer, please to keep a little closer to the tune in the last line, where it repeats; and observe the 'crescendo,' all of you."

With fresh courage and renewed zeal, they all—grandma just like the little girls—sprang at the hymn, increasing the speed at the first word of every line, like a stone going down hill.

The repeat was redoubled *ad libitum*, and with increased rate and energy.

"They may say what they may, Mrs. Ayscough, about Mendelssohn and Rossini," quoth Mr. Cobham, "and brag of their new-fangled Hymnals with their stiff white notes like a row of parsons in their surplices, and tunes with unpronounceable names of very orthodox saints— no doubt!—as if we hadn't now more saints of our own in the Calendar than we exactly know what to do with; but give me good, old, solid Psalmody which you can tackle at with all your might and make a merry noise. When I sing I like to pull out all my stops, and put both feet on the pedals. None of your wishy-washy lullaby ditties for me, when I rise to praise my God! I would sweep them all away like chaff before the wind."

And there he stood like a war-horse that "paweth in the valley and rejoiceth in his strength," and "smelleth the battle afar off."

School, choir, and Church were all different manifestations of the same one fact. The way it worked is illustrated in the devotedness of Mrs. Pollock, for many years the leading contralto. She was one of the little girls gathered and taught by Mrs. Mary Warren at old St. Paul's, and had been brought to the Holy Cross when ten years of age. She became a pupil of the Mary Warren Institute, and was brought up under the care and supervision of the saintly Rector. She had a beautiful voice, much admired by Prof. Hopkins and by all.

A self-sacrificing chorister, she fulfilled her duties twice on a very stormy Sunday. Thereafter she took sick. Concerning the time, one writes: " Our dear Dr. Tucker came every morning before school and towards evening. He made every suggestion and provided everything he could think of. In two weeks she left us, just as the chimes were ringing for ten o'clock. She had asked the Sunday before to have the window raised, that she might hear the bells. I opened it again. Dr. Tucker thought, and we all thought, that she heard. She would always recognize him when he first came in. That morning she looked so happy and said, ' I will sing " Rock of Ages." ' He helped her, but had to finish it alone." She was only thirty-one years of age when called away, leaving a sorrowing community at the Holy Cross.

The Rector made all preparations, providing things needful for the burial. He placed the body in the ante-chapel, to remain there all night before the funeral. Again the letter: " I went over Tuesday morning. People were going in and out. Mr. S. stood at the head of the casket. I heard people remarking, ' It is a Church rite; he is chief mourner.' I remember hearing that he stood there all through the service."

The gifted contralto was at the same time a faithful Christian, type of the sort of culture resulting from the labors of Doctor Tucker in his school.

21

So it happened time and again. Acts of direct benevolence were associated with the administration of school affairs. Another instance may be adduced.

During a considerable length of time the Rector had been visiting a sick parishioner. He called regularly once each day. He would drop in at the noon hour, and then hurry back to his school. In the last period of the sickness the pastor called twice in each twenty-four hours.

Just when the patient had been given up by the physicians his wife became dangerously ill. A lawyer was sent for. Doctor Tucker was present; there was likewise in attendance a little daughter of the house. After the will had been executed, the father turned to Doctor Tucker, asking him in case the wife should not recover whether he would see that arrangements were made for their child to go to boarding-school; there had been talk between the parents of a project to send the daughter, when she should have grown old enough, to St. Agnes' School at Albany. The father stated that there would be money enough to give his child a good education, and that after such a course she would be able to look out for herself. The Doctor put his arms around the little one, at once promising that the request should be remembered, and making himself responsible for her education.

The little one, now grown to womanhood, tells me: " My father died and my mother recovered; but, nevertheless, he (Dr. Tucker) watched over me with a father's care until death claimed him.

As he himself expressed it, the parsonage was ever to me a second home."

The child was placed in the Mary Warren Institute, where she developed such capabilities for music that she was given opportunities for advanced study. In truth the parsonage was made a second home for her; there she was accustomed to play upon the piano on certain afternoons of each week. After a while a new grand piano made its appearance at the Rectory, which was serviceable for these musical days. When the ward was married the Doctor gave her away, acting *in loco parentis.* So the pastor's vow was fulfilled. After his death it was found that the grand piano was bequeathed to the ward whose education he had promised to supervise.

Was there ever such a principal who had the ability and the will to make his pupils happy to such a degree as this? Doctor Tucker used to retain for the season a box at Music Hall, as well as seats in the balcony. Here he would take a considerable number of girls to attend upon public performances. Often he would send away—at his expense—one or more of his pupils to enjoy a vacation. He would frequently provide private lessons upon the piano.

For a time, each summer he gave a picnic for all, but as the weather was uncertain he changed that to an evening dance at the school-room, for which cards of invitation were distributed to pupils, to be issued by them. Doctor Tucker himself was present. Moreover, the supper was of the very

best. Near the close of his career he started a
string quartet among pupils, furnishing instruments
where needed.

At Christmas the gifts from the head of the
school to the individual members were such as
friend would give to friend. Indeed, his holiday
greetings in concrete form extended to a wide
circle, including young and old; just before the
festive season his study would be changed into a
storehouse of packages of all sorts and sizes.

In the history of the school St. John's Day has
always been a feast of high esteem. Long ago
patron and Rector invented a plan which should
afford an outing to the scholars under circumstances which would make the occasion a thing of
itself. Summer having arrived, on the day of the
Nativity of St. John Baptist there were two morning services at the Church. In the afternoon
teachers and pupils would march in procession, one
carrying the school banner. I have heard it said
that formerly there used to be a band of music.
Until within the last four or five years Doctor
Tucker was accustomed to march at the head of
the line. When all had arrived at Mount Ida, the
day was passed *en fête* about the cottage. Here
many such festival occasions have been made
memorable by dramatic or musical performances.

Dr. Warren writes concerning the permanent
connection between the Holy Cross and the
grounds or park about his home: " The Church
and this place seem to be twin institutions. I
broke ground here in 1839 by planting a cabbage

garden, the same year that the day school originated at St. Paul's.   The two institutions advanced
side by side, even as the cabbage plant which has
progressed into a cauliflower."

The unfailing interest of the principal is further
witnessed by his voluntary expenditure in behalf
of school and choir.   He furnished all the music
for the school.   Similarly, he paid a large proportion of the expenses pertaining to the musical department of service.   The considerable proceeds
derived from the sale of his first Church Hymnal
were devoted to the needs of the choir.

Take it altogether, is there aught of marvel in
the fact that when one meets anywhere a former
pupil of the Warren Free Institute he finds a
woman who is enthusiastic in her praises of its
ecclesiastical head?

And yet with most people the position would
have been counted of small moment, possessing
only a temporary influence.   At the beginning the
new pastor was elected only for one year.   Thereafter nobody thought of the formality of a renewal,
and the appointment simply held over.   But think
what he made of the place!   Think what a rolling stream of undying influence went out from
this post, of what men would consider an uncertain tenure!   One reason for this, no doubt, is to
be found in the simple-mindedness and straight-
forwardness of his aim.   He never changed; he
never lost the spirituality of his beginning.   Many
young men who enter the ministry start out with
motives as religious as those cherished by the

youthful Tucker; but after a while they find that the practice varies from the theory, that to serve God through wardens and vestries is a very different thing, more secular, more political, and time-serving than the simple self-consecration, the devotion of soul and body to the direct service of the Lord with which they commence.

Doctor Tucker had neither warden nor vestry, but he knew troubles not few nor feigned. Nevertheless he kept up his purity and sincerity of intention all through. His motives were fair and clear at the end as at the beginning.

Reference has been made to a New Year's reception at the parsonage. On this one day the Rector recalled the customs of his youth; in so far did he perpetuate the fashion of his New York circle. Then he received; he kept open house for all. Friends came from far, and not merely parishioners of the Holy Cross. There was an ample and substantial spread, and there was an unfailing hospitality manifested at all times in private, but on New Year's day in a brilliant and more public assembling. The celibate showed that he had a home and that he knew how to entertain.

As to the question of celibacy in connection with the Rector, Dr. Warren writes again: " I think that our Missionary enterprise of the Holy Cross depended much on the fact of there being three old bachelors concerned in it; for I am sure that if any one of them had ever married, it would have been disastrous to the others and to the enterprise."

XIX

THE END WHICH IS THE BEGINNING

The earthly end was drawing nigh, although the ones nearest to the central personality knew it not; they had no premonition.

The Jubilee had been celebrated, and all had settled down to the routine of Church and school life, looking forward to a sequence of happy years. There was one severe attack of illness, but the sufferer rallied well and soon dismissed the thought of it from his mind.

When the heavy blow had fallen, after the first shock was over, people began to recall the last things precedent to that sad event. Upon the streets of Troy it was not unusual to see the erect figure of the Rector in a barouche or carriage, but his final appearance is now spoken of as characteristic.

There was in his parish a woman, not counted among the rich, unable to get about with convenience to herself, who had often expressed a desire to visit Oakland, a picturesque bit of landscape to which good Trojans are carried after they depart this life. Doctor Tucker asked Mrs. —— to be ready on a certain day. The barouche came;

he handed her in and took his seat alongside; had
she been a queen he could not have treated her
with greater consideration or more unfeigned politeness. The Rector's last ride constituted a scene yet
recalled in vivid remembrance.

During Lent, on a week-day evening, it had
been the custom of the Pastor to deliver a course
of lectures upon a special subject. In the spring
of 1895, at the beginning of the fast, Doctor Tucker
asked the larger girls about the choice of a topic.
He desired their preference—whether he should
give his own reminiscences, including the telling
of many things known to himself alone, or deliver
a course of instruction in some department of doctrine. Strange to say, they chose the latter. The
cause seemed to be that they would tolerate no
thought which involved the idea of his departure.
They could not bear even the suggestion.

So, at a rehearsal, when the conductor made the
remark that they must learn self-dependence, for
that the day was coming when they must go on
without him, tears were the speedy response.

On another practice night, occurring about the
middle of August, Culley's Anthem, " I will wash
my hands in innocency," was in course of study.
As it was midsummer, men-singers were few. The
organist was on the other side of the water. Doubt
was expressed whether the anthem would " go
well " in service. Doctor Tucker turned to the
temporary organist, saying: " I think we shall be
able to get through all right." At one point in
the anthem the basses made the attack, starting

alone. Just here the Rector's voice was particularly helpful.

The Sunday following, at Morning Prayer—the very last of his life—when the anthem was sung all went well. That evening, at the residence of a parishioner, some one remarked to him, " I never heard you sing better than you did to-day." "Yes," replied the Doctor, " I did pull out all my stops," recalling the phraseology adopted in the story which he had dictated.

The very next day—the fateful Monday—the Rector was engaged in his ordinary round of duty. He had left the school, had gone into the Church, thence entering the Rectory, to partake of his luncheon at noon. He had just seated himself at the table when he was stricken with the blow which meant the last of earth for him.

Tuesday morning he rallied slightly from the paralysis. During a short period he recognized those about him, but he spoke no word to any. Gradually he relapsed into unconsciousness, which continued until the end, which was peace. He died at ten minutes before noon on Saturday, the 17th of August, 1895. Near relatives, dear friends, were gathered at his bedside.

At noon the bell of the Holy Cross was tolled, announcing to the citizens of Troy the passing of this pure soul. It was a fact in which they all had living interest. Then there began a long-continued expression of universal regret, of wide-spreading sorrow, manifested in many ways. The *Daily Times*, in its issue of that Saturday afternoon, voiced the popular idea and feeling when it headed its column, " A Saint of Modern Days Translated." Tributes of highest esteem, of stronger significancy than the ordinary newspaper notice, appeared in various journals.

Troy's oldest clergyman, the Rev. Peter Havermans, was pastor of a Roman Catholic congregation. He had come to Troy in 1843, one year earlier than Doctor Tucker. The two soon became friends. While the Rector of the Holy Cross lay ill the Pastor of St. Peter's called often, to make inquiry at the parsonage. When the latter learned that the end had come he was deeply moved. At the time, Father Havermans was ninety years of age, the oldest priest of his communion in America. Other clergy, of diverse titles, united in one expression of sorrow and affection.

The Bishop of the Diocese had been away—in residence at his summer home at North East Harbor, Maine. He came on at once to attend the services. Arriving about three o'clock on Monday afternoon, Bishop Doane entered the Church where lay the body of the much loved and honored priest, clad in a vestment of white embroidered with gold —a valued offering made months before by one of the guilds of the parish. The coffin was placed in the ante-chapel. There, through Monday afternoon, some twenty-five hundred parishioners and other friends came to look upon the familiar, classic features.

At the hour of the Bishop's arrival—about three o'clock in the day—there appeared a boy nine or ten years of age, clad plainly but neatly, evidently belonging to a family—not of this faith—which had been blessed by the benefactor, whose alms had been unseen, unknown, but measureless. The boy passed into the sacred enclosure, stepped to the side of the oaken coffin and looked upon the quiet face. Then he knelt by the side of the dead, crossed himself, and prayed. All the onlookers, standing round, bowed their heads in unison with the child's devotion.

At that moment the Bishop stepped in. He saw at once the state of the case. First he laid his hand upon the head of the boy, giving his blessing; then he, chief pastor, knelt to take part in the intercession, ever mindful of his loyal priest.

Mr. W. W. Rousseau is the organist of the Church—the devoted friend and faithful coworker of the Rector so highly valued. Mr. Rousseau had been abroad during the summer. He reached his home only on Saturday—the day of the Rector's death—not in time to see his dear friend yet alive, yet in season to take the musical direction of the Burial Office. It was a sorrowful but sweet undertaking for him. Like the members of his choir, his affections were so enlisted that they were overwrought.

Mr. Rousseau wrote me about the one subject: " You will observe that the last care he had in mind was his Church, as he had but just come from it and gone into his dining-room and seated himself for his usual noon lunch when he was stricken with the fatal malady. . . . So has departed one whose like we shall never see on earth." The organist pays his own heartfelt tribute in a few paragraphs published in the Troy *Times:*

After an absence of six weeks, the writer returns to find a desolate house, a bereaved community, a void in a Church-life that can never be filled, and the hand I know would have been most warmly extended to welcome me home cold in death; while the great pleasure we both anticipated in recounting together the results of my visits to the many European Cathedrals has been suddenly banished. But it is a satisfaction beyond expression to know that Dr. Tucker died as he wanted to die —in the harness.

And it is a gratifying fact that the Church he loved so well, and at which he had ministered so faithfully, was perhaps the last object of his care, as he had just left the Church and entered his home when he was stricken. But the day before (Sunday), he waited upon the Lord in His holy temple as usual.

But all is over. No more shall we be greeted with his ever-kindly smile; never again on earth shall we listen to the voice that we all had learned to love and revere. Noblest, truest, best of friends, farewell! How truly has been fulfilled the motto that adorned his private room: " Be thou faithful unto death, and I will give thee a crown of life! "

During the time in which the cherished form lay in state there were palm branches about him, placed, as it were, within reach of his hand. Members of St. Stephen's Guild kept faithful watch during the night preceding the burial.

On Sunday morning there had been a Celebration held at eight o'clock, at which the Rev. Dr. Maxcy was celebrant. The whole Church was filled absolutely. Each worshipper present received the Holy Communion at this especial service. It was a great congregation of loving, sorrowing, and praying friends.

Thereafter no service was held in the Church until the Office of Burial on Tuesday morning. Then Bishops Doane and Potter were in attendance, with some forty vested clergy. The space within the Church was insufficient to accommodate the throngs of people who strove to enter; many waited without.

Although the service was of tenderest feeling, yet the scene was bright and joyous, just as he who had gone would have liked to have had it. The altar was vested in white. There was an abundance of lights in the chancel. Doctor Tucker was accustomed to say, " Let us have plenty of light." Beautiful flowers were on every side. Fresh roses shed fragrance. The palm branches still foretold triumph. Violet hangings were apparent only within the limits of the choir. The first hymn was the exultant strain, " Ten thousand times ten thousand "—a favorite of the one remembered.

The choir of the Church, devoted every soul of them to the Pastor, were so moved by their personal sorrow that, at the Burial Office, they could scarcely sing plain chants and hymns. The organist was so persuaded beforehand of their unusual attachment and feeling that he did not venture to place even a single anthem upon the programme for the day—this with reference to a choir which is accustomed to sing anthems all the time.

Was there ever such a Burial Service as this? When, after the office, the treasured body was carried along the alley-way, the singers broke down on account of their grief. The congregation joined them in audible sobs. What a tribute of affection it was! All along the street there were constant manifestations of respect and true grief. It might appear that, after all, the great mass cares more for its true saints than for princes or conquerors.

A line of fifty coaches was filled with actual mourners. Arrived at Oakwood, after the body had been committed to the earth, nearly every member of the multitude cast fresh flowers into the open grave. Throughout the time occupied by service and procession, the bell of St. Paul's—the mother Church—was tolled.

Trojans are glad that their saint lies buried close at hand, within the confines of their own interesting city, of that which had become his true home by adoption and long residence.

The place of resting for his body is, as he wished it, in a spot " where the sun might shine upon his grave." He lies in the midst of a plot, with space about him in which, according to his own request, any of the poor of the Church, who so desire, may be buried.

The feeling of Church musicians outside of his own city is summed up in a letter which arrived soon after the burial, addressed to a musical friend in Troy. Dr. George William Warren, organist of St. Thomas' Church, New York, writes from his summer home:

BOLTON-ON-LAKE-GEORGE,
NEW YORK,
Aug. 22, 1895.

DEAR MRS. MARY:

It was an added sorrow to my constant grief for the death of our sainted friend, that I could not be at Holy Cross Church last Tuesday, but it was entirely impossible to leave home either on Monday or Tuesday. Today I could have been with all you mourners.

I feel so lost now that I never can see him again in this world. His regard and sympathy, and the consolation of being with him at the parsonage as occasion allowed me, was everything to me, and now I am desolate indeed; and if so for me, think of you who could see him every day. Truly we are afflicted. . . .

On the 26th of August Dr. Warren writes again:

Many, many thanks for your letter of Saturday, every item of which I read with a melancholy interest, almost morbid.

I hope some consolation will come to us by and by, yes, and to the Parish and School of the Holy Cross. All good things end in this world, and our minds should be trained to meet trouble, and yet we are never ready for these appalling changes; and when I think of the parsonage without him, I am desolate. We are, however, comforted, for our dear saint is at rest and in bliss everlasting. Amen.

Truly your friend
GEO. WM. WARREN.

One-half hour after the return from the cemetery a message was received by cable, from Tours in France, conveying an order for flowers for the burial. It was followed by a letter from Mrs.

Percy Alden, stating that, in the Paris *Herald*, she had just seen the announcement of the death. She expressed her great sorrow, and hoped that her " cable " would be in time.

The Rev. Arthur B. Moorhouse wrote from Boston: " Doctor Tucker was a most remarkable man; none like him in my estimation. He was always deeply sympathetic, in musical matters particularly. I used to steal away from Boston on every opportunity, to come to the Holy Cross to hear that wonderful service. I had a most delightful visit with the Doctor just after Easter. Although he did not seem so strong as usual, yet I did not think he was really breaking down. His loss will be felt all over the country."

J. D. Shaw of Irvington, N. J., wrote 28th August, 1895:

I have seen the *Churchman*. It has a short account of his life with a good portrait, but in no way does it go into all the particulars that a paper from Troy would. Every word of eulogy was truthful.

He was my Sunday-school teacher 55 years ago, and in every way took great interest in me. If you had seen his father, you would not have forgotten him. He was Major Tucker, President of one of the Wall St. banks, N. Y. He was nearly seven feet in height, with a strong military air. You could not but observe him in passing.

Of the son, Rev. Dr. Tucker, we may well say

> Servant of God, well done!
> Rest from thy loved employ.
> The battle fought, the victory won,
> Enter thy Master's joy.

The Standing Committee at once met and adopted a minute:

The Standing Committee of the Diocese of Albany, N. Y., assembled on this the 20th day of August, 1895, to attend upon the funeral obsequies of the Rev. John Ireland Tucker, D.D., desire to place on record the following minute:

Born 1819—Died 1895. These are the periods that mark the earthly pilgrimage of our associate, wherein were fulfilled the Psalmist's promise: "With long life will I satisfy him and show him my salvation." . . .

In the formation of the Diocese of Albany he took a prominent and active part, and ever since that time he has given of his time, advice, labor and aid to further its progress. His pride in the prosperity of the same was great; the honors heaped upon its first Bishop caused him more joy than had they been his own, so unselfish was his nature; interest in diocesan institutions never flagged; loyalty to his Bishop was strong and continuous; honors did not have to be conferred on him before he would rouse himself to higher thought and generous deed; to him honors were as mere accidents, for the reason he himself was above, beyond and greater than them all.

From the formation of the Diocese he has been a member of the Standing Committee and since the death of the Rev. William Payne, D.D., four and one-half years ago, its honored and revered president. It has been the lot of few dioceses as old as ours, to have had only two presidents and those two such saintly characters as were Drs. Payne and Tucker. It is not our place to linger with detail in the various spheres of activity wherein our departed brother exercised his gifts so conspicuously and so successfully, but rather to think of him as our associate in the Standing Committee of this Diocese. . . .

In our councils we saw at work in him constantly the strong intellect and the warm heart; in him mercy and

22

truth met together; righteousness and peace kissed each
other; impetuous, yet so calm; gentle, yet so strong;
modest, yet so brave; retiring, yet so conspicuous; simple,
yet so learned; manly, yet so Christlike. His whole life
was a sweet song, which as the days flew by grew sweeter
and stronger, as though it was a preparedness for leadership in the choirs of the New Jerusalem.

Dear Dr. Tucker, we, thine associates of the Standing
Committee, bid thee " Farewell," knowing it will not be
so long a time before we shall have the joy of reunion
and of thy welcome to become partakers with thee of
those blessings prepared for those who love God, and
upon which thou art entered. " Farewell! " but only for
a brief time, for that strange voice of thine that so fascinated us in our earthly worship will yet in louder and
clearer and sweeter tones help us the better to sing the
song of the redeemed—" Blessing and glory and wisdom
and thanksgiving and honor and power and might be
unto our God forever and ever. Amen." " Mark the
perfect man, and behold the upright, for the end of that
man is peace."

JAMES CAIRD,
For the Committee.

At the Diocesan Convention holden a few
months later, the Bishop, in his address, recalled
the vivid scene of the burial:

I received on Saturday, the 17th of August, in North
East Harbor, news of the death of dear Dr. Tucker,
for which I was somewhat prepared by Dr. Ferguson's
thoughtfulness in telegraphing me of his sudden illness.
I came at once of course to Troy and took my part in
the solemn and touching office of his burial, the Bishop
of New York being with me, and about forty clergymen,
many of whom had come long distances, and all of whom
had come out of the deep sense of personal love and per-

sonal loss. I print, in the appendix of this address, the minute of the Standing Committee, the minute adopted by the Bishops and clergy present, all too faint and feeble utterances of our true and reverent affection for this holy man. It is a strange coincidence, that this same address should contain the notice of the Jubilee, which we kept on Christmas eve, in the Church of the Holy Cross, with proud and thankful hearts. And I am sure that you will agree with me, that our sorrow ought to be unselfish enough and full enough of faith, to realize that if we called that golden, we ought to call this the jewel jubilee for him. It is idle to attempt to put in words the estimate of such a life and such a character. He was so many-sided that the sense of his loss touches hundreds of people; who knew him, from the far outside, only as the reverent priest, the rare musician, the composer and com-piler of what I believe to be the best musical hymnal in the Anglican Communion; who knew him, in the closer relations, either of official counsel or of close and in-timate personal friendship; who loved him and looked up to him as their guide and teacher in spiritual things, their devoted pastor, their friend, so prompt and keen in sympathy with every joy and sorrow of their lives; his fellow-citizens, whose leader and example he was in all that made for righteousness and truth and honor; his own immediate family, whose personal bereavement we may not forget in the great sorrow of our own loss.

I am sure none who were there that day, either in the Church or about the grave, can ever forget the well-won tribute poured out, by every sign and token of grief and love. As we passed out between the double file of sing-ing men and girls, bearing the body for the last time from the Church which he had created and served, while the voices of the choir half sang, half sobbed, the words of the " Paradise hymn "—keeping their sobs in tune and time—I said to the Bishop of New York: " It was worth living to have won such a tribute as that." I am free to say after a friendship of forty years, the latter half of

which has been filled with constant and intimate intercourse, that I have never known a priest in whom God
had so beautifully combined all gifts of nature and of
grace, that go to make a rounded and completed man.
He was a theologian, one of very few, accurate in all the
definitions of the truth, keeping his mind fresh with all
the newest publications of the day; and staunch and true
in his convictions of the Catholic faith. He was a gentleman with every instinct of kindly courtesy, and with all
the grace and finish and polish which a rare and fine nature gets from the manners of a gentleman. And in his
inner life, into whose sacred places the eyes of man could
only imperfectly look, he showed by every unstudied
and instinctive act and word, that he was one of the men
who " walk with God." He has left behind him many a
memory and many a memorial which will only freshen
and brighten as time goes on.

XX

AFTERWARD

It was on a Sunday, not long after the day of the memorable burial, that two persons walked in Oakwood, near to the place of his resting. They noted the bank of flowers there preserved. Said one of the visitors: "Is that Doctor Tucker's grave?"

Being answered in the affirmative, the woman continued:

I am no Episcopalian; but Dr. Tucker was one good man. I knew him thirty years ago. My husband was a real-estate agent; he rented a house to a man who came here with his family, and tried to make a living by teaching music. He did not get on very well here, and finally went to Hoosack Falls, leaving his family in the house. Not long afterwards he came home late one night, and his wife soon came to our house, asking my husband to go for Dr. Vincent, as her husband was very ill.

Dr. Vincent came, and said there was no hope for the man; then, at their request, my husband went for Dr. Tucker. I remember it was just at the break of day when he came. After a few words with the sick man, he knelt down by his bed, and offered up the best prayer I ever heard in my life.

The man died soon after. Dr. Tucker paid the expenses of the funeral, took the girls into his school, found employment for the boys, and in fact raised that family until they could care for themselves. There is no doubt about it—he was really a good man.

On the 15th of September a memorial Celebration was held at the Church of the Holy Cross, the Bishop of the Diocese being Celebrant and Preacher. The sermon consisted of a brief address, in a part of which the Bishop said:

You and I are here today for the first Communion Service since this pulpit became empty. I am not seeking to fill it, and I thank God that no man can fill it. When God raises us individuals, He is not as cheap and mean as you and I. Dr. Tucker's place can never be filled, and we would not have it filled. But it would be a dishonor to him and a discredit to God if the work he began should go into unworthy hands, for he was too good a workman. You and I are here, for the first time since the burial service never to be forgotten. We came then to share our common sorrow. Today we come for a memorial Celebration of the Eucharist, and the Eucharist is a thanksgiving. He had faith, love, hope; and because he believed and loved whatever God told him, he gained the increase. What can we find depicted more grand than his beautiful character?

So there began a series of offices in memory.

On the 29th of the same month the Rev. H. R. Freeman delivered a discourse at St. John's Church, in memory of Doctor Tucker. Other memorial services were held elsewhere.

On the recurrence of the Feast of All Saints, the loving ones, remembering ever, could not but give chief place to this high saint of God. Under the auspices of parish guilds, a service was held in the open air, at Oakwood, about the new-made grave. Parishioners and visiting clergy were present. The faithful choir was on duty; each member carried a bunch of flowers; later these were laid upon the mound of earth. Large floral crosses and other offerings had been sent by the four guilds of the parish.

Dr. Maxcy chanted the especial office. Among the hymns there were two having tender significance and association. One was

> The Saints of God! Their conflict past,
> And life's long battle won at last,

which was sung to Stainer's setting; the other was the elder Bishop Doane's hymn, "Thou art the way," set to one of the tunes the authorship of which is marked in the Hymnal by the modest initials "J. I. T." So two friends who had loved long, parted for a while but now reunited in Paradise, were associated in this office of All Saints at Oakwood: the one as the author of a hymn, the other the composer of the tune to which the words were sung.

Doctor Tucker's composition for the 425th Hymn will no doubt come into use more and more as it becomes the better known. It is eminently proper for this particular wording, and it is a noble sacred song.

Yet one year later, when All Saints' came round again, the good people might not yet forget; so long as they live they are bound to remember and pray for him, with reference to whom they give God thanks. A memorial service was held " for all the saints," but with especial remembrance of the names associated with the parish. This time the office was said in Church, on the afternoon of the Feast. Bishop Doane made the address. Again his father's hymn was sung to the tune by " J. I. T." A large number of local clergy were in attendance. Other music composed by the late Rector had place in the festival services.

A few months after the day of parting, the present writer stepped within the confines of the " parsonage," as it was ordinarily styled in Troy. The place was forsaken—no one dwelling therein. Yet there was enough about the walls and rooms to convey an indefinable sense of the presence which had passed away. Books were everywhere, not only in the two libraries, but in unexpected localities, such as in the entry passages far up on the third floor. All the volumes, except the hymnals, had been willed to St. Stephen's College, long served by Doctor Tucker. At the time of my visit a few books were already in packing boxes, ready for transshipment; but enough remained to indicate the character of the late owner. There were fine editions of *belles lettres*. One would read the title " Hawthorne's ' Our Old Home,' " and of many another favorite. Good editions were the rule. Encyclopædias appeared in the original English print, likewise standard books of theology.

Dr. Maxcy once made the remark that the Rector

of the Holy Cross was an omnivorous reader, rapid but accurate, making the book his own. He was also great in the preparation of indexes of that which had been read.

The furnishing of the house was liberal; it all gave token of culture. But in the Doctor's bedroom on the third floor—the apartment which concerned only himself and which entered not into the service of others—one would be struck by the extreme simplicity. Here asceticism found play— in this case, sign of unselfishness and generosity.

Below, in the drawing-room, there was a grand piano, as became the home of a musician. And, like the books, paintings were manifest at every turn.

In the hallway, at first entrance one would note colored prints of the Vatican and St. Peter's, Rome. In the dining-room, at the right, etchings have place, including a striking picture by Haig of the Cathedral of Toledo, in which a procession is just entering the choir. Over the sideboard is an etching of Canterbury. In another frame, monks are at a Friday refection; there is much fish, but large flasks are also brought in. Sir Walter Scott appears in one corner; beneath this the Kaulbach engraving of Goethe's " Lottie " cutting bread for the children. Beside the mantelglass Salisbury comes into view.

Mount to the second story by the broad stairway; pass before the many books lining the entryway, and you find yourself in the front study, having the solid cases of black walnut built up into the structure of the apartment. Here are the large standard works of theology, for reference. This was the original study, used years ago. Over the mantel-shelf there is a colored print, " Le Recit de Missionaire," who sits and tells his story—about his serious work—to monks that care not; they are heedless, attending to lighter affairs.

Beside this is the drawing-room, with the grand piano and a library of valuable music. Paintings in oils hang on the walls. There is a great canvas showing " Ruth and Naomi "; another, " The Early Mass "; yet again, " Isaac and Rebecca." The " Mater Dolorosa " is prominent, but St. Cecilia presides over the precincts largely devoted to her art.

At the back of the building was located the second study, occupied by the Doctor for a number of recent years. Here was the working plant for every-day use: a writing-table, large files of manuscripts, of papers; also books, photographs, engravings. The portraits of friends hang within reach—Bishop Doane of New Jersey and Bishop Henry C. Potter, apparently taken when Dr. Potter was a young Rector in Troy.

A small anteroom opens next to the study. Here is the varied assortment of two hundred different musical hymnals, bequeathed to the friend and organist, Mr. Rousseau. There is just room for a lounge; nevertheless over that hangs a fine etching.

Above, *au troisième*, one notes the Bishop's room which was set apart in the times when Bishop

Horatio Potter used to come on from New York and to stay a while. Beside this was Doctor Tucker's own apartment, where he lay down to nightly rest and where he lay down for the last sleep. Upon the wall is a drawing of the Church of the Holy Cross as it appeared in its childhood; also over the couch an illuminated sentence—the only text inscribed anywhere in all the house—" Be thou faithful unto death, and I will give thee a crown of life."

Yet later, a few months farther on, I made a brief stay at the Warden's home, located on the leafy and lovely campus of St. Stephen's College. There Dr. Fairbairn—old friend of the Rector of the Holy Cross—said to me:

From time to time Doctor Tucker had stayed here with me.

I sent for him to come spend the night before Commencement. He wrote that he had ceased to be away from home over night. It was a genial letter. A few days after I went to see him.

In the old time, I was Rector of Christ Church in Troy. The first four years of Tucker's ministry we lived together under the same roof. We were peculiarly intimate, constant friends. Frequently we used to go to his father's house; we dined there often. His father was kind to me; Tucker was kind to me.

Then the Warden told the story, quoted elsewhere, about the one friend procuring a nurse for the other through a spell of sickness. Dr. Fairbairn continued:

He married me, married my daughter and baptized my son. He buried my wife; to the grave he carried some flowers, and laid them there after he had read the service.

He used to complain sometimes about the condition of the Church in general. It was pretty bad at that time. He was tempted to give it up. But he balanced the question, and settled it once for all.

Some people used to think that he might be persuaded to renounce his Church. Deshon was an army officer in the ordnance department. He used to come to me and say, " You hold on to Tucker, or he'll go to Rome." But Deshon went and he didn't. Dr. Rider, President of a R. C. College at Worcester, Mass., came to Troy, delivering addresses and making some converts, among them Deshon, who became a priest. Dr. Tucker remained a faithful Anglican to the end.

He always set apart a portion of the day for regular study. Besides this he gave attention to lighter reading, especially on Church subjects. No important work of fiction, such as Mrs. Ward's book, escaped him. Bull's works he read in Latin, just after he went to Troy. He told me that he found it a little laborious; but he stuck to it. He was a studious man.

He gave the afternoon to pastoral visiting. In his pastoral work, a remarkable trait was his care of the girls; he looked after them and their parents; he went into the school and taught them.

Intellectually he was not a brilliant man, but he had a good mind; wrote a good sermon. He confined himself to the Holy Cross. He was rarely absent; never exchanged. Once he had an engagement to exchange with the chaplain at West Point, but when the time came, he got me to go and do it for him. He was regular and faithful in the writing of his sermons. I think they kept progressing most of the week.

In social life, he loved company; he entertained a great deal after he got in his own house, and he received many even when in apartments. Gibson used to come down from Cohoes nearly every week. Dr. Muhlenberg came up and preached.

Among the books [bequeathed to St. Stephen's College] we found a lot of receipted bills, many of them for jewelry. I began to find out. These things had been given to the children of that school. It only shows with what affection he dealt with them. He gave them not only books, he set before them not only religion, but he gave them things which would make them feel at home with themselves, make them feel good and comfortable.

Dr. Fairbairn talked further about the musical abilities of his friend; also about the effect produced by his personal presence. " Few were as graceful as he."

The Warden had published a paper in the *St. Stephen's College Messenger*. In this he urged the young men at college to become acquainted with Doctor Tucker's life, and to find in his career a stimulus and encouragement. " Dr. Tucker lived in Troy," he wrote, " for fifty-one years; and at the end of that period, he was probably more respected, more influential, and more loved than at any portion of it. His life would be a great study for young men."

The writer referred to propriety of conduct as one of the elements of a true success.

His conduct was always proper. I have attempted to recall some improper action or word which escaped him during the four years that we stood in such intimate relations. But I do not recall any such. The picture before my mind is a man of the utmost propriety. His manners and his dress were of such a character as always to impress one. One could not fail to feel that he was in the presence of a superior person. No vulgar expression or story ever escaped from his lips. No slovenliness was ever seen in him. This neatness was natural to him. It was not assumed or put on, but it became part of him. There are plenty of clergymen who are as learned, and as vigorous in their work, but it is rare to find one as graceful as he. That was one of the elements of character which made Dr. Tucker. He exemplifies in a grand sense what William of Wyckham said, " Manners maketh man."

There might be written a discourse on the manners of Dr. Tucker, which would be a great lesson to young men. Such cultivation would be in any one a real element of success.

So the head of a college talks to the youth under his care; he calls attention to the shining example which has been set before them.

He emphasizes a feature characteristic of the entire earthly career which we have contemplated. Doctor Tucker never outlived that to which he was born and bred.

Says Thackeray: " What is it to be a gentleman? Is it to have lofty aims; to lead a pure life; to keep your honor virgin; to have the esteem of your fellow citizens and the love of your fireside; to bear good fortune meekly; to suffer evil with constancy; and through evil and good to maintain truth always? Show me the happy man whose life exhibits these qualities, and him will we salute as gentleman."

And so it is that a bright and wholesome memory abides of him who liked always a sufficiency of light, having no fellowship with darkness either in his chancel or in his every-day living, and whose body sleeps now " where the sun may shine upon it."

———

The story here told had just been completed, its manuscript was ready for the press, when a telegram came to hand announcing the sudden death of William W. Rousseau, whose name appears more than once in the foregoing pages. He was the organist at Holy Cross during the latter half of Doctor Tucker's rectorship, also the constant co-worker with his Rector, especially in the editorship of all the hymnals.

The two were linked together, like David and Jonathan, in bonds of affection. For his chief the younger cherished a reverential admiration. Further, there existed in both a oneness of sentiment, as, for example, about the absolute desirability of the adoption of the lovely art into the direct service of God. Each worked as hard as he could for the accomplishment of this end.

Fitting it seemed that the one friend should follow so soon the other into the world beyond. That was a joyful reunion.